FUTURE WORKSCAPES

INTERNATIONAL PERSPECTIVES ON EQUALITY, DIVERSITY AND INCLUSION

Series Editor: Mustafa F. Özbilgin

Recent Volumes:

Volume 1:	*Practical and Theoretical Implications of Successfully Doing Difference in Organizations*, Edited by Donnalyn Pompper
Volume 2:	*Gender, Careers and Inequalities in Medicine and Medical Education: International Perspectives*, Edited by Maria Tsouroufli
Volume 3:	*Management and Diversity: Perspectives from Different National Contexts*, Edited by Mustafa F. Özbilgin and Jean-François Chanlat
Volume 4:	*Management and Diversity: Thematic Approaches*, Edited by Mustafa F. Özbilgin and Jean-François Chanlat
Volume 5:	*The Strength of Difference: Itineraries of Atypical Bosses*, Edited by Norbert Alter
Volume 6:	*Race Discrimination and Management of Ethnic Diversity and Migration at Work: European Countries' Perspectives*, Edited by Joana Vassilopoulou, Julienne Brabet and Victoria Showunmi
Volume 7:	*Lived Experiences of Exclusion in the Workplace: Psychological & Behavioural Effects*, Edited by Kurt April, Babar Dharani and Amanda Ronita April
Volume 8:	*Management and Organizational Studies on Blue & Grey Collar Workers: Diversity of Collars*, Edited by Joanna Paliszkiewicz and Demet Varoğlu
Volume 9:	*Contemporary Approaches in Equality, Diversity and Inclusion: Strategic and Technological Perspectives*, Edited by Berk Kucukaltan
Volume 10:	*Care and Compassion in Capitalism*, Edited by Cagri Yalkin and Mustafa F. Özbilgin
Volume 11A:	*Future Workscapes: Strategic Insights and Innovations in Human Resources and Organizational Development*, Edited by Joanna Paliszkiewicz, Demet Varoğlu and Olena Kulykovets

INTERNATIONAL PERSPECTIVES ON EQUALITY, DIVERSITY AND INCLUSION   VOLUME 11B

FUTURE WORKSCAPES: EMERGING BUSINESS TRENDS AND INNOVATIONS

EDITED BY

JOANNA PALISZKIEWICZ
Warsaw University of Life Sciences, Poland

DEMET VAROĞLU
TOBB University of Economics and Technology, Türkiye

AND

OLENA KULYKOVETS
Warsaw University of Life Sciences, Poland

United Kingdom – North America – Japan
India – Malaysia – China

Emerald Publishing Limited
Emerald Publishing, Floor 5, Northspring, 21-23 Wellington Street, Leeds LS1 4DL.

First edition 2025

Editorial matter and selection © 2025 Joanna Paliszkiewicz, Demet Varoğlu, and Olena Kulykovets.
Individual chapters © 2025 The authors.
Published under exclusive licence by Emerald Publishing Limited.

Reprints and permissions service
Contact: www.copyright.com

No part of this book may be reproduced, stored in a retrieval system, transmitted in any form or by any means electronic, mechanical, photocopying, recording or otherwise without either the prior written permission of the publisher or a licence permitting restricted copying issued in the UK by The Copyright Licensing Agency and in the USA by The Copyright Clearance Center. Any opinions expressed in the chapters are those of the authors. Whilst Emerald makes every effort to ensure the quality and accuracy of its content, Emerald makes no representation implied or otherwise, as to the chapters' suitability and application and disclaims any warranties, express or implied, to their use.

British Library Cataloguing in Publication Data
A catalogue record for this book is available from the British Library

ISBN: 978-1-83662-177-5 (Print)
ISBN: 978-1-83662-176-8 (Online)
ISBN: 978-1-83662-178-2 (Epub)

ISSN: 2051-2333 (Series)

INVESTOR IN PEOPLE

*To my friends: Magda, Marzena, Kasia, Dominika, Lucy, Beata
Thank you for always being there, for your endless inspiration,
and for believing in me* — J. P.

To my parents Zerrin and Kadri Bacacı – D. V.

For my sister Veronika, for her support and peace of mind – O. K.

CONTENTS

List of Figures and Tables	ix
About the Editors	xi
About the Contributors	xiii
Foreword by Ireneusz Dąbrowski	xix
Foreword by Fatih Çetin	xxi
Preface	xxiii

SECTION I
EMERGING BUSINESS TRENDS

Chapter 1   Spiritual Branding Attributes and Consumer Buying Intention: The Proposal of Conceptual Model
Ngoc Bich Do, Y Nhu Nguyen Luu, Vi Thai Huyen Kim and Viet Chi Duong — 3

Chapter 2   Factors Affecting Career Commitment of Public Servants in Vietnam: Perspectives of Investment Model and Moderation Effects of Perceived Economic Conditions
Quang-An Ha — 13

Chapter 3   Effects of Working Motivation on Efficiency and Work Satisfaction: Case of Employees at the Software Company
Pham Duc Chinh, Yen Nguyen Thi and Ma Thi Ngan — 27

Chapter 4   Rethinking Organizational Hierarchy: A Critical Analysis of Strategic Management Schools
Mehmet Barca and Semih Ceyhan — 45

Chapter 5   Placing Non-managerial Employees in the Management Theories: Toward a Theoretical Advancement
Mehmet Barca — 59

SECTION II
INNOVATIONS AND BUSINESS PRACTICES

Chapter 6   A Study on Environment, Social and Governance Disclosure in the Case of the Packaging Sector in Romania
*Anca Draghici, Gabriela Banaduc,
Roxana Mihaela Sirbu and Tamas-Szora Attila*   *91*

Chapter 7   Is Digitalization Bad for Trade Union Density in OECD Countries in the Age of Globalization?
Orhan Cengiz and Ömer Demir   *113*

Chapter 8   The Role of Internal Communication and Employee Participation in Creating Health and Safety Climate: A Monographic Study
Elif Sungur, Nevin Kılıç and Çiğdem Vatansever   *129*

Chapter 9   Importance of Corporate Social Responsibility (CSR) in the Global Food Processing Industry
Małgorzata Wiktoria Paprocka   *143*

Index   *155*

LIST OF FIGURES AND TABLES

FIGURES

Fig. 1.1.	Proposed Conceptual Model.	7
Fig. 2.1.	A Conceptual Model Proposed Main Factors Affecting Career Commitment of Public Servants in Vietnam Public Organizations.	20
Fig. 3.1.	Proposed Research Model.	32
Fig. 3.2.	CFA (Modification) Model Outcomes.	35
Fig. 3.3.	Results of SEM Model Research (Modified).	37
Fig. 6.1.	The Theoretical Framework of the IVC Process.	96
Fig. 6.2.	Study Stages.	98
Fig. 6.3.	The Conceptual Model Design of the Study.	99
Fig. 7.1.	Digital Competitiveness Ranking 2023.	116
Fig. 7.2.	Trade Union Density: Percentage of Employees in OECD Countries.	117
Fig. 7.3.	Estimation Techniques.	120
Fig. 8.1.	Hierarchical Code–Subcode of Communication Map.	139
Fig. 8.2.	Safety Climate Model as Grounded Theory.	139
Fig. 9.1.	Documents by Year.	146
Fig. 9.2.	Documents by Subject Area.	147

TABLES

Table 3.1.	Assessment Criteria and CFA Results.	36
Table 3.2.	Testing the Discrimination Between Concepts From the Critical Model.	36
Table 3.3.	Relationships Between Concepts in the Research Model.	38
Table 3.4.	Bootstrap.	39
Table 6.1.	Synthesis of the Data on ESG and/or Sustainability Reports of the Packaging Companies Considered in the Research.	99
Table 6.2.	Total Code Units Over the Data Set (Code System).	102
Table 6.3.	Total Code Units in the Data Set Sorted by Descending Frequency Per Each Company.	104
Table 6.4.	Synthesis of the Research Findings From the Content Analysis.	107
Table 6.5.	Synthesis of the Research Findings From the Validation Stage.	107

Table 7.1.	Summary of Literature Review.	118
Table 7.2.	Data Description.	119
Table 7.3.	Descriptive Statistics.	122
Table 7.4.	The CSD and Slope Heterogeneity Tests Results.	123
Table 7.5.	The CIPS Unit Root Test Results.	123
Table 7.6.	Generalized Panel Quantile Regression Results.	124
Table 7.7.	The D–H Panel Causality Test Results.	124
Table 8.1.	Code Frequency Matrix of FG Interviews.	137

ABOUT THE EDITORS

Joanna Paliszkiewicz works as a Full Professor at the Warsaw University of Life Sciences (WULS–SGGW). She is the Director of the Management Institute. She is also an Adjunct Professor at the University of Vaasa in Finland. She obtained the academic title Full Professor from the International School for Social and Business Studies in Slovenia. She is well recognized in Poland and abroad for her expertise in management issues: knowledge management and trust management. She has published over 250 papers/manuscripts and is the author/co-author/editor of 21 books. Currently, she serves as the Deputy Editor-in-Chief of the *Management and Production Engineering Review*. She is an Associate Editor for the *Journal of Computer Information Systems, Expert System With Applications, Issues in Information Systems, Przegląd Organizacji,* and *Intelligent Systems With Applications*. She serves as the President of the International Association for Computer Information Systems in the United States.

Demet Varoğlu received her B.Sc. (1983) and MBA (1986) degrees from Middle East Technical University (METU), Department of Business Administration. She completed her Ph.D. (1993) at Ankara University, Department of Business Administration and earned her Associate Professor degree in the field of Organizational Behavior in 2000. Starting from the position of Research Assistantship (1984), she was among the academic staff of METU Department of Business Administration for more than 20 years. Between 2004 and 2006, she served as the Chairperson of the Gender and Women Studies Program at METU. Since 2006, she has been working at TOBB University of Economics and Technology, Department of Business Administration. She is the first female academician who received the full professor title (March 2018) in her department and is currently a member of the university senate. Besides introductory and/or must courses on business administration, management, organizational behavior, and human resource management, she has taught and continues to teach undergraduate and graduate level courses on power and politics in organizations, gender issues in organizations and negotiation. She has national and international publications on power and politics, gender, conflict management, information sharing, leadership, and employee selection decisions. Her current research interests are diversity and discrimination at the workplace, counterproductive work behaviors, and emotions in organizations. Together with two colleagues, she received the Turkish Education Association's 1999 National Award on Education Research.

Olena Kulykovets is an Assistant Professor at the Management Institute at the Warsaw University of Life Sciences. She obtained her PhD in 2022 in the discipline of Management and Quality Sciences at the University of Warsaw, Faculty of Management. Her scientific interests focus on topics related to non-standard marketing tools, as well as the use of modern technologies in the field of scientific research, and the use of artificial intelligence to support the marketing activities of enterprises.

ABOUT THE CONTRIBUTORS

Tamas-Szora Attila is a Full Professor at "1 Decembrie 1918" University of Alba Iulia, Romania, where he also serves as President of the University Senate. He specializes in finance and accounting, with expertise in consultancy, auditing, evaluation, and financing programs. He has been a faculty member since 1993 and is currently an Associate Lecturer at UBB Cluj-Napoca and the West University of Timisoara. He is a member of several professional organizations, including the Body of Expert and Licensed Accountants of Romania, where he served as President of the Alba Branch from 2013 to 2015, and the Chamber of Tax Consultants of Romania. He is also affiliated with ANEVAR, the Chamber of Financial Auditors, and the National Union of Insolvency Practitioners.

Gabriela Banaduc is PhD student at the Politehnica University of Timisoara under the supervision of Professor Anca Draghici. Her research field of interest is sustainability management in the case of designing, planning, and implementing great investment projects (financed by structural funds) for local development. She is also a public servant in charge of the Projects and Planning Department at the Caransebes City Hall, in Romania.

Mehmet Barca is a Professor of Management and Organization at the Social Sciences University of Ankara, Turkey. He earned his MBA and PhD from Leicester University, UK. His research areas include strategic management, human resource management (HRM), knowledge management, and change management, with publications in prestigious journals such as *Strategic Organization* and the *Journal of Strategy and Management*. He authored *Economic Foundations of Strategic Management* (Ashgate, 2003; Routledge, 2017). With nearly 30 years of academic experience and over 20 years in professional consultancy, he has developed strategic plans and HRM functions for public, private, and nonprofit organizations. He has also held leadership roles as dean, vice rector, and rector and currently serves as an independent board member for several companies, including those listed on the stock market.

Orhan Cengiz is an Associate Professor at Çukurova University, Pozanti Vocational School, Department of Accounting and Taxation, Adana/Türkiye. He received his Bachelor's, Master's, and PhD degrees in Economics from Çukurova University. His research focuses on globalization, the role of the state, the international political economy, and economic development.

Semih Ceyhan works as Associate Professor at the Management Department of Ankara Yildirim Beyazit University Business School. He completed his PhD in

2019 on the subject of "Dominant Management Logics in Siyasetnamas." His interest areas include management, spirituality and religion, Islamic management, strategic management, and entrepreneurship. Some of his work appeared in high-ranked journals such as *The International Journal of Human Resource Management, International Journal of Emerging Markets, Kybernetes,* and *Journal of Business and Industrial Marketing.*

Ömer Demir is an Assistant Professor at Şırnak University, Silopi Vocational School, Department of Management and Organization, Sirnak, Türkiye. He studied engineering for two years at Çukurova University, Adana, Türkiye, and received an associate degree in Law from Anadolu University, Eskişehir, Türkiye. He earned his Bachelor's, Master's, and Doctorate degrees in Economics from Çukurova University. During his undergraduate studies in Economics, he spent a semester as a visiting student at the Europa-Flensburg University in Flensburg, Germany, and its partner, the University of Southern Denmark in Odense, Denmark. His research in international economics focuses on international political economy with a special emphasis on globalization, digitalization, international trade, capital flows, geopolitical risk, and economic development.

Ngoc Bich Do is a Lecturer at the School of International Business and Marketing, Ho Chi Minh City. Her research interests include brand crisis management, consumer behavior, sustainability, and innovation.

Anca Draghici has a MSc degree in Machine Tool Design (1989, Transilvania University of Brasov, Romania), a BSc degree in Business Management (2001, Babes-Bolyai University of Cluj-Napoca, Romania), and a PhD degree in the Research Field of Machine Tool Ergonomics (2001, Transilvania University of Brasov, Romania). She is a Full Professor and PhD Supervisor at Politehnica University Timisoara, Romania. Her teaching subjects are related to human resources management, ergonomics, occupational health and safety, leadership and sustainability, and knowledge management. Her research field of interest is related to organizational dynamics. She has a great international experience in different Erasmus+ projects (developing innovative learning resources for higher education and vocational training), and she is General Chair of the ErgoWork conferences series (being President of the Romanian Ergonomics and Workplace Management Society, ErgoWork) and Program Co-chair of the International Symposium in Management conferences series. Also, she is a prestigious member of the Romanian Academic Society of Management.

Pham Duc Chính is a Lecturer at the University of Economics and Law of Vietnam National University. His major and main research interests are human resources management.

Viet Chi Duong is an undergraduate student at University of Economics Ho Chi Minh City, Vietnam. He has achieved two prizes in research competition namely "UEH Youth Researcher 2023" and KQM-AR 2023, respectively, at his university and an accepted paper in Second International Congress on Blue and Gray Collar Workers hosted by Warsaw University of Life Sciences, Management Institute Warsaw, Poland. His main research field focuses on marketing management, international business, and technology innovation.

Quang-An Ha is currently a Full-time Lecturer at the University of Economics Ho Chi Minh City. He received a PhD in Business Administration from the College of Management, National Cheng Kung University, Taiwan. His researches are published in *Behaviour and Information Technology*, *Computers in Human Behaviour*, *International Journal of Human–Computer Interaction*, *Journal of Global Information Technology Management*, *International Journal of Mobile Communications*, and several outstanding international conference proceedings such as Decision Science Institute (DSI), Pacific Asia Conference on Information Systems (PACIS). His research interests include knowledge management, organizational performance, social commerce, and human–computer interaction.

Nevin Kılıç is an Assistant Professor of the Department of Psychology at Fatih Sultan Mehmet Foundation University. After graduating from Middle East Technical University, Psychology, she completed her Master's degree at the same university at Social Psychology Graduate Program and Doctorate degree at Marmara University, Department of Organizational Behavior. She has worked as a Psychologist at Traffic Foundation and specialized in the traffic psychology area. She specialized in driver selection and evaluation. At the same time, she carried out training and awareness programs on traffic safety and the development of safe driver attitudes and behaviors in the traffic and transportation sector. She works as Vice President and Lecturer in the Department of Psychology at Fatih Sultan Mehmet Foundation University and gives Social Psychology, Social Gender, Environmental Psychology, and Industrial-Organizational Psychology courses. Employee well-being, employee health and safety, environmental sustainability, behavioral safety, and attitudes and behaviors related to traffic are her main interests.

Vi Thai Huyen Kim is a student majoring in International Business at University of Economics Ho Chi Minh City, Vietnam. With main research interest in international business management and marketing strategies, she has a research paper that won an award in the KQM-AR 2023 competition at her university and an accepted paper at the Second International Congress of Blue and Gray Collar Workers organized by Warsaw University of Life Sciences, Management Institute Warsaw, Poland.

Y Nhu Nguyen Luu is a student majoring in Marketing at Ho Chi Minh City University of Economics (UEH), Vietnam. She has participated in many research articles related to consumer behavior and marketing strategies for businesses. Among them, one research paper won an award in the KQM-AR 2023 competition at UEH and one accepted paper at the Second International Congress of Blue and Gray Collar Workers organized by Warsaw University of Life Sciences, Management Institute Warsaw, Poland.

Ma Thi Ngan is a Lecturer at the Thai Nguyen University of Economic and Technology, Vietnam. Her major and main research interests are research methods in educational studies.

Małgorzata Wiktoria Paprocka graduated in Philosophy and Finance and Banking. Currently, she is continuing her studies at the Doctoral School of WULS in Warsaw in the discipline of Economics and Finance. She is professionally involved in banking since 2019, in the area of Environmental, Social and Governance (ESG) risk and sustainable finance. She is interested in business ethics, sustainable development, sustainable finances, and new technologies. She is privately fascinated by wildlife and photography and documentary film.

Roxana Mihaela Sirbu is PhD Assistant at Politehnica University of Timisoara, Romania, and Manager of the Structural Fund Projects Office. She has a PhD in the field of green investments from the same university (2021). She recently finalized a postdoc program at the "1 Decembrie 1918" University, Alba Iulia, Romania, developing studies on the sustainability of companies based on the analysis of environmental aspects presented in nonfinancial statements under the supervision of Prof. Attila Tamas-Szora.

Elif Sungur is an Assistant Professor of the Department of Public Relations and Publicity at İstanbul Maltepe University, also Vice Dean of Communication Faculty. Graduated from the Department of Journalism and Public Relations Faculty of Communication at Istanbul University (BA), she completed the MBA program of Istanbul University, Institute of Business Administration. She completed her Doctorate degree at Maltepe University, Department of Business Administration. She has worked as training manager in the hotel and consultancy sectors. Her academic and professional scope of interest consists of corporate social responsibility, organizational communication, and health and safety culture in organizations. She conducted and participated in several projects and also designed and developed training contents in the area of health and safety culture communication, behavioral-based safety for companies, nongovernmental organizations, and government. She is giving lectures on corporate communication, management and organization, human resources management, etc. She is a member of TAOM-Turkish Academy of Management Association.

Yen Nguyen Thi is a Lecturer at the University of Economics and Law of Vietnam National University. Her major is International Business, and her main research interests are human resources management, corporate social responsibility, and consumer behavior.

Çiğdem Vatansever after graduating from Boğaziçi University, Department of Psychology, she completed her Master's and Doctorate degrees at Marmara University, Department of Organizational Behavior. She has worked as HR manager and specialized in recruitment, training development, and internal communication in the banking, food, and consultancy sectors. She works as a Professor at the Labor Economics and Industrial Relations Department in Namık Kemal University of Türkiye. She serves as Coordinator for FEAS University–Industry Collaboration and also develops social innovation projects through the university's R&D and technology development zone. People and culture management, employee health and safety, work and non-work life balance, social sustainability, and leadership development are her main interest areas.

FOREWORD BY IRENEUSZ DĄBROWSKI

In an era of unprecedented technological advances and rapidly changing economic landscapes, organizations face many challenges and opportunities. In this dynamic context, *Future Workscapes: Emerging Business Trends and Innovations* provides a timely and insightful exploration of the trends shaping the future of business. This volume is a testament to the collaborative efforts of leading scholars and practitioners who delve deeply into the nuances of contemporary business practices and strategies.

The first section, "Emerging Business Trends," sets the stage with a compelling examination of the latest developments in the business world. It begins with an insightful analysis of spiritual brand attributes and their influence on consumer purchase intentions. Subsequent chapters offer a detailed study of the factors influencing career commitment among civil servants in Vietnam and an exploration of the impact of work motivation on efficiency and satisfaction in the software industry. In addition, a critical analysis of strategic management schools argues for a more inclusive approach by integrating non-managerial employees into management theories.

The second section, "Innovations and Business Practices," shifts the focus to practical strategies and innovative approaches that companies can adopt to maintain their competitive edge. This section includes an in-depth examination of environmental, social, and governance disclosures in the Romanian packaging sector, highlighting the importance of transparency and accountability. It also addresses the controversial issue of the impact of digitalization on trade union density in Organisation for Economic Co-operation and Development (OECD) countries, providing critical insights into how technology and globalization are reshaping labor dynamics. In addition, this book presents a monographic study on the role of internal communication and worker participation in fostering a health and safety climate in organizations. The final chapter highlights the importance of corporate social responsibility in the global food processing industry, emphasizing the need for sustainable and ethical business practices.

This book provides a comprehensive overview of emerging trends and innovative practices, making it a valuable resource for anyone seeking to understand and navigate the future of business. *Future Workscapes: Emerging Business Trends and Innovations* is not just a collection of academic insights; it is a guide for business leaders, policymakers, and academics who want to understand the evolving business landscape. The rigorous research and diverse perspectives presented in this book make it essential reading for those seeking to stay ahead in an increasingly complex and competitive global marketplace.

This book provides forward-looking knowledge based on practical realities. I hope that readers will find it enlightening and inspiring, and that it will serve as a catalyst for continued innovation and strategic growth in their respective fields.

Associate Professor, Dr Ireneusz Dąbrowski
SGH Warsaw School of Economics

FOREWORD BY FATIH ÇETIN

In today's era of rapid digital transformation in the workplace, the book *Future Workscapes: Emerging Business Trends and Innovations* provides valuable views into the future of work, exploring significant changes in a timely manner. This book is a joint effort, leveraging the knowledge of experts from various disciplines and regions. It is divided into two primary sections, each carefully designed to explore essential elements of the business trends and innovative business practices.

The first section investigates current business trends, including spiritual branding, career development, motivation of information technology (IT) professionals, organizational hierarchy, and the dynamics of non-managerial employees. These topics are crucial for understanding how modern businesses operate and thrive in a competitive environment. The discussions in this section offer a nuanced view of the challenges and opportunities that businesses face today. The second section focuses on innovative business practices. It addresses environmental sustainability, social responsibility, digitalization, effective communication, and corporate social responsibility. These practices are increasingly becoming the cornerstone of successful business strategies, as companies recognize the importance of integrating these elements into their core operations. This section not only highlights best practices but also provides practical guidance for implementation.

As the business world continues to evolve, the insights and strategies presented in this book will serve as a valuable resource for scholars, practitioners, and anyone interested in staying ahead in the ever-changing business landscape. The collaborative nature of this work, combined with the expertise of its contributors, ensures that readers will gain a comprehensive understanding of both the current trends and the innovative practices shaping the future of business.

Prof. Dr Fatih Çetin
Baskent University

PREFACE

The world of business is evolving, driven by technological advancements, globalization, and shifting societal expectations. Organizations must stay ahead of emerging trends to thrive in this dynamic environment and continually innovate their practices. With this objective in mind, we present *Future Workscapes: Emerging Business Trends and Innovations*.

This book is a collaborative effort of scholars and experts from diverse fields, offering a comprehensive examination of contemporary business trends and the innovative practices that are shaping the future. The contributors have provided valuable insights into the challenges and opportunities that modern businesses face and how they can strategically navigate this complex landscape.

The first section, "Emerging Business Trends," explores the latest developments and theoretical advancements in the business world. It begins with an in-depth analysis of spiritual branding attributes and their impact on consumer buying intentions. It presents a conceptual model that sets the stage for understanding the nuanced ways consumer behavior evolves. This is followed by a detailed study of the factors affecting the career commitment of public servants in Vietnam, highlighting the perspectives of investment models and the moderation effects of perceived economic conditions. Complementing these discussions is an examination of working motivation and its effects on efficiency and work satisfaction in the software industry. Additionally, there is a critical analysis of strategic management schools, advocating for the inclusion of non-managerial employees in management theories. These discussions provide a robust foundation for rethinking traditional organizational hierarchies and fostering more inclusive management practices.

The second section, "Innovations and Business Practices," focuses on practical strategies and innovative approaches that businesses can adopt to stay competitive. This includes an exploration of environmental, social, and governance disclosure in the packaging sector in Romania, underscoring the growing importance of transparency and accountability. The contentious issue of digitalization's impact on trade union density in OECD countries is tackled, offering critical insights into how globalization and technological advancements are reshaping labor dynamics. This is followed by a monographic study on the role of internal communication and employee participation in creating a health and safety climate within organizations. Finally, the significance of corporate social responsibility in the global food processing industry is discussed, emphasizing the need for businesses to integrate sustainable and ethical practices into their operations.

Immense gratitude is extended to all the contributors for their rigorous research and thought-provoking analyses, which have made this book a valuable resource for academics, practitioners, and policymakers alike. Deep appreciation is also extended to the readers, whose engagement and interest drive the continuous exploration of business innovation and trends.

As you delve into the chapters of *Future Workscapes: Emerging Business Trends and Innovations*, it is hoped that you find inspiration, practical knowledge, and strategic insights to navigate in the rapidly evolving business landscape.

Joanna Paliszkiewicz, Demet Varoğlu, and Olena Kulykovets
Editors

SECTION I
EMERGING BUSINESS TRENDS

CHAPTER 1

SPIRITUAL BRANDING ATTRIBUTES AND CONSUMER BUYING INTENTION: THE PROPOSAL OF CONCEPTUAL MODEL

Ngoc Bich Do, Y Nhu Nguyen Luu,
Vi Thai Huyen Kim and Viet Chi Duong

School of International Business and Marketing, University of Economics Ho Chi Minh City, Vietnam

ABSTRACT

Spirituality serves as an ethical benchmark for shaping human and brand identity. Only a few studies have recently attempted to examine the impact of spiritual attributes on customer behavior. This study extends the current literature and aims to develop a research model to investigate spiritual brand attributes toward customers' behavior. The study employs the stimulus–organism–response (SOR) model as a theoretical signpost to construct the research model. Driven by this chapter, future research opportunities are presented, and the opportunity for empirical research is also illustrated.

Keywords: Spiritual brand attributes; spirituality; SOR theory; purchase intention; brand love

1. INTRODUCTION

Spirituality has been receiving a lot of attention from researchers. Many studies have proven that spirituality has an impact on businesses and markets all over the world (Brownstein, 2008; Fernando & Jackson, 2006; Heintzman, 2003); several studies have been conducted in areas such as tourism (Andriotis, 2009; Cochrane, 2009), cosmetics (Aoun & Tournois, 2015), and banking (Ab Hamid et al., 2019; Setiawan & Sahara, 2022). Notably, the current study highlights the growing popularity of spirituality adoption in branding (Sardana et al., 2018).

The spiritual attribute is closely related to religion, but it is more than just a ritual, as it is deeply ingrained in the faith and belief system (Ab Hamid et al., 2019; Setiawan & Sahara, 2022). The spiritual brand attributes are jointly linked to religion and are embedded in faith and belief systems (Ab Hamid et al., 2019; Setiawan & Sahara, 2022). It indicates that businesses that invest in spirituality can develop a distinctive value proposition and set themselves apart from competitors (Mohamad et al., 2023). Additionally, Pirnazarov (2020) stated that businesses may attract their customers' spiritual ideals to raise community engagement perception or consolidate brand prestige.

Previous studies revealed the core elements of spiritual brand attributes, including ethics, beliefs, and corporate social responsibility (CSR) (Ab Hamid et al., 2019; Aoun & Tournois, 2015). Those factors were positively associated with brand image and behavioral response single-religion focused (Ab Hamid et al., 2023). Yet little attention is drawn to countries in which different cultures coexist. In addition, prior literature suggested that brand love and trust are vital determinants of the purchase behavior of consumers (Aydin et al., 2014; Eagly & Chaiken, 1993; Grewal et al., 1998; Sanny et al., 2020). However, the relationship between spiritual brand attributes and those affective states of brand love and trust still needs further examination.

Therefore, to close the aforementioned gaps, this research aims to suggest a model that investigates the influence of spiritual brand attributes on brand love, trust, and purchase intention. The rest of this chapter is organized into three parts as follows: First, the theoretical background is presented. Second, the literature review and research model are elaborated. Finally, the conclusion and future research are shown.

2. THEORETICAL BACKGROUND

2.1. Spiritual Brands

Deepak Sardana (2018) defined spiritual brands as brands promoted by spiritual leaders, emphasizing the role of spiritual leaders in promoting brands. For example, in Indian culture, spiritual leaders have played an impeccable role and play a vital role in bridging the gap between consumers and spiritualism (Bhatia & Rathore, 2020). Meanwhile, in the study of Gnanakumar (2020), spiritual brands are referred to as brands inspired by faith, assuming that spiritual foundations give rise to these brands. In the realm of Islamic culture, research has proposed the concept of spiritual brand attributes (Aoun & Tournois, 2015; Mourad &

El Karanshawy, 2013), which can be interpreted as the connection of the brand with an individual's system of beliefs or religion (Aoun & Tournois, 2015). In the study of Gad and Nicholas (2003), brand's spiritual dimension suggests the perception of the social responsibility of the higher education institute and its role in upgrading and enhancing the society.

Overall, it can be inferred that spiritual brands encompass a spectrum of meanings, ranging from those associated with spiritual leaders to brands inspired by faith and aligned with personal beliefs or social responsibility. In the scope of this research, since we focus on the integration of spiritual attributes into the branding approach, thus spiritual brands could be understood as brands whose attributes go beyond the functional and emotional, offering insights into a spiritual dimension, reflecting the holistic attributes and the brand's worldview stemming from a belief system (Aoun & Tournois, 2015).

2.2. Impact of Spiritual Brands

Previous literature has validated that spirituality and religion contribute to establishing trust and impact consumer purchasing decisions. In marketing academia, brands created by spiritual foundations that are faith based are given immense significance and appreciation (Einstein, 2007). In India, spiritual brands focus on CSR activities like building schools, donations and charity, blood donation camps, etc. to create a better public image. Through these actions, they have established themselves in the market as dependable, trusted, secure, eco-friendly, ayurvedic, and economical. Consequently, consumers previously dedicated to foreign brands are shifting toward spiritual brands like Patanjali, Sri Tattva, Isha Shoppe, etc., as they feel a stronger connection to their culture and nation. The marketing of products through spiritual leaders and their connection with consumers makes it easy for them to tap the market (Kumar et al., 2016). Some luxury brands have incorporated spirituality into their brand identity by using spiritual symbols in their designs. Vetements released a range of star sign tees and raincoats, catering to the growing interest in astrology and spiritual practices, while Christian Dior showed zodiac motifs in their design to appeal to youngsters.

Consumers regard spiritual brands or faith-marketed products as a means to articulate their beliefs, while sellers regard these products, along with their religious practices, as a vehicle for promoting their religion (Rathore & Bhatia, 2020). The more spiritual an individual consumer is, the more likely that consumer is to be ethically predisposed (Vitell et al., 2016). Adoption of spiritual marketing activities can elevate the emotional engagement of customers. This, in turn, fosters the relationship between the company and its customers, creating a deep connection that can lead to brand love (Al-Hadrawi et al., 2022).

2.3. Previous Studies of Spiritual Brands

Many researchers have enriched the field of spirituality in consumerism. For example, Sardana et al. (2018) explored consumer preference for spiritual brands by discovering that spirituality does not impact purchasing spiritual brands. Still, intrinsic and extrinsic religiosities are what lead to the buying decision.

Moreover, when choosing such products/services, consumers consider the product's functional aspect, price, and social, cognitive, and affective factors (Ladhari & Tchetgna, 2017). However, Sardana et al.'s (2018) study can only be interpreted and understood in the social context of India, where spiritual leaders (such as Baba Ramdev and Sri Ravishankar) promoting their self-branded products have essentially called themselves "spiritual gurus" yet their primary disposition is religious. Another study in this field stated that normative community pressure is another vital purchase driver (Sardana et al., 2021); aligning with societal norms often influences an individual's choices and behavior (Ajzen, 2005). When it comes to Islamic banks, which are differentiated from conventional banks in terms of spiritual dimensions, ethics, CSR, and beliefs, they are variables that define corporate brand image in customers' perceptions, leading to brand loyalty. In tourism, spiritual experiences enhance the positive effect of religious travel benefits through the brand image (Shirmohammadi & Abyaran, 2019).

While previous research has primarily examined spirituality from a religious perspective, marketing scholars are now exploring how individuals interact with spiritual products, services, and locations. Yet, only a few studies have been found to incorporate the spiritual dimension into branding strategies (El-Amir & Burt, 2010). Moreover, a comprehensive review of the literature indicates that despite several studies on the SOR model in branding approach, its application in the context of spiritual branding, in particular, is limited. We propose to fill this gap by applying the SOR theory model and reading the spirituality aspect applied to branding, with a comprehensive outlook of integrating spiritual attributes into Fast Moving Consumer Goods (FMCG) brands and how they interact with customers' attitudes and behavioral intentions.

3. SOR THEORY

The SOR theory, suggested by Mehrabian and Russell (1974), provides a theoretical framework for understanding consumer behavior responses. According to the theory, the external environment and factors act as stimuli that will evoke cognitive or emotional states in the individual, which, in turn, ultimately lead to specific behavioral outcomes (Wang et al., 2023). Specifically, the first part of the SOR framework, stimulus (S), derives from outer variables, including sense modality variables and information rate or load (Mehrabian & Russell, 1974). In the second part of the SOR model, the organism component represents individuals' emotional reactions to an environmental stimulus. These emotions change with different intensities, degrees of pleasure, or activation (Russell & Pratt, 1980) or even in specific cases (Russell & Barrett, 1999).

Researchers have started to employ the SOR framework to explain consumer behavior. In advertising, Moon et al. (2017) used the SOR model to elucidate the mediation role of eco-labeling as an environmental stimulus that leads to confusion and results in customers' negative Word of mouth (WOM). Regarding branding, drawing on the SOR model, Kamboj et al. (2018) examined branding co-creation in brand communities on social media. In their study, Anisimova et al.

(2019) applied the SOR model to investigate the mediating effects of controlled and uncontrolled communications of corporate brand perceptions on consumer satisfaction and loyalty.

A thorough examination of existing literature reveals that despite numerous studies on the SOR model in the context of branding, its application in the realm of spiritual branding is limited. Based on the assessment of prior research, we assert that the SOR model serves as the most suitable theoretical framework for our investigation for two primary reasons. First, it presents a conceptual framework for exploring the consumer decision-making process when it comes to purchasing spiritual brands. Second, by employing the model, what external attributes trigger those spiritual brands' buying decisions can be defined.

4. RESEARCH MODEL PROPOSAL

The proposed research model inherits from previous theoretical models and research, including the SOR theory model of Mehrabian and Russel (1974). The SOR theory demonstrates that external environmental cues act as a stimulus (S) that can trigger individuals' internal cognitive and emotional organism (O), thereby inspiring their behavioral responses (R) (Mehrabian & Russell, 1974).

This study identifies spiritual brand attributes as an innovative and emerging form of corporate brand image (Ab Hamid et al., 2019). Hence, three factors, including ethics, belief, and CSR, belong to Block S. These elements remain within the brand and constitute components of the consumer's external environment. It comes from the internal core values of the brand and reflects the business's image before customers; thus, these elements belong to stimuli.

Brand love and trust express users' affective outcomes toward the brand; therefore, they will be categorized in the organism cluster. Finally, the intention is the sign showing the customer's response, which will be in the response cluster. Fig. 1.1 illustrates the proposed research model.

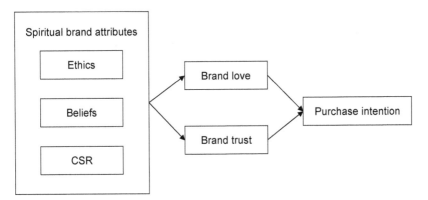

Fig. 1.1. Proposed Conceptual Model. *Source*: Research team's proposal.

4.1. Cluster 1: Spiritual Brand Attributes

Three factors included in spiritual brand attributes are beliefs, ethics, and CSR.

First, theoretically, the characteristics of institutions' religious beliefs are said to illustrate the corporate brand image (Aoun & Tournois, 2015). Hence, beliefs refer to the business practices or product lines that align with the religious beliefs of the target customer, making them religiously correct (Aoun & Tournois, 2015). Beliefs can also be linked to a sense of presence or connectedness with the creator' norms and rules, influencing customers' perceptions of the brand (Dasti & Sitwat, 2014; Yousef et al., 2021). In other words, it could be argued that religiously correct products and services that align with an individual's well-being in the world and the hereafter contribute significantly to the brand's image (Moberg, 1984).

Second, ethics is one of the critical determinants of corporate brand image, sometimes related to God-consciousness (Osman-Gani et al., 2010). Ethics refers to "the science of conduct," which deals with two opposing moral questions such as good or bad, right or wrong, and virtues or vice. It involves moral practices and is defined as ethical values and moral ailments or ills (Dasti & Sitwat, 2014). This study defines ethics as a brand's conduct or actions consistent with societal moral values. As a result, any decision regarding financing, operation, production, or investment must consider the impact on society (Mansour et al., 2015). From that point of view, to reflect brand ethical virtues such as justice, transparency, and honesty, their products are also expected to reflect through the quality of the product, the way they produce, and the consequences afterward.

Finally, the concept of CSR was first introduced in the 1950s by an American economist concerned with a corporation's goodwill producing a positive and productive impact on stakeholders (Jusoh & Ibrahim, 2018). In the context of FMCG, we evaluate CSR's brand based on four responsibilities toward the society that corporations could fulfill, including economic, legal, ethical, and discretionary or philanthropic (Carroll, 2000). CSR generally requires businesses to go beyond profit maximization by incorporating corporate activities such as sound environmental practices, philanthropic contributions, socially responsible programs, and occupational safety (Dusuki, 2008).

4.2. Cluster 2: Organism – Brand Love and Brand Trust

Brand love is defined as a satisfied customer's enthusiasm and emotional attachment to a specific brand name (Carroll & Ahuvia, 2006). Brand love is more than just fondness or liking; it is the brand a customer chooses for a specific reason (Maxian et al., 2013). It is clear that brand love is more intense than simple liking and results from a strong emotional connection (Ahuvia, 2005; Bazi et al., 2023). In a seminal article on brand love, Batra et al. (2012) defined the following components: self-brand integration, attitude valence and strength, positive emotional connection, anticipated separation distress, long-term relationship, and passion-driven behavior.

According to Arjun and Holbrook (2001), brand trust is a consumer's willingness to trust their initiative and the product that the brand provides. Trust is a belief, so there is a possibility that it will lead to a positive outcome, but at the same time, a negative outcome is also not denied (Worchel, 1979). However, brand trust can reduce the consumer's uncertainty because the consumer knows that the brand can be worth trusting and believes that a dependable, safe, and honest consumption scenario is the vital link of brand trust (Flavián et al., 2006).

In the FMCG sector, consumers perceive more significant risk in usage than in other frequently purchased items, and it is emphasized that consumers will rely on the brand image, which is built on spiritual attributes, as part of a risk reduction process to manifest higher brand trust. Previous studies suggest that brand love is largely determined by parasocial interaction, a perceived relationship between an individual and a subject that creates the illusion of a two-way relationship (Zhang et al., 2020). Thus, in the FMCG context, spiritual brand attributes (ethics, beliefs, and CSR) that improve corporate brand image through various social interaction ways of businesses, such as quality, charity work, and religious advocacy of business contribute to brand loyalty.

4.3. Cluster 3: Response – Purchase Decision

Purchase intention can be defined as "what consumers think they will buy." Halim and Hamed (2005) explain purchase intention as the number of patrons that have a proposal to buy the products in the future, make repeat purchases, and contact again to the specific product. Purchase intention is positively influenced by some independent variables such as brand image, product quality, product knowledge, product involvement, product attributes, brand loyalty, etc. In this study, purchase intention is defined as the readiness of consumers to purchase spiritual attributes and products belonging to ethical brands.

Previous research (Kim & Ko, 2012; Kumar et al., 2021; Martín-Consuegra et al., 2018; Navaneethakrishnan & Sathish, 2020; Verma, 2021) found a strong correlation between purchase intention and brand or product attitudes and preferences. There was a relationship between brand trust and purchase intention, implying that if brand trust grows, so will the rate of purchase intention (Aydin et al., 2014; Dam, 2020; Sanny et al., 2020). Hence, we suppose that purchase intention is largely associated with brand trust, love, and positive relationships.

5. CONCLUSION

The study was conducted to understand the impact of spiritual brand attributes on purchase intention for ethical and unethical brands. From the SOR theory, we have built a research model examining the effect of spiritual brands on consumer's cognitive behavior.

Future studies can further develop from the current conceptual model by including further research on the impact of spiritual brand attributes on other factors such as customer delight, positive brand referral, etc. In addition, future studies can also carry out empirical studies on a larger scale or in other countries and with other religions.

ACKNOWLEDGEMENT

This research is fully funded by the University of Economics Ho Chi Minh City (UEH) under grant number 2024-10-01-2581; University of Economics Ho Chi Minh City.

REFERENCES

Ab Hamid, S. N., Maulan, S., & Wan Jusoh, W. J. (2023). Brand attributes, corporate brand image and customer loyalty of Islamic banks in Malaysia. *Journal of Islamic Marketing*, *14*(10), 2404–2428.

Ab Hamid, S. N., Wan Jusoh, W. J., Maulan, S., & Taib, C. A. (2019). Measuring the spiritual brand attribute of Islamic banks. *Journal of Business Management and Accounting (JBMA)*, *9*(2), 51–70.

Ahuvia, A. C. (2005). Beyond the extended self: Loved objects and consumers' identity narratives. *Journal of Consumer Research*, *32*(1), 171–184.

Ajzen, I. (2005). *EBOOK: Attitudes, personality and behaviour*. McGraw-Hill Education.

Al-Hadrawi, B. K., Al-Surf, A. R., & Hussein, H. G. (2022). Spiritual marketing and brand love: A study in Noor Al-Kafeel Corporation for animal and food products. *Webology (ISSN: 1735-188X)*, *19*(6), 446.

Andriotis, K. (2009). Sacred site experience: A phenomenological study. *Annals of Tourism Research*, *36*(1), 64–84.

Anisimova, T., Weiss, J., & Mavondo, F. (2019). The influence of corporate brand perceptions on consumer satisfaction and loyalty via controlled and uncontrolled communications: A multiple mediation analysis. *Journal of Consumer Marketing*, *36*(1), 33–49.

Aoun, I., & Tournois, L. (2015). Building holistic brands: An exploratory study of Halal cosmetics. *Journal of Islamic Marketing*, *6*(1), 109–132.

Arjun, C., & Holbrook, M. B. (2001). The chain of effects from brand trust and brand affect to brand performance: The role of brand loyalty. *Journal of Marketing*, *65*, 81–93.

Aydın, G., Ar, A. A., & Taşkın, Ç. (2014). The role of brand trust on parents' purchase intentions of baby-care products. *Doğuş Üniversitesi Dergisi*, *15*(2), 165–180.

Batra, R., Ahuvia, A., & Bagozzi, R. P. (2012). Brand love. *Journal of Marketing*, *76*(2), 1–16.

Bazi, S., Filieri, R., & Gorton, M. (2023). Social media content aesthetic quality and customer engagement: The mediating role of entertainment and impacts on brand love and loyalty. *Journal of Business Research*, *160*, 113778.

Bhatia, A., & Rathore, A. (2020). Brands inspired by spiritual leaders: Exploring Indian FMCG market and new age consumers. *International Journal on Emerging Technologies*, *11*(3), 759–764.

Brownstein, B. (2008). Profitability and spiritual wisdom: A tale of two companies. *Business Renaissance Quarterly*, *3*(3), 137–138.

Carroll, A. B. (2000). Ethical challenges for business in the new millennium: Corporate social responsibility and models of management morality. *Business Ethics Quarterly*, *10*(1), 33–42.

Carroll, B. A., & Ahuvia, A. C. (2006). Some antecedents and outcomes of brand love. *Marketing Letters*, *17*(2), 79–89.

Cochrane, J. (2009). Spirits, nature and pilgrimage: The "other" dimension in Javanese domestic tourism. *Journal of Management, Spirituality & Religion*, *6*(2), 107–119.

Dam, T. C. (2020). Influence of brand trust, perceived value on brand preference and purchase intention. *The Journal of Asian Finance, Economics and Business (JAFEB)*, *7*(10), 939–947.

Dasti, R., & Sitwat, A. (2014). Development of a multidimensional measure of Islamic spirituality (MMIS). *Journal of Muslim Mental Health*, *8*(2), 137–144.

Dusuki, A. W. (2008). What does Islam say about corporate social responsibility. *Review of Islamic Economics*, *12*(1), 5–28.

Eagly, A. H., & Chaiken, S. (1993). *The psychology of attitudes*. Harcourt Brace College Publishers.

Einstein, M. (2007). *Brands of faith: Marketing religion in a commercial age*. Routledge.

El-Amir, A., & Burt, S. (2010). A critical account of the process of branding: Towards a synthesis. *The Marketing Review, 10*(1), 69–86.

Fernando, M., & Jackson, B. (2006). The influence of religion-based workplace spirituality on business leaders' decision-making: An inter-faith study. *Journal of Management & Organization, 12*(1), 23–39.

Flavián, C., Guinalíu, M., & Gurrea, R. (2006). The role played by perceived usability, satisfaction and consumer trust on website loyalty. *Information & Management, 43*(1), 1–14.

Gad, T., & Nicholas, I. (2003). Leadership branding. In Nicholas Ind. (Ed.), *Beyond branding: How the new values of transparency and integrity are changing the world of brands* (pp. 183–198). Kogan Page.

Gnanakumar, B. (2020). Reinforcement of brands of faith with the paradox of cultural divergence in Indian perspective. *European Business Review, 32*(3), 513–530.

Grewal, D., Krishnan, R., Baker, J., & Borin, N. (1998). The effect of store name, brand name and price discounts on consumers' evaluations and purchase intentions. *Journal of Retailing, 74*(3), 331–352.

Halim, W. Z. W., & Hamed, A. B. (2005). *Consumer purchase intention at traditional restaurant and fast food restaurant.* Consumer Behavior.

Heintzman, P. (2003). The wilderness experience and spirituality: What recent research tells us. *Journal of Physical Education, Recreation & Dance, 74*(6), 27.

Jusoh, W. N. H. W., & Ibrahim, U. (2018). *Corporate social responsibility of Islamic banks in Malaysia: Arising issues.* SSRN.

Kamboj, S., Sarmah, B., Gupta, S., & Dwivedi, Y. (2018). Examining branding co-creation in brand communities on social media: Applying the paradigm of stimulus-organism-response. *International Journal of Information Management, 39*, 169–185.

Kim, A. J., & Ko, E. (2012). Do social media marketing activities enhance customer equity? An empirical study of luxury fashion brand. *Journal of Business Research, 65*(10), 1480–1486.

Kumar, S., Murphy, M., Talwar, S., Kaur, P., & Dhir, A. (2021). What drives brand love and purchase intentions toward the local food distribution system? A study of social media-based REKO (fair consumption) groups. *Journal of Retailing and Consumer Services, 60*, 102444.

Kumar Mishra, M., Kesharwani, A., & Das, D. (2016). The relationship between risk aversion, brand trust, brand affect and loyalty: Evidence from the FMCG industry. *Journal of Indian Business Research, 8*(2), 78–97.

Ladhari, R., & Tchetgna, N. M. (2017). Values, socially conscious behaviour and consumption emotions as predictors of Canadians' intent to buy fair trade products. *International Journal of Consumer Studies, 41*(6), 696–705.

Mansour, W., Ben Jedidia, K., & Majdoub, J. (2015). How ethical is Islamic banking in the light of the objectives of Islamic law? *Journal of Religious Ethics, 43*(1), 51–77.

Martín-Consuegra, D., Faraoni, M., Díaz, E., & Ranfagni, S. (2018). Exploring relationships among brand credibility, purchase intention and social media for fashion brands: A conditional mediation model. *Journal of Global Fashion Marketing, 9*(3), 237–251.

Maxian, W., Bradley, S. D., Wise, W., & Toulouse, E. N. (2013). Brand love is in the heart: Physiological responding to advertised brands. *Psychology & Marketing, 30*(6), 469–478.

Mehrabian, A., & Russell, J. A. (1974). *An approach to environmental psychology.* The MIT Press.

Moberg, D. O. (1984). Subjective measures of spiritual well-being. *Review of Religious Research, 25*(4), 351–364.

Mohamad, V., Abdul, S. A., Putit, L., Osman, A. A., & Dwita, V. (2023). The success factor of spirituality towards customer satisfaction. *International Journal of Entrepreneurship and Management Practices, 6*(21), 20–45.

Moon, S. J., Costello, J. P., & Koo, D. M. (2017). The impact of consumer confusion from eco-labels on negative WOM, distrust, and dissatisfaction. *International Journal of Advertising, 36*(2), 246–271.

Mourad, M., & El Karanshawy, H. (2013). Branding Islamic studies: Exploratory study in the Middle East. *Journal of Islamic Marketing, 4*(2), 150–162.

Navaneethakrishnan, K., & Sathish, A. S. (2020). It's all about brand love-expressing through purchase intention, brand trust and brand attitude. *Journal of Critical Reviews, 7*(4), 313–318.

Osman-Gani, A. M., Hashim, J., & Ismail, Y. (2010, November). Effects of religiosity, spirituality, and personal values on employee performance: A conceptual analysis. In M. Osman-Gani (Ed.), *9th international conference of the academy of HRD (Asia chapter)* (pp. 11–14). Academy of Human Resource Development (AHRD), in collaboration with East China Normal University.

Pirnazarov, N. (2020). Philosophical analysis of the issue of spirituality. *International Journal of Advanced Science and Technology*, *29*(5), 1630–1632.

Rathore, A., & Bhatia, A. (2020). Evaluating success factors of spiritual brands inspired by faith: Customer satisfaction and brand loyalty. *International Journal of Advanced Science and Technology*, *29*(11s), 1154–1164.

Russell, J. A., & Barrett, L. F. (1999). Core affect, prototypical emotional episodes, and other things called emotion: Dissecting the elephant. *Journal of Personality and Social Psychology*, *76*(5), 805.

Russell, J. A., & Pratt, G. (1980). A description of the affective quality attributed to environments. *Journal of Personality and Social Psychology*, *38*(2), 311.

Sanny, L., Arina, A. N., Maulidya, R. T., & Pertiwi, R. P. (2020). Purchase intention on Indonesia male's skin care by social media marketing effect towards brand image and brand trust. *Management Science Letters*, *10*, 2139–2146.

Sardana, D., Cavusgil, E., & Gupta, N. (2021). The growing popularity of spiritual brands: what drives purchase intent?. *International Business Review*, *30*(4), 101777.

Sardana, D., Gupta, N., & Sharma, P. (2018). Spirituality and religiosity at the junction of consumerism: Exploring consumer preference for spiritual brands. *International Journal of Consumer Studies*, *42*(6), 724–735.

Setiawan, D., & Sahara, M. A. (2022). The effect of ethical values on Islamic banking performance. *Corporate and Business Strategy Review*, *3*(2), 34–42.

Shirmohammadi, Y., & Abyaran, P. (2019). The influence of spiritual experience on the brand of religious place. *International Journal of Tourism, Culture & Spirituality*, *4*(1), 33–55.

Verma, P. (2021). The effect of brand engagement and brand love upon overall brand equity and purchase intention: A moderated–mediated model. *Journal of Promotion Management*, *27*(1), 103–132.

Vitell, S. J., King, R. A., Howie, K., Toti, J. F., Albert, L., Hidalgo, E. R., & Yacout, O. (2016). Spirituality, moral identity, and consumer ethics: A multi-cultural study. *Journal of Business Ethics*, *139*, 147–160.

Wang, Y., Zhang, W., & Chu, J. (2023). What drives citizen's participate intention in smart city? An empirical study based on stimulus-organism-response (SOR) theory. *Journal of the Knowledge Economy*, 1–23.

Worchel, P. (1979). Trust and distrust. In W. G. Austin & S. Worchel (Eds.), *Social psychology of intergroup relations* (pp. 174–187). Broks/Cole.

Yousef, W., Foroudi, P., Hussain, S., Yousef, N., Melewar, T. C., & Dennis, C. (2021). Impact of the strength of religious beliefs on brand love in the Islamic market. *Corporate Reputation Review*, *25*, 1–18.

Zhang, H., Xu, H., & Gursoy, D. (2020). The effect of celebrity endorsement on destination brand love: A comparison of previous visitors and potential tourists. *Journal of Destination Marketing & Management*, *17*, 100454.

CHAPTER 2

FACTORS AFFECTING CAREER COMMITMENT OF PUBLIC SERVANTS IN VIETNAM: PERSPECTIVES OF INVESTMENT MODEL AND MODERATION EFFECTS OF PERCEIVED ECONOMIC CONDITIONS

Quang-An Ha

School of International Business and Marketing, University of Economics Ho Chi Minh City, Vietnam

ABSTRACT

This study proposes the factors influencing career commitment among public servants in Vietnam. By applying perspectives of the investment model with the moderating effects of perceived economic conditions, this study suggests that commitment to a career of public servants depends on career satisfaction, career alternatives, career investment, and professional self-efficacy. Additionally, the study proposes that perceived economic conditions moderate the relationships between these factors and career commitment. As economic instability may influence job satisfaction, turnover intentions, and investment decisions, understanding its interaction with career dynamics is crucial for public sector management. Overall, this study contributes to a better understanding of the complexities of career commitment among Vietnamese public servants and provides policymakers with more insights on how to improve employee commitment.

Keywords: Career commitment; career alternatives; career investment; career satisfaction; perceived economic conditions; public servants

1. INTRODUCTION

Public servants play an important role in the government's activities (Eldor, 2018; Gruening, 2001; Hodgkinson et al., 2018; Osborne, 2006). From the healthcare workers to an apolitical public official who is in charge of implementing the government's programs and policies, it is inevitable that the roles played by civil servants in the modern community have been diversified along with the development of the society (Bason, 2017; Hood, 2000; Peters, 2010; Sabharwal et al., 2014).

The roles of modern public servants have been highlighted in the two popular public management theories which explain how the governments operationalize to deliver the best services to their people (Young et al., 2020). The New Public Management (NPM) theory (Gruening, 2001), while focusing on the outcome of the service with an intra-organizational perspective, strongly believes in the efficiency of competition between independent individuals within a public organization. According to NPM, the public servants are approached to be more customer centric and sensitive to the performance. The New Public Governance (NPG) theory, which appeared after the NPM framework, on the other hand, emphasizes both the process and the outcome of the service (Osborne, 2006) with an inter-organizational point of view. According to NPG, the roles of the public servants are described to be more complex with the collaboration across the working units. The public servants, therefore, are required to obtain more soft skills related to effective communication, critical and analytical thinking, co-production expertise in working with citizens and international collaboration as well (Dickinson, 2016).

Either NPM or NPG, the research around these frameworks indicates the same idea that service quality significantly influences the satisfaction of citizen with public services (Andrews & Van de Walle, 2013; Ashill et al., 2008; Howlett et al., 2017; Kakouris & Meliou, 2011; Osborne et al., 2013). The work performance of public servants therefore simultaneously creates the public service's image and promotes trust to citizens (Eldor, 2018). Career commitment is especially important to employees because it associates with their work performance (Aryee & Tan, 1992). People who are committed to their careers are found to have less turnover intention to leave their workplaces (Lin, 2020) and more likely to overcome the obstacles to pursue the established career goals (Colarelli & Bishop, 1990). Research by Fu and Chen (2015) defined career commitment as "the degree to which someone identifies with and values his or her profession or vocation." According to this definition, the term career commitment seems to be relevant with professional identities and benefits that motivate people to work. Factors influence career commitment of a worker in general are organizational commitment, career satisfaction, organizational support and work difficulties (Aryee & Tan, 1992), locus of control, career socialization, role states, career benefit (Jones et al., 2006), career identity, and work-to-personal life fulfillment (Cicek et al., 2016). However, only few previous studies have examined the career commitment of public servants in the influence of bad economic conditions. Therefore, the purpose of this study is to investigate the impacts of career satisfaction, alternatives of current career, perceived economic conditions, and professional self-efficacy on career commitment of public servants in Vietnam.

2. LITERATURE REVIEW

2.1. Career Commitment

Career commitment relates to how much occupational experiences an individual is aiming to achieve because it has connection with career development (Aryee & Tan, 1992) and salary levels (Ballout, 2009) in a particular profession. In the career commitment literature, this concept is examined as having three subconcepts including career identity, career resilience, and career planning (Carson & Bedeian, 1994; Hartmann et al., 2020; Singh et al., 2018). Career resilience measures the level of constant willingness a worker has when facing vocational difficulties. Career identity represents the affective commitment or emotional attachment of an employee to work in an organization. The other dimension of career commitment is career planning which explains how the workers plan for the future when developing a set of required skills to match with their career goals (Arora & Rangnekar, 2016b; Carson & Bedeian, 1994; Steffy & Jones, 1988; Wilson et al., 2016).

Research suggested that career commitment has a positive relation with organizational commitment (Major et al., 2013), job involvement (Huang et al., 2019; Kasemsap, 2013), and professional identity (Arora & Rangnekar, 2016a) and, therefore, increases the chance for career success. However, so far, no research found in the occupational commitment databases investigated the influence of political aspects on career commitment of public servants and its influence in the relationship between professional investment and one's career commitment in the public sector.

2.2. Investment Model Theory

The investment model was originally built by Rusbult (1980). The investment theory has an underlying assumption that in a relationship, individuals are motivated to act based upon their expected rewards (for example, happiness) and costs (for example, time and effort). The investment model also postulates that people decide to stay or to leave their partners mainly depending on their own commitment to the relationship. The commitment would increase over time as the amount of resources invested in that relationship increases. The theory helps to predict that people with high investment volume and high relational affective satisfaction will be more committed. Empirical studies in different scientific aspects have tested and supported this theory (Etcheverry et al., 2013; Fu, 2011; Fu & Chen, 2015; Lehtman & Zeigler-Hill, 2020; Paul & Seward, 2016; Wieselquist, 2009).

According to the theory, the interdependence feature of a relationship is characterized by focal elements: dependence and satisfaction (Rusbult et al., 1998). Dependence is the state of relying on a particular romantic partner for affection or support (the value), which they cannot be contented in other relationships (Andaleeb, 1996; Tan et al., 2018). Satisfaction is the result from the personal evaluation of benefits people can gain and expected costs they need to invest in the relationship. People feel satisfied when the benefit exceeds the cost (Rusbult, 1980; Rusbult et al., 1994). The appearance of an attractive alternative might influence the stability (both satisfaction and dependence) of the relationship because people see potential beneficial investment elsewhere (Farrell & Rusbult, 1992; Pollack et al., 2015).

The concept investment in the investment model refers to the assets or resources that people has placed in a relationship (Farrell & Rusbult, 1992; Sternberg & Lubart, 1991). The investment serves as a psychological stimulation to commitment because the act of investment involves the feeling of attachment, therefore increasing the costs of leaving a relationship (Akkermans et al., 2019; Caryl, 2011; den Boer et al., 2019).

As we can see, the theory was initially developed to explain the phenomenon related to interpersonal relationship (Rusbult, 1980; Rusbult et al., 1986); it is possible that this theory can be applicable for the organizational working environment (Akkermans et al., 2019; den Boer et al., 2019; Fu, 2011; Fu & Chen, 2015). Therefore, if the investment model can explain the situation when a person chooses to remain in an unhealthy relationship, it may also provide the explanation for why workers persist in contributing in a career path they do not want (Fu, 2011; Fu & Chen, 2015). The specialty of this model provides us the framework to understand the conditions encouraging people to stay in an unfavorable association.

3. DEVELOPMENT OF THE PREPOSITION

3.1. The Impact of Career Satisfaction on Career Commitment

Career commitment is a strong aspect related to career development. A successful career development requires a sustainable commitment and skills expertise (Sambunjak et al., 2010). In the public sector, the quality of the public service is important because it reflects how effectively the government operates. A public servant who commits to work a long time for the public organizations tends to perform better than the one who plans to spend just a short period of time in the public service and then moves to the private one (Stephenson, 2020).

Empirical research on the public sector in the developing country revealed that job satisfaction has a positive significant influence on career commitment of the public servants (Shah, 2011). Valickas and Pilkauskaitė Valickienė (2019) in an investigation on career development of Lithuanian civil servants have found that job satisfaction and career satisfaction both have positive influence on career commitment, in which career satisfaction predicates a stronger impact than job satisfaction in particular. In alignment with the recommended findings, a proposition states that career satisfaction significantly influences career commitment of public servants as below:

P1. Career satisfaction has a positive impact on career commitment of public servants.

3.2. The Impact of Career Alternatives on Career Commitment

The investment theory posits that the instability of a relationship is influenced by the readiness of other alternatives that seem attractive to the partner. People get along well when the individual feels satisfied with what they have from the relationship, the amount of investment they put in to build up the relationship, and at the same time, there are not many attractive alternatives available.

When applying to vocational research, the career alternatives are defined as the accessibility of other career options, which the individual believes that she can start a new path with higher chances of success (Fu & Chen, 2015). The career alternative concept explains how the employees perceive the attractiveness of other career paths they have compared to the current one. In the case the individuals think that the present job satisfied their career goals and personal needs, if they change the jobs, they probably would have wasted the time and efforts invested in this current career. It is possibly true that the person might choose to commit to the chosen career, showing a higher level of career commitment. Therefore, the following proposition can be assumed:

P2. Career alternatives have a negative impact on career commitment of public servants.

3.3. The Impact of Career Investment on Career Commitment

Career investment is all the efforts and hours of time a person decides to invest in a career for career enhancement purposes. The investment would be considered as the worthless resources in one's career that would be deemed worthless or lost if one decided to switch to another career. Civil servants devote significant time and effort to learning new knowledge in administrative procedures, legal frameworks, policy analysis, and government systems. However, these skills are too specific and may not be easy to transfer to other industries. Therefore, even in cases where a civil servant is not happy with their current career path, the substantial investment made in acquiring these skills may unintentionally tie them to it. Further immersion in specialized knowledge and administrative techniques may strengthen their commitment to this particular career path. In contrast, considering a career change entails giving up one's invested professional identity and years of honed expertise. Consequently, the greater the investment, the higher the career commitment that the civil servants have.

P3. Career investment has a positive impact on career commitment of public servants.

3.4. The Impact of Professional Self-efficacy on Career Commitment

Self-efficacy is the belief of one person in her own capacity to succeed or perform a task or a set of different tasks (Vancouver & Kendall, 2006). According to the self-efficacy theory (Bandura & Adams, 1977; Maddux, 1995), this concept explains why people who have higher magnitude of self-efficacy are able to handle more difficult tasks with a higher pressure level. In a professional career, the level of how strong an individual's self-efficacy is to reflect his/her resoluteness of believing in the success of his/her works. The generality dimension of self-efficacy indicates how confident an individual is to perform another challenge once she already succeeds in performing the previous task. Study by Fu and Chen (2015) confirmed that employees with a higher level of professional self-efficacy are more determined to commit in their careers.

Hsieh et al. (2016) found that for public servants, self-efficacy is highly related with job satisfaction. Research by Caillier (2016) suggested that self-efficacy positively influences the extra-role behaviors of a public servant (helping coworkers and serving for the greater benefit of the organization) and negatively affects the turnover intentions of the public workers. Therefore, it can be rational to predict that for public servants, a higher level of professional self-efficacy would increase the career commitment as presented in the following proposition:

P4. Professional self-efficacy has a positive impact on career commitment of public servants.

3.5. The Moderation Effect of Perceived Economic Conditions

Chirumbolo et al. (2020) discussed that the combination of the overall highly competitive and dynamic economic trends with an unstable government is prone to prefer more flexible arrangements in the workforce with short-term contracts and profits. The long-term employments in both private and public sectors, therefore, are at risk. Shoss (2017) mentioned about job insecurity as the perceived threat to the career progression and vocational steadiness, which regarding to the public sector is considered to be safer compared to the private sector. The study by Shoss (2017) also summarized that job insecurity has a negative influence on both job satisfaction and commitment belief of the employees, explained by a psychological contract infringement mediating mechanism. In this study, it can be argued that drawing upon perspectives of public servants, perceiving of unfavorable economic conditions would activate the threat of job instability, leading to weakening the relationship between their career satisfaction and career commitment as shown in the following proposition:

P5. Perceived economic conditions moderate the relationship between career satisfaction and career commitment of public servants, such that the positive relationship is weaker when perceived economic conditions are worse.

Shoss (2017) pointed out in her study that when people feel insecure about their jobs, they tend to have the extraorganizational behaviors like looking for new vocational opportunities to preserve the employment status. We argue that in the public sector, when civil servants perceive that there is a high chance the bad economic condition could influence their career, they would be proactively coping with the situation by looking for new alternatives outside and, therefore, reduce the level of career commitment. A proposition can be developed as follows:

P6. Perceived economic conditions moderate the relationship between career alternatives and career commitment of public servants, such that the negative relationship is stronger when perceived economic conditions are worse.

From the corporate-level perspective, companies in general are afraid of investing their money and resources to a politically unstable environment (Giambona et al., 2017). So instead of investing in a country with high risk of political instability, the companies decided to spend their fundings to other countries with less worrisome problems. From the individual point of view, research findings by Piatak (2017) about public servants in the United States show that during the stable economic periods, there were significantly less job switching behaviors witnessed between sectors (private, public, or nonprofit sector). However, in the time of economic instability, public employees are more likely to move their jobs to the private sector. In alignment with the previous research, we argue that in the time of economic instability, the public servants who are more risk-averse will be less likely to invest their money and other resources on career and, therefore, lower the commitment to the ongoing career.

P7. Perceived economic conditions moderate the relationship between career investment and career commitment of public servants, such that the positive relationship is weaker when perceived economic conditions are worse.

Based on seven propositions, we proposed a research model in Fig. 2.1.

4. CONCEPTUAL MODEL AND RESEARCH METHODOLOGY

4.1. Conceptual Model

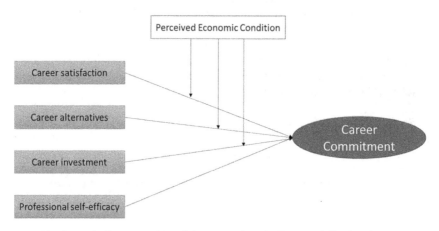

Fig. 2.1. A Conceptual Model Proposed Main Factors Affecting Career Commitment of Public Servants in Vietnam Public Organizations.

4.2. Sampling and Measuring

The on-site survey will be conducted to investigate around 200 public servants working in public service organizations located in Vietnam. Respondents in the study are both anonymous and voluntary; they will be informed that any information provided would be only used for academic purposes. Descriptive analysis and the structural equation modeling approaches will be used to validate the data set and to test the proposed hypotheses. The measurement items of each construct are for the most part adopted or adopted from previous related studies; some are self-developed. The preliminary version of the questionnaire is generated after conducting literature reviews and in-depth discussions with some public servants: managers or leaders of Vietnamese public organizations. Following measures are suggestions of construct measurements with a 5-point Likert-like scale format with a response ranging from strongly disagree to strongly agree.

Career satisfaction: The five-item Career Satisfaction Scale developed by Greenhaus et al. (1990) will be adopted in this study. These five items are "I am satisfied with the success I have achieved in my career," "I am satisfied with the progress I have made toward achieving my overall career goals," "I am satisfied with my rate of promotion during my career," "I am satisfied with the pay level I have achieved during my career," and "I am satisfied with the status that I have achieved during my career."

Alternatives of current career: Three items that can be consumed for measuring the accessibility of other career options are adopted from previous studies (Fu & Chen, 2015; Van Dam, 2005). For instance, they are "I can obtain another comparable/better career opportunity easily if I want to," "There are a sufficient number of career options for me in the labour market that I can do," and "It will be difficult for me to change to another career."

Investment to career: The six measuring items for Career Investment, which are adopted from a prior study by Van Dam (2005), are as follows: "I have invested a lot in my professional career," "I have invested specific and non-portable training in my professional career," "I have made many adjustments in the private sphere in my professional career," "I have to refrain from certain things in life in my professional career," "I have invested job tenure in my professional career," and "I have an invested length of service in my professional career."

Professional self-efficacy: Professional self-efficacy will be assessed using the four-item measure adopted from Fu and Chen (2015) and Kossek et al. (1998). For example: "Compared with others in the workplace, I am confident of my expertise," "Compared with others in the workplace, I am confident of my professional skills," "I have faith in my ability to learn new expertise constantly," and "I have faith in my ability to learn new professional skills constantly."

Perceived economic conditions: There are two self-developed questions to measure respondent's perceived economic conditions in the country at the present and the coming years: "How do you perceive the economic position of the Vietnam next year in comparison with this year?" and "How do you perceive the economic position of your household next year in comparison with this year? Respondents will answer the 5-point Likert-like questions with a response ranging from very unfavorable to very favorable.

Career commitment: It will be constructed as a second-order construct that includes career identity, career planning, and career resilience. These latent variables are applied from a previous study by Fu and Chen (2015). For career identity, there are three measuring items such as "The current job is an important part of who I am," "I do not feel 'emotionally attached' to a career in the current job," and "I strongly identify with the idea of a career in the current job." For career planning, there are three items such as "I have created a plan for my development as a professional in current job," "I have a strategy for achieving my career goals in the current job," "I have identified specific goals for my own personal development in the current job." For career resilience, there are three reversed items including "Given the problems I encounter in the workplace, I sometimes wonder if I get enough out of it," "Given the problems in the current job, I sometimes wonder if the personal burden is worth it," and "The discomforts associated with the current job sometimes seem too great."

Control variables: Some demographical variables such as age and gender, position, and work experiences of subjects will be included in the research model as control variables.

5. CONCLUSION

The current study is primarily to examine what influences the commitment of Vietnamese public employees to their career paths. This research has applied the investment model theory to investigate the key antecedents of employees' career commitment in the field of organizational behavior studies, more specifically the investment model might first extend its scope of the theoretical implications into the context of public organization in a developing country such as Vietnam. This study proposes that career satisfaction, career alternatives, career investment, and professional self-efficacy are main determinants of the public servants' commitment to their careers. Additionally, the study proposes that perceived economic conditions can effectively moderate the relationships between these factors and career commitment. This study has an ultimate purpose to advance our understanding of the complexities of career commitment among developing countries' public servants and provides the policymakers with new insights into how to improve employee commitment. The author hopes that this conceptual research will be timely conducted to successfully validate these proposed propositions in order to make further confirmations to the theoretical contributions and practical implications and further deeply dig into the extent of literature of career commitment in a typical context of a public service business environment. Consequently, the findings of this study would better assist public managers or leaders as well as the policymakers as a meaningful reference in planning a more feasible effective strategies in human resource and organizational performance so as to enhance employee's career commitment which in turn can bring about several favorable outcomes in job performance within public organizations in Vietnam as well as other developing countries.

REFERENCES

Akkermans, J., Tims, M., Beijer, S., & De Cuyper, N. (2019). Should employers invest in employability? Examining employability as a mediator in the HRM–commitment relationship. *Frontiers in Psychology*, *10*, 717.

Andaleeb, S. S. (1996). An experimental investigation of satisfaction and commitment in marketing channels: The role of trust and dependence. *Journal of Retailing*, *72*(1), 77–93.

Andrews, R., & Van de Walle, S. (2013). New public management and citizens' perceptions of local service efficiency, responsiveness, equity and effectiveness. *Public Management Review*, *15*(5), 762–783.

Arora, R., & Rangnekar, S. (2016a). Linking the Big Five personality factors and career commitment dimensions. *Journal of Management Development*, *35*(9), 1134–1148.

Arora, R., & Rangnekar, S. (2016b). Towards understanding the two way interaction effects of extraversion and openness to experience on career commitment. *International Journal for Educational and Vocational Guidance*, *16*(2), 213–232.

Aryee, S., & Tan, K. (1992). Antecedents and outcomes of career commitment. *Journal of Vocational Behavior*, *40*(3), 288–305.

Ashill, N. J., Rod, M., & Carruthers, J. (2008). The effect of management commitment to service quality on frontline employees' job attitudes, turnover intentions and service recovery performance in a new public management context. *Journal of Strategic Marketing*, *16*(5), 437–462.

Ballout, H. I. (2009). Career commitment and career success: Moderating role of self-efficacy. *Career Development International*, *14*(7), 655–670.

Bandura, A., & Adams, N. E. (1977). Analysis of self-efficacy theory of behavioral change. *Cognitive Therapy and Research*, *1*(4), 287–310.

Bason, C. (2017). *Leading public design: Discovering human-centred governance*. Policy Press.

Caillier, J. G. (2016). Linking transformational leadership to self-efficacy, extra-role behaviors, and turnover intentions in public agencies: The mediating role of goal clarity. *Administration & Society*, *48*(7), 883–906.

Carson, K. D., & Bedeian, A. G. (1994). Career commitment: Construction of a measure and examination of its psychometric properties. *Journal of Vocational Behavior, 44*(3), 237–262.

Caryl, E. (2011). The investment model of commitment processes. In P. A. M. Van Lange, E. T. Higgins, & A. W. Kruglanski. *Handbook of theories of social psychology* (pp. 218–231). SAGE.

Chirumbolo, A., Callea, A., & Urbini, F. (2020). Job insecurity and performance in public and private sectors: A moderated mediation model. *Journal of Organizational Effectiveness: People and Performance, 7*(2), 237–253.

Cicek, I., Karaboga, T., & Sehitoglu, Y. (2016). A new antecedent of career commitment: Work to family positive enhancement. *Procedia-Social and Behavioral Sciences, 229,* 417–426.

Colarelli, S. M., & Bishop, R. C. (1990). Career commitment: Functions, correlates, and management. *Group & Organization Studies, 15*(2), 158–176.

den Boer, L., Klimstra, T. A., Branje, S. J., Meeus, W. H., & Denissen, J. J. (2019). Personality maturation during the transition to working life: Associations with commitment as a possible indicator of social investment. *European Journal of Personality, 33*(4), 456–467.

Dickinson, H. (2016). From new public management to new public governance: The implications for a 'new public service'. In J. Butcher & D. Gilchrist (Eds.), *The three sector solution: Delivering public policy in collaboration with not-for-profits and business* (pp. 41–60). Australian National University Press.

Eldor, L. (2018). Public service sector: The compassionate workplace – The effect of compassion and stress on employee engagement, burnout, and performance. *Journal of Public Administration Research and Theory, 28*(1), 86–103.

Etcheverry, P. E., Le, B., Wu, T. F., & Wei, M. (2013). Attachment and the investment model: Predictors of relationship commitment, maintenance, and persistence. *Personal Relationships, 20*(3), 546–567.

Farrell, D., & Rusbult, C. E. (1992). Exploring the exit, voice, loyalty, and neglect typology: The influence of job satisfaction, quality of alternatives, and investment size. *Employee Responsibilities and Rights Journal, 5*(3), 201–218.

Fu, J.-R. (2011). Understanding career commitment of IT professionals: Perspectives of push–pull–mooring framework and investment model. *International Journal of Information Management, 31*(3), 279–293.

Fu, J.-R., & Chen, J. H. (2015). Career commitment of information technology professionals: The investment model perspective. *Information & Management, 52*(5), 537–549.

Giambona, E., Graham, J. R., & Harvey, C. R. (2017). The management of political risk. *Journal of International Business Studies, 48*(4), 523–533.

Greenhaus, J. H., Parasuraman, S., & Wormley, W. M. (1990). Effects of race on organizational experiences, job performance evaluations, and career outcomes. *Academy of Management Journal, 33*(1), 64–86.

Gruening, G. (2001). Origin and theoretical basis of new public management. *International Public Management Journal, 4*(1), 1–25.

Hartmann, S., Weiss, M., Newman, A., & Hoegl, M. (2020). Resilience in the workplace: A multilevel review and synthesis. *Applied Psychology, 69*(3), 913–959.

Hodgkinson, I. R., Hughes, P., Radnor, Z., & Glennon, R. (2018). Affective commitment within the public sector: Antecedents and performance outcomes between ownership types. *Public Management Review, 20*(12), 1872–1895.

Hood, C. (2000). Paradoxes of public-sector managerialism, old public management and public service bargains. *International Public Management Journal, 3*(1), 1–22.

Howlett, M., Kekez, A., & Poocharoen, O.-O. (2017). Understanding co-production as a policy tool: Integrating new public governance and comparative policy theory. *Journal of Comparative Policy Analysis: Research and Practice, 19*(5), 487–501.

Hsieh, C.-W., Hsieh, J.-Y., & Huang, I. Y.-F. (2016). Self-efficacy as a mediator and moderator between emotional labor and job satisfaction: A case study of public service employees in Taiwan. *Public Performance & Management Review, 40*(1), 71–96.

Huang, W., Yuan, C., & Li, M. (2019). Person–job fit and innovation behavior: Roles of job involvement and career commitment. *Frontiers in Psychology, 10,* 1134.

Jones, M. L., Zanko, M., & Kriflik, G. (2006). On the antecedents of career commitment. In J. Kennedy & L. Di Milia (Eds.), *Proceedings of the Australian and New Zealand Academy of Management Conference* (pp. 1–22). Australian and New Zealand Academy of Management.

Kakouris, A. P., & Meliou, E. (2011). New public management: Promote the public sector modernization through service quality. Current experiences and future challenges. *Public Organization Review*, *11*(4), 351–369.

Kasemsap, K. (2013). Practical framework: Creation of causal model of job involvement, career commitment, learning motivation, and learning transfer. *International Journal of the Computer, the Internet and Management*, *21*(1), 29–35.

Kossek, E. E., Roberts, K., Fisher, S., & Demarr, B. (1998). Career self-management: A quasi-experimental assessment of the effects of a training intervention. *Personnel Psychology*, *51*(4), 935–960.

Lehtman, M. J., & Zeigler-Hill, V. (2020). Narcissism and job commitment: The mediating role of job-related attitudes. *Personality and Individual Differences*, *157*, 109807.

Lin, C.-P. (2020). Exploring career commitment and turnover intention of high-tech personnel: A socio-cognitive perspective. *The International Journal of Human Resource Management*, *31*(6), 760–784.

Maddux, J. E. (Ed.). (1995). Self-efficacy theory. In *Self-efficacy, adaptation, and adjustment* (pp. 3–33). Springer.

Major, D. A., Morganson, V. J., & Bolen, H. M. (2013). Predictors of occupational and organizational commitment in information technology: Exploring gender differences and similarities. *Journal of Business and Psychology*, *28*(3), 301–314.

Osborne, S. P. (2006). The new public governance? *Public Management Review*, *8*, 377–388. https://doi.org/10.1080/14719030600853022

Osborne, S. P., Radnor, Z., & Nasi, G. (2013). A new theory for public service management? Toward a (public) service-dominant approach. *The American Review of Public Administration*, *43*(2), 135–158.

Paul, K. A., & Seward, K. K. (2016). Place-based investment model of talent development: A proposed model for developing and reinvesting talents within the community. *Journal of Advanced Academics*, *27*(4), 311–342.

Peters, B. G. (2010). *Still the century of bureaucracy? The roles of public servants* (Chapter 7) in *Public management in the postmodern era*. Edward Elgar Publishing.

Piatak, J. S. (2017). Sector switching in good times and in bad: Are public sector employees less likely to change sectors? *Public Personnel Management*, *46*(4), 327–341.

Pollack, J. M., Coy, A. E., Green, J. D., & Davis, J. L. (2015). Satisfaction, investment, and alternatives predict entrepreneurs' networking group commitment and subsequent revenue generation. *Entrepreneurship Theory and Practice*, *39*(4), 817–837.

Rusbult, C. E. (1980). Commitment and satisfaction in romantic associations: A test of the investment model. *Journal of Experimental Social Psychology*, *16*(2), 172–186.

Rusbult, C. E., Drigotas, S. M., & Verette, J. (1994). The investment model: An interdependence analysis of commitment processes and relationship maintenance phenomena. In D. J. Canary & L. Stafford (Eds.), *Communication and relational maintenance* (pp. 115–139). Academic Press.

Rusbult, C. E., Johnson, D. J., & Morrow, G. D. (1986). Predicting satisfaction and commitment in adult romantic involvements: An assessment of the generalizability of the investment model. *Social Psychology Quarterly*, *49*(1), 81–89.

Rusbult, C. E., Martz, J. M., & Agnew, C. R. (1998). The investment model scale: Measuring commitment level, satisfaction level, quality of alternatives, and investment size. *Personal Relationships*, *5*(4), 357–387.

Sabharwal, M., Hijal-Moghrabi, I., & Royster, M. (2014). Preparing future public servants: Role of diversity in public administration. *Public Administration Quarterly*, *38*(2), 206–245.

Sambunjak, D., Straus, S. E., & Marusic, A. (2010). A systematic review of qualitative research on the meaning and characteristics of mentoring in academic medicine. *Journal of General Internal Medicine*, *25*(1), 72–78.

Shah, N. (2011). Investigating employee career commitment factors in a public sector organisation of a developing country. *Journal of Enterprise Information Management*, *24*(6), 534–546.

Shoss, M. K. (2017). Job insecurity: An integrative review and agenda for future research. *Journal of Management*, *43*(6), 1911–1939.

Singh, R., Zhang, Y., Wan, M., & Fouad, N. A. (2018). Why do women engineers leave the engineering profession? The roles of work–family conflict, occupational commitment, and perceived organizational support. *Human Resource Management*, 57(4), 901–914.

Steffy, B. D., & Jones, J. W. (1988). The impact of family and career planning variables on the organizational, career, and community commitment of professional women. *Journal of Vocational Behavior*, 32(2), 196–212.

Stephenson, M. C. (2020). The qualities of public servants determine the quality of public service. *Michigan State Law Review*, 2019(5), 1177.

Sternberg, R. J., & Lubart, T. I. (1991). An investment theory of creativity and its development. *Human Development*, 34(1), 1–31.

Tan, K., Arriaga, X. B., & Agnew, C. R. (2018). Running on empty: Measuring psychological dependence in close relationships lacking satisfaction. *Journal of Social and Personal Relationships*, 35(7), 977–998.

Valickas, A., & Pilkauskaitė Valickienė, R. (2017). Relationship among individual level factors in career development system of civil service. *Global journal of guidance and counseling in schools: current perspectives*, 7(1).

Vancouver, J. B., & Kendall, L. N. (2006). When self-efficacy negatively relates to motivation and performance in a learning context. *Journal of Applied Psychology*, 91(5), 1146.

Van Dam, K. (2005). Employee attitudes toward job changes: An application and extension of Rusbult and Farrell's investment model. *Journal of Occupational and Organizational Psychology*, 78(2), 253–272.

Wieselquist, J. (2009). Interpersonal forgiveness, trust, and the investment model of commitment. *Journal of Social and Personal Relationships*, 26(4), 531–548.

Wilson, M. E., Liddell, D. L., Hirschy, A. S., & Pasquesi, K. (2016). Professional identity, career commitment, and career entrenchment of midlevel student affairs professionals. *Journal of College Student Development*, 57(5), 557–572.

Young, S. L., Wiley, K. K., & Searing, E. A. (2020). "Squandered in real time": How public management theory underestimated the public administration–politics dichotomy. *The American Review of Public Administration*, 50(6–7), 480–488.

CHAPTER 3

EFFECTS OF WORKING MOTIVATION ON EFFICIENCY AND WORK SATISFACTION: CASE OF EMPLOYEES AT THE SOFTWARE COMPANY

Pham Duc Chính[a], Yen Nguyen Thi[a] and Ma Thi Ngan[b]

[a]*Faculty of Business Administration, University of Economics and Law, Vietnam National University, Ho Chi Minh City, Vietnam*
[b]*Faculty of Basic Sciences, Thai Nguyen University of Economics – Technology, Vietnam*

ABSTRACT

The study was conducted to determine the relationship between three factors: work motivation (intrinsic and extrinsic), work efficiency, and job satisfaction of employees at the software company in Ho Chi Minh, Vietnam. Survey data collected from 300 employees working at the software company show that with the specific work characteristics of the information technology industry, the stronger the employee's motivation to work, especially the intrinsic motivation, the greater efficiency and job satisfaction. At the same time, the higher the work efficiency, the more positive the employee's job satisfaction will be. This study also draws some managerial implications that are valuable for reference for information technology enterprises to find solutions to increase work motivation, efficiency, and staff satisfaction, thereby minimizing layoffs, stabilizing personnel, and increasing competitiveness.

Keywords: Work motivation; work efficiency; job satisfaction; the software company; work environment; organizational policy

1. INTRODUCTION

The self-determination theory studies the classification of motivational factors and the impact of environmental conditions on individuals. Accordingly, the work outcomes of employees are influenced by numerous factors: intrinsic factors such as job performance ability, job satisfaction, and alignment of personal and organizational values; external factors impacting employees, including internal relationships such as direct managers, colleagues, human resource (HR) managers, organizational policies, and the work environment; external influences from outside the organization, such as customers, partners, communities, and regulatory agencies. This research aims to identify the impacts of internal and external motivations on employees' job satisfaction and work efficiency at the software company.

2. THEORETICAL FRAMEWORK AND RESEARCH MODEL

Work motivation is succinctly understood as the stimuli and impetuses that generate the individual positive tendencies to manage actions to reach an anticipated goal. The manifestations of motivation are readiness, effort, and enthusiasm to achieve the goals for the organization and employees. Work motivation originates within the intrinsic thoughts of the employee, manifested through the specific tasks that they are responsible for and their attitude toward the organization. Different employees undertake different tasks and may have different work motivations to perform more positively (Deci & Ryan, 1985; Lin, 2007; Mujah et al., 2011).

2.1. Work Motivations

There are two types of work motivation: intrinsic and extrinsic. Intrinsic motivation is an activity that satisfies the employee's inherent desire to understand their abilities and autonomy in work and to have challenging work (Amabile, 1993; Deci, 1975; Warr et al., 1979).

Ryan and Deci (2000) argue that intrinsic motivation involves performing an activity for its inherent satisfaction rather than for separable outcomes. Intrinsic motivation drives an employee to act for the enjoyment or challenge it brings rather than for external incentives, pressures, or rewards. Intrinsic motivation is the extent to which a person wants to do their job well to achieve genuine satisfaction (Warr et al., 1979). Intrinsic motivation leads to high job quality, timely task completion, meeting challenges, and outstanding performance. Intrinsic motivation is behavior that lacks clear external rewards except for the satisfaction inherent in the activity itself or the satisfaction of engaging in an activity more than any other outcome beyond the activity itself (Ryan & Deci, 2008). The self-determination theory research began to focus on intrinsic motivation (Ryan & Deci, 2020), which may be responsible for the excellence of human work throughout life, as opposed to externally imposed work and guidance (Ryan & Deci, 2017). Howard et al. (2020) posit that intrinsic motivation describes entirely self-determined behaviors and characteristics of the highest reservoir of perceived causality orientation.

Meanwhile, external motivation is propelled by all factors and sources from the outside to stimulate individuals' work efficiency. External factors may include rewards, recognition, job feedback, deadlines, job demands, supervisory activities, salary bonuses, and promotions (Kluger & DeNisi, 1996; Whang & Hancock, 1994). External motivation is a construct closely linked whenever an activity is undertaken to achieve some separable outcomes. Thus, external motivation contrasts with intrinsic motivation, which refers to engaging in an activity for the enjoyment of the activity itself rather than its instrumental value (Ryan & Deci, 2005). External motivation is driven by external forces pushing individuals to perform or achieve something with the aim of gaining rewards or avoiding negative consequences. This type of motivation relies on the fact that if human behavior is positively rewarded for completed tasks, it tends to be repeated. However, such behavioral rewards must be strong and long-lasting to enhance its likelihood of recurrence. It involves the expectation to achieve rewards or avoid punishments or any undesirable consequences (Kingful & Nusenu, 2015). Ryan and Deci (2020) argued that external motivation pertains to behaviors performed for reasons other than their inherent satisfaction. External motivation relates to behaviors driven by rewards and punishments imposed from the outside and is a form of motivation often experienced as controlled and not autonomous. Some internal motivation is related to external motivation that has been internalized to some extent; behavior is regulated by internal rewards of self-esteem for success and by avoiding anxiety, shame, or guilt for failure. While intrinsic motivation represents autonomous forms of motivation, external motivation can also be enacted autonomously. Autonomous external motivations share with intrinsic motivation the quality of having high volition but differ mainly in that intrinsic motivation is based on interest and enjoyment – individuals engage in these behaviors because they find them appealing or even enjoyable, whereas identified and integrated motivations are based on a sense of value – people view activities as worthwhile, even if not inherently enjoyable.

2.2. Work Efficiency

Work efficiency is the completion of tasks that include the employee's work. (Porter & Lawler, 1968). Based on their research, Locke et al. (1976) have suggested that performance is a function of employee capabilities, goal acceptance, level of goal, and interaction of target with their abilities. Motowidlo and Kell (2013) define work efficiency as the total expected value for the organization of the phases of discrete behavior that an individual performs over a standard period. The most important result of motivation is personal achievement. In this respect, internal motivation is set to respond to the fact that employees with high internal motivations will get the best work outcomes (Meyer et al., 2004), as it relates to enthusiasm (Ryan & Deci, 2008) and perseverance (Vallerand & Blssonnette, 1992). In addition, internal motivation is positively associated with enthusiasm and attachment (Van den Broeck et al., 2013), prosperity (Spreitzer & Grant, 2005), and happiness (Ryan & Deci, 2000). These positive influence states are theorized to motivate employees and focus their attention on work in a way that integrates them. In addition to being actively related to work performance and physical fields (Cerasoli et al., 2016), internal motivation has also been shown to positively affect work efficiency in context and creativity (Gagné & Deci, 2005). Therefore, it may be suggested that:

Hypothesis 1 (H1): The more robust the intrinsic motivation, the more favorable it will be to boost work efficiency.

Studies on extrinsic motivation affecting work efficiency, more specifically for employees, conducted by different researchers also show similarities. For example, a study by Smith et al. (1969) at Cornell University developed job description indicators (JDIs) to measure a person's job satisfaction through factors such as (1) the nature of the job, (2) salary, (3) promotion, (4) colleagues, and (5) supervision by superiors. The relationship between extrinsic motivation and employee efficiency that was studied suggests that tangible external dynamics depending on performance will result in higher performance in the case of simple and standardized tasks that are easy to measure and attribute (Bareket-Bojmel & Ariely, 2014; Lazear, 2000). Moreover, the synthesis of experimental studies by Weibel et al. (2010) found that such external incentives have a relatively strong positive impact on performance for uninteresting tasks and a small but significant negative impact on exciting tasks. Finally, an aggregate analysis by Jenkins and Shaw (1998) demonstrated that extrinsic motivation positively relates to work efficiency for quantitative tasks. However, they are unrelated to quality work efficiency for qualitative tasks because quality is more difficult to measure. Therefore, it may be suggested:

Hypothesis 2 (H2): The more external motivators influence, the more positive they influence the employee's work efficiency.

2.3. Job Satisfaction

Spector (1997) argues that job satisfaction is how people feel about the job and the aspects of their work. Since it is a general judgment, it is an attitude variable. Kotler et al. (2001) argue that job satisfaction is the state of a person's feelings derived from comparing the results obtained from his or her expectations. According to Hulin et al. (2003), job satisfaction can be measured by cognitive, emotional, and behavioral measures. For Kreitner et al. (2007), job satisfaction primarily reflects how much an individual loves his or her job. That is the employee's feelings for his job.

A study by Timothy et al. (2001) qualitatively and quantitatively assessed the relationship between work efficiency and job satisfaction. The previously studied qualitative assessment lists seven models that characterize the relationship between job satisfaction and performance. The bright point of this study is that it has provided a program for future research into the relationship between satisfaction and efficiency.

Storey et al. (2019) argue that when employees feel productive, it increases employee job satisfaction for software companies. Increasing employee satisfaction can improve employee attraction and retention, while higher work efficiency will reduce costs and increase customer satisfaction through faster software improvements. Job satisfaction is shaped by factors such as pay and salary distribution, new levels of work, career opportunities that work brings, the contribution of work to professional advancement, the attitude of the superior to the staff, and the friendship within the organization (Gibson et al., 1997). Gannon and Noon (1971) found that 60.7% of the 168 managers revealed higher job satisfaction due to higher efficiency and productivity. Moreover, work efficiency is essential in human relationships and their involvement in decision-making (Antoni, 2009). High-efficiency employees will be satisfied with their work and attach importance to communicating and sharing knowledge with colleagues and superiors, which will play an essential role in improving job satisfaction. Thus, it may be suggested that:

Hypothesis 3 (H3): The higher the work efficiency, the more positive the employee's satisfaction is.

Küskü (2003) argues that job satisfaction reflects individual needs and desires for satisfaction and the level of employee perception of their work. This definition comes from Maslow (1943) that workers are satisfied when they meet their needs from low to high. Wright and Kim (2004) also argue that job satisfaction matches what employees expect and feel from work. Some other researchers argue that job satisfaction is the positive emotional state of a worker's work that reflects his/her behavior and beliefs (Locke, 1976; McGehee & Tullar, 1979; Weiss et al., 1967).

Intrinsic motivations have been shown to influence job satisfaction more than extrinsic motivations (Erciş, 2010). Individuals who are satisfied with their internal motivation can easily assume responsibility within the organization, and these responsible individuals tend to sacrifice for the organization (Xie et al., 2017). So, you can see that intrinsic motivation directly impacts job satisfaction. Highly motivated employees are more satisfied with higher jobs and are less likely to give up. On the contrary, low-motivated employees tend to be satisfied with lower jobs and always intend to relocate. It is possible to hypothesize the extrinsic motivation that affects job satisfaction and productivity. Therefore, it may be suggested:

Hypothesis 4 (H4): The more robust the intrinsic motivation, the more direct and positive the impact that increases employee job satisfaction.

Job satisfaction is a positive perception of the outcome of a job through the evaluation of the job characteristics (Price & Mueller, 1981; Robbins & Judge, 2013). When external sources generate factors that increase job satisfaction, they lead to specific behaviors related to the individual's external environment. More than individual determination, willingness and skill to succeed are needed for job satisfaction. The environmental factors to support these factors must also be quantified and of high quality because some of the elements individuals need can only be met by the external environment. This is a physically fit working environment, being part of a cohesive collective, appreciated by colleagues and superiors, and subject to project-oriented control rather than oppressive control. Internal satisfaction can only be achieved through complete and effective external means. If external means are insufficient or nonexistent, internal satisfaction decreases and eventually disappears. Intrinsic motivation refers to an employee's adaptation to working through external factors. These factors relate to goals such as receiving rewards, avoiding punishment, and improving professional careers. Individuals who are interested in a job can get tangible or invisible benefits from the activity involved. Money rewards, job assurances, relationships with superiors, and relations with colleagues form an external reward system (Panagiotis & Petridou, 2008). The leader's essential task is to ensure satisfaction in external work. Leaders should find and use the best means to get people to work. The theories of demands need to be considered at this point. It is an accepted approach that external motivation drives the employee's "needs" for job satisfaction. Therefore, it may be suggested that:

Hypothesis 5 (H5): The higher the impetus of extrinsic motivation, the higher the employee's job satisfaction.

Based on the above information, the following research model was constructed (Fig. 3.1).

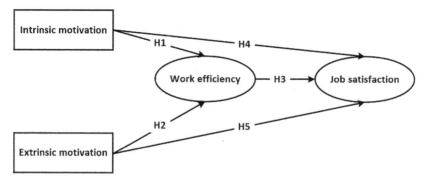

Fig. 3.1. Proposed Research Model. *Source*: Created by author.

3. RESEARCH METHODOLOGY

3.1. Scale

This study will measure an employee's intrinsic and extrinsic motivation by measuring performance and job satisfaction. From the research mentioned above hypotheses and reference research papers, the author has synthesized and constructed a scale of research variables but renamed the elements accordingly. Although the name differs, the content has been inherited and developed to suit the research context at the software company, Ho Chi Minh City, Vietnam.

The renaming of these factors, as well as their constituent aspects, is considered based on the definition of the factor itself and related studies, namely, the internal motivation scale (6 observations) and the external motivation (4 observations), based on Gagné et al. (2015); a efficiency scale of 10 observational variables based on references from Kuvaas and Dysvik's scale (2009); a job satisfaction scale with 10 observations from Scott and MacIntyre's (1997) results.

3.2. Participants

With an amount of 300 pounds of inputs for those who are directly employed in the software production at the software company, Ho Chi Minh City, Vietnam. All feedback data will be checked, recorded, and processed with the support of SPSS and AMOS 20 software. The SPSS 20 software is used to encrypt, input, and clean data with the following steps: descriptive statistics, verification of the reliability of the scale using Cronbach's alpha coefficient, exploratory factor analysis (EFA), affirmative factor analysis, model and research hypothesis (structural equation modeling (SEM)), and Bootstrap research model estimates.

4. DATA ANALYSIS AND RESULTS

Given that the software company has more male employees (61%) than female employees (39%), the gender ratio in the sample is similar to that of the software company. The subjects in the sample were highly educated, with the highest percentage being university with 86%. The postgraduate group was 17 with 5.7%, the college group with 8.3%, and no intermediate qualifications. This is also the specialty of the general educational level of the software company employees. The software company has a relatively young staff; this characteristic is also reflected in the study sample. The age group in the most surveyed sample was 25 and under 35, accounting for 72.3%. The age group under 25 accounted for 15.7%. The percentage of people over the age of 35 is 12%. The number of working years of the company employees in the survey sample is 3–5 years, accounting for 31%, and from 1 to 3 years, accounting for 28.7%. Twenty-three percentage of employees work for over five years. Subjects working under one year accounted for the lowest percentage, 17%. Given the number of employees of younger ages, single persons (63.7%) also account for a billion more than married persons (36.3%). Thus, the ratio of subjects allocated to different gender groups, educational level, age, working age, and marital status of the sample is balanced. This ensures that the results of the study are representative.

4.1. Cronbach's Alpha

The results of Cronbach's alpha (Table 3.1) indicate that all coefficients are more significant than 0.6. Specifically, the reliability coefficient of the internal motivation scale is relatively large, 0.907 > 0.6; the external motivation scale is 0.802 > 0.6. After re-running the data when excluding three variables, *HQ3*, *HQ6*, and *HQ7*, the reliance coefficient for the work satisfaction scale measurement is 0.0935 > 0.6. The variable correlation coefficient – the total is more significant than 0.3, so no variable is excluded from the scale. Scale performance and job satisfaction are reliable for subsequent analysis. That would satisfy the scale's reliability requirement. Finally, all 25 observed variables are included in the EFA detection factor analysis.

4.2. Exploratory Factor Analysis

The test results showed that the factor analysis indicators of the scale of independent variables and dependent variables were both satisfactory. The results of the EFA analysis showed that after the removal of waste variables from Cronbach's alpha analysis, no variables were eliminated during the analysis of EFA. The factors derived from 25 variables are renamed as follows:

Group 1 consists of the six observational variables BT1, BT2, BT3, BT4, BT5, and BT6, which are called the "Intrinsic Motivation."

Group 2 consists of four observational variables, BN1, BN2, BN3, and BN4, called "Extrinsic Motivation."

Group 3 consists of seven observational variables, HQ1, HQ2, HQ4, HQ5, HQ8, HQ9, and HQ10, which are named "Work Efficiency."

Group 4 consists of eight observational variables, HL1, HL2, HL3, HL4, HL6, HL7, HL8, and HL10, which are called "Work Satisfaction."

Extract four factors with Kaiser–Meyer–Olkin (KMO) and Bartlett's test = 0.917 > 0 for independent variables. Five meaningful EFA analyses. Out of 25 observed variables, four factors are obtained with the equivalence of 61.9% > 50%, the value of Eigenvalue =1.938 > 1. Factor loading coefficients are more significant than 0.5. The above proves that these scales explain the concepts of research significantly.

4.3. Confirmatory Factor Analysis

To test the difference between the four components from the EFA analysis in Section 4.4, build a critical model in which all components will be freely linked. CFA results of the critical model are shown in Fig. 3.2.

The above analysis shows that the values of the model's evaluation indicators all meet the acceptance threshold from previous studies (Table 3.1), so it can be concluded that the model is suitable for the market data. There is no need to carry out model adjustment measures, so it can be concluded that the scale is

Effects of Working Motivation on Efficiency and Work Satisfaction 35

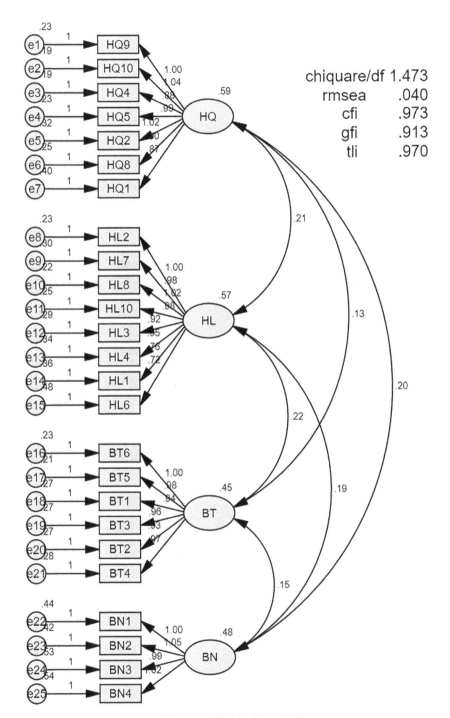

Fig. 3.2. CFA (Modification) Model Outcomes.

Table 3.1. Assessment Criteria and CFA Results.

STT	Criteria	Acceptable Threshold Level	Standard Value	CFA Value
1	Chi-square test	$p > 0.05$	Carmines and McIver (1981)	$\chi^2 = 396.281$; $p = 0.000$
2	Chi-square adjusted for degrees of freedom. (χ^2/df)	<2: good; <3 can be acceptable	Carmines and McIver (1981)	χ^2/df = 1.473
3	Comparative fit index (CFI)	>0.9	Bentler and Bonett (1980)	CFI = 0.973
4	Tucker and Lewis index (TLI)	>0.9	Bentler and Bonett (1980)	TLI = 0.970
5	Root mean square error approximation (RMSEA)	<0.08	Steiger (1990)	RMSEA = 0.040

Source: Results of data synthesis and analysis by the author.

unidirectional. In addition, Table 3.2 shows the results of testing the discrimination between concepts from the critical model: all correlation indices (*r*) of the concepts have values other than 1, equal to 1. Meanwhile, the standard errors all have a *p*-value < 0.05. Therefore, with 95% confidence, it can be concluded that the concepts of the components in the CFA (standardization) of the critical model achieve discriminant value.

Table 3.2. Testing the Discrimination Between Concepts From the Critical Model.

			Estimate	SE	CR	*p*-Value
HQ	←	BT	0.176	0.073	2.419	0.016
HQ	←	BN	0.366	0.079	4.659	***
HL	←	BN	0.204	0.075	2.742	0.006
HL	←	BT	0.368	0.070	5.258	***
HL	←	HQ	0.202	0.060	3.364	***
HQ9	←	HQ	1.000			
HQ10	←	HQ	1.039	0.053	19.757	***
HQ4	←	HQ	0.884	0.048	18.377	***
HQ5	←	HQ	0.990	0.053	18.656	***
HQ2	←	HQ	1.016	0.059	17.331	***
HQ8	←	HQ	0.901	0.052	17.270	***
HQ1	←	HQ	0.874	0.059	14.748	***
HL2	←	HL	1.000			
HL7	←	HL	0.979	0.058	16.925	***
HL8	←	HL	1.019	0.055	18.616	***
HL10	←	HL	0.981	0.055	17.765	***
HL3	←	HL	0.924	0.056	16.461	***
HL4	←	HL	0.946	0.059	16.042	***
HL1	←	HL	0.758	0.056	13.504	***
HL6	←	HL	0.717	0.062	11.640	***
BT6	←	BT	1.000			
BT5	←	BT	0.977	0.061	15.906	***
BT1	←	BT	0.940	0.064	14.774	***

Table 3.2. (Continued)

			Estimate	SE	CR	p-Value
BT3	←	BT	0.960	0.064	14.927	***
BT2	←	BT	0.930	0.064	14.612	***
BT4	←	BT	0.970	0.065	14.887	***
BN1	←	BN	1.000			
BN2	←	BN	1.051	0.097	10.835	***
BN3	←	BN	0.992	0.098	10.143	***
BN4	←	BN	1.016	0.100	10.214	***

Source: Results of data synthesis and analysis by the author.
Note: Estimate: estimated value; SE: standard error; CR: critical value; *p*-value: significance level.
***$p < 0.001$.

4.4. Testing Models and Research Hypotheses (SEM)

From the results of testing the suitability of the critical model above, the scales that meet the requirements will be included in the hypothesis testing model. The results of linear structural analysis in Fig. 3.3 show that the research model is compatible with market data with the indexes $\chi^2 = 396.281$, df = 269 ($p = 0.000$), $\chi^2/df = 1.493 < 2$, TLI = $0.970 > 0.9$, CFI = $0.973 > 0.9$, and RMSEA = $0.040 < 0.07$.

The estimation results in Table 3.3 show that most relationships are statistically significant (with $p < 0.05$); these relationships can be accepted with confidence at the 95% level.

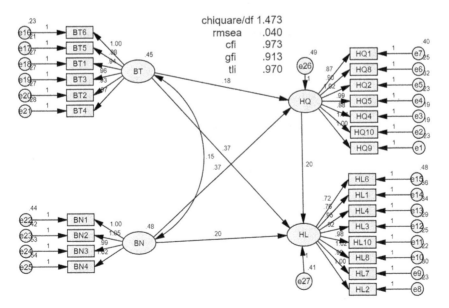

Fig. 3.3. Results of SEM Model Research (Modified). *Source*: Author's analysis results.

Table 3.3. Relationships Between Concepts in the Research Model.

The Relationship			ML (B)	SE	CR	p-Value	Standardized ML (β)
Work efficiency	←	Intrinsic motivation	0.176	0.073	2.419	0.016	0.154
Work efficiency	←	Extrinsic motivation	0.366	0.079	4.659	***	0.329
Work satisfaction	←	Extrinsic motivation	0.204	0.075	2.742	0.006	0.186
Work satisfaction	←	Intrinsic motivation	0.368	0.07	5.258	***	0.326
Work satisfaction	←	Work efficiency	0.202	0.06	3.364	***	0.205

Note: Estimate: estimated value; SE: standard error; CR: critical value; *p*-value: significance level. ***$p < 0.001$.

Thereby, analyze the results of testing these relationships through the SEM model as follows:

Hypothesis H1 with the statement "The more robust the intrinsic motivation, the more favorable it will be to boost employee efficiency," with test results showing *p*-value = $0.016 < 0.05$ and SE = 0.073, indicating that the relationship is statistically significant at the 95% confidence level or this hypothesis is accepted. It can be concluded that the higher the internal motivation, the more positively it will affect employee performance.

Hypothesis H2 with the statement, "The more external motivators influence, the more positive they influence the employee's efficiency." The estimation results show that the standard deviation value SE = 0.079 and *p*-value < 0.001, with 95% confidence, can consider accepting this hypothesis. This means that when extrinsic motivation increases, work efficiency also increases and vice versa. At the same time, the standardized estimate value of the impact level reached 0.366, higher than that of intrinsic motivation, implying that the impact of extrinsic motivation on work performance is higher than that of intrinsic motivation.

Hypothesis H3 with the statement "The higher the work efficiency, the more positive the employee's satisfaction is." This hypothesis is accepted with the specified results showing that *p*-value < 0.001 with SE value = 0.060. This means that when employee performance increases or decreases, their job satisfaction increases or decreases.

Hypothesis H4 with the statement "The stronger the internal motivation, the more direct and positive impact it will have on increasing employee job satisfaction." The test results show that the *p*-value < 0.001 with SE = 0.070, thereby showing that this hypothesis is accepted and statistically significant when considered at the 95% confidence level. At the same time, the standardized estimated value of this relationship reaches 0.368, more significant than that of external motivation. This implies that intrinsic motivation is crucial and has the most substantial positive impact on job satisfaction.

Hypothesis H5 with the statement, "The higher the impetus of extrinsic motivation, the higher the employee's job satisfaction is." The test results show that *p*-value = $0.006 < 0.05$ and SE = 0.075, showing that this relationship is statistically significant at the 95% confidence level; this hypothesis can be accepted.

4.5. Test the Research Model Estimates With Bootstrap

The Bootstrap method of estimation of the study model with the number of replications of the sample $N = 1,000$ is according to Kline (2005) and Pattengale et al. (2010), based on the results of the estimates presented in Table 3.4, the deviation may appear. However, the value is not significant; the absolute value of the CR deadline value is small compared to 2, so it is possible to conclude that estimates in the model are reliable with a slight deviation and have no statistical significance at a 95% reliability.

4.6. Policy Implications of the Research Results

4.6.1. Policy Implications of Intrinsic Motivation

Among the 300 employees questioned, the highest average value belongs to BT1: "I feel that what I am doing is the driving force behind my work" (mean = 3.95). Employees understand expressly what work they are doing and what needs to be done. Next is BT5 (mean = 3.94) – the work of the software industry itself creates inspiration and promotes employees' internal motivation, making them satisfied and work more effectively.

To make workers' work rich, meaningful, and essential to the company's operations, we can give workers more freedom. Decide on issues such as choosing working methods, work order, and work pace, and work according to flexible hours for them. Second, encourage low-level workers' participation in decisions and coordination among workers. Leaders can encourage employees to participate in many ways. They can ask for employees' opinions and aspirations through informal conversations, questions related to company issues, or leadership. Leaders can ask employees to give suggestions on an issue in the company that employees and management are interested in. Third, make employees feel responsible for their work and show them that their role is essential. Ensure employees can see that their tasks have contributed significantly and meaningfully to the overall results of the entire company. Fourth, provide timely and accurate feedback on employee task completion.

However, to implement this solution successfully and effectively, the company must do well to give power to its employees, and leaders need to understand what their employees need. Make employees know what they will benefit from

Table 3.4. Bootstrap.

Relationships Parameter			\multicolumn{6}{c}{Bootstrap Estimation}
			SE	SE–SE	Mean	Bias	SE–Bias	CR
HQ	←	BT	0.064	0.003	0.148	−0.006	0.005	−1.2
HQ	←	BN	0.073	0.004	0.336	0.007	0.005	1.4
HL	←	BN	0.072	0.004	0.184	−0.002	0.005	−0.4
HL	←	BT	0.061	0.003	0.312	−0.013	0.004	−3.25
HL	←	HQ	0.063	0.003	0.215	0.01	0.004	2.5

Note: SE: standard error, SE–SE: standard error of standard error, Mean: mean value, Bias: bias, SE–Bias: standard deviation of bias, CR: critical value.

working efficiently, explain to employees what they are doing and why they have to do so, and regularly evaluate and record the results of their work. In the current situation, the company needs to enrich its work according to the following principles: increased job demands: the job should change in a way that increases the difficulty and responsibility of the job; Increased accountability of employees: allowing for more executive responsibilities in the execution of work. Please create a free and reasonable work schedule within the limits that allow the company to allow employees to do their work according to their schedules, limit the working time – try to give employees the most challenging jobs so they can feel their importance to the company. Provide feedback on employees and vice versa; employees should also report the situation of work performance regularly to the supervisor.

4.6.2. Policy Implications of Extrinsic Motivation
According to survey data, the highest consensus rate belongs to BN2 (mean = 3.25) – "In order to strive to do the job well, there must always be an important external factor influencing me." This means that for employees, the current reward and gift policy positively impacts their motivation and gives them satisfaction. However, BN3 has the lowest consensus in the four questions (mean = 2.53) and emphasizes more than one thing. With young people, rewards and accompanying elements can boost motivation for employees to work more efficiently but not as a prerequisite for them to do their jobs.

Four types of actions require attention to be adjusted to influence extrinsic motivation. Frist is externally adjusted behavior: This is the least automatic form of extrinsic motivation. This type of behavior is based only on reward, encouragement, or external pressure. Second, internalization: In this case, the cause of the behavior is external but individual at the time of the activity to increase self-esteem and reduce guilt or anxiety. Third, regulation through identification: In this type of behavior, the individual has previously analyzed objectives or rewards imposed from outside and understood that they are essential to him. Fourth is integrated regulation: This is the most autonomous form of external motivation. In this type of regulation, people receive external incentives as if they were their own. This phase differs from external motivation, in which the goals to be achieved do not belong to the individual's internal capacity but remain external.

4.6.3. Policy Implications of Work Efficiency
The most consensual working efficiency factor is HQ7 (mean =3.27) – "I always put the quality of work first" – which reflects the company's quality policy. When employees join the company, they are continuously trained in quality, understanding that a quality job must come with efficiency. There is always a quality management department to follow each project to ensure the employees' results are both efficient and high quality. However, most employees disagree with HQ4 (mean = 2.16) – which means that the employee understands that he needs to put in enough effort to get the job done correctly, not necessarily more than the

current effort. This point needs to be considered in order to formulate the right policy for employees to make more effort.

Several policy implications help improve employee efficiency: First is to create a friendly, cooperative, and respectful working environment where all employees have a joyful attitude and cooperate. At the same time, there is a need for a proper management framework to create initiative in each employee's work and reduce the management role significantly. Second, the work needs to be allocated to each employee with the right expertise and skills, and the effectiveness of the work will then be improved. In order to generate leverage in improving employee productivity, the company should apply target management methods and evaluate employee achievements to motivate them to move forward. Third, focus on the development and creation of staff, constant care, and equipment: just like humans, if you always follow the old way, after a while, the efficiency will not be as good as it was at first. We should focus on investing machinery in management.

4.6.4. Policy Implications of Job Satisfaction

The most consensual working efficiency factor is HQ7 (mean =3.27) – "I always put the quality of work first" – which reflects the company's quality policy. When employees join the company, they are continuously trained in quality, understanding that a quality job must come with efficiency. There is always a quality management department to follow each project to ensure the employees' results are both efficient and high quality. However, most employees disagree with HQ4 (mean = 2.16) – which means that the employee understands that he needs to put in enough effort to get the job done correctly, not necessarily more than the current effort. This point needs to be considered in order to formulate the right policy for employees to make more effort.

Several policy implications help improve employee efficiency: First is to create a friendly, cooperative, and respectful working environment where all employees have a joyful attitude and cooperate. At the same time, among the questions asked about satisfaction among employees, the majority are satisfied with their colleagues with HL9 (mean = 3.13). This is perfectly logical because this software company is a company with several young people who are always dynamic, enthusiastic, and willing to cooperate in a spirit to accomplish the assigned work competently; this is a strength to be noted in the right team policy.

Through fulfilling their responsibilities, the company's collective members cooperate directly with each other and always have mutual relevance and impact. So, the first thing that the leadership of the software company needs to do is improve the working environment and create close relationships and bonds between colleagues to increase motivation. Specifically:

The first is to create sharing, rhythmic, and compelling coordination between colleagues. Create an atmosphere of working collectively that is always joyful and social, form the attitude of people to work, friends, colleagues, and leaders enthusiastically, and create harmony and solidarity.

The second is to build a spirit of solidarity, mutual affection, and collaboration to help each other progress in work and life. In the labor collective, emotions are always spread from one person to another; this will have a perfect effect on the psychological state and attitude toward the worker's work. This affects labor productivity and business production efficiency.

Third, it is necessary to organize more awards competitions between employees and between departments in the company to create more excitement in the work process, such as creative competitions, flower shows, cooking, literature, sports.

5. CONCLUSION

The practical research on factors affecting work motivation at the software company has the following results: First, from the research model after preliminary research (including 4 factors and 25 observed variables), through an actual survey, a research model of factors affecting employees' work motivation at the software company was identified. These factors are (1) internal motivation, measured by six observed variables; (2) external motivation – there are four observed variables; (3) work efficiency – there are seven observed variables; and (4) job satisfaction – there are eight observed variables. Second, when the above four factors were included in multiple regression analysis, the statistical results showed that all factors had beta coefficients other than zero, with a p-value < 0.05, meeting statistical requirements. It can be concluded that these four factors all measure the work motivation of employees at the software company. Third, most employees' ratings on the criteria of the scales affecting work motivation and work efficiency are at an average level and relatively good. This proves that the level of motivation among employees in the company is not high. Fourth, variance analysis also shows differences in assessments in groups with different personal characteristics for factors affecting work motivation. Therefore, when developing policies, paying attention to these factors is necessary.

REFERENCES

Amabile, T. M. (1993). Motivational synergy: Toward new conceptualizations of intrinsic and extrinsic motivation in the workplace. *Human Resource Management Review*, *3*(3), 185–201.

Antoni, G. D. (2009). Intrinsic extrinsic motivations to volunteer and social capital formation. *KYKLOS*, *62*(3), 359–370.

Bareket-Bojmel, L., Hochman, G., & Ariely, D. (2014). It's (not) all about the Jacksons: Testing different types of short-term bonuses in the field. *Journal of Management*, *43*(2), 1–21.

Bentler, P. M., & Bonett, D. G. (1980). Significance tests and goodness of fit in the analysis of covariance structures. *Psychological Bulletin*, *88*(3), 588.

Carmines, E. G., & McIver, J. P. (1981). *Analyzing models with unobserved variables: Analysis of covariance structures*. In G. W. Bohrnstedt & E. F. Borgatta (Eds.), *Social measurement: Current issues* (pp. 65–115). Sage Publications, Inc.

Cerasoli, C. P., Nicklin, J. M., & Nassrelgrgawi, A. S. (2016). Performance, incentives, and needs for autonomy, competence, and relatedness: A meta-analysis. *Motivation and Emotion*, *40*(6), 781–813.

Deci, E. L. (1975). *Intrinsic motivation*. Plenum Press, Springer.

Deci, E. L., & Ryan R. M. (1985). *Intrinsic motivation and self-determination in human behavior.* Springer.

Erciş, M. S. (2010). The importance of motivation in marketing communication and multinational shopping center example. *Gazi Üniversitesi İletişim Fakültesi, 30*(1), 165–180.

Gagné, M., & Deci, E. L. (2005). Self-determination theory and work motivation. *Journal of Organizational Behavior, 26*, 331–362.

Gagné, M., Forest, J., Vansteenkiste, M., Crevier-Braud, L., Broeck, A. V. d., Aspeli, A. K., Bellerose, J., Benabou, C., Chemolli, E., Güntert, S. T., Halvari, H., Indiyastuti, D. L., Johnson, P. A., Molstad, M. H., Naudin, M., Ndao, A., Olafsen, A. H., Roussel, P., Wang, Z., & Westbye, C. (2015). The multidimensional work motivation scale: Validation evidence in seven languages and nine countries. *European Journal of Work and Organizational Psychology, 24*(2), 178–196.

Gannon, M. J., & Noon, J. P. (1971). Management's critical deficiency: Executives unaware of applicable research. *Business Horizons, 14*(1), 49–56.

Gibson, J.L., Ivancevich, J.M., & Donnelly, J.H. (1997). *Organizations* (9th ed.). McGraw-Hill.

Howard, J. L, Gagné, M., & Morin, A. J. S. (2020). Putting the pieces together: Reviewing the structural conceptualization of motivation within SDT. *Motivation and Emotion, 44*(4), 1–16. https://doi.org/10.1007/s11031-020-09838-2

Hulin, C. L., & Judge, T. A. (2003). Job attitudes. In W. C. Borman, D. R. ligen, & R. J. Klimoski (Eds.), *Handbook of psychology: Industrial and organizational psychology* (pp. 255–276).

Jenkins, G. D., & Shaw, J. D. (1998). Are financial incentives related to performance? A meta-analytic review of empirical research. *Journal of Applied Psychology, 83*(5), 777–787.

Kingful, S., & Nusenu, A. A. (2015). Teachers motivation in senior high schools in Ghana: A case of Ghana senior high school. *Journal of Education and Practice, 6*(16), 110–121.

Kline, R. B. (2005). *Principles and practice of structural equation modeling* (2nd ed.). Guilford.

Kluger, A. N., & DeNisi, A. (1996). The effects of feedback interventions on performance: A historical review, a meta-analysis, and a preliminary feedback intervention theory. *Psychological Bulletin, 119*(2), 254–284.

Kotler, P., Armstrong, G., Saunders, J., & Wong, V. (2001). Principles of marketing, 2nd edition. *Corporate Communications: An International Journal, 6*(3), 164–165.

Kreitner, R., Kinicki, A., & Buelens, M. (2007). *Organizational behaviour.* McGraw-Hill.

Küskü, F. (2003). Employee satisfaction in the higher education: The case of academic and administrative staff in Turkey. *Career Development International, 8*(7), 347–356.

Kuvaas, B., & Dysvik, A. (2009). Perceived investment in employee development, intrinsic motivation and work performance. *Human Resource Management, 19*(3), 217–335. https://doi.org/10.1111/j.1748-8583.2009.00103.x

Lazear, E. P. (2000). Performance pay and productivity. *The American Economic Review, 90*(5), 1346–1361.

Lin, P. Y. (2007). Meta-analysis of the association of serotonin transporter gene polymorphism with obsessive-compulsive disorder. *Progress in Neuro-Psychopharmacology and Biological Psychiatry, 31*(3), 683–689.

Locke, E. (1976). Nature and causes of job satisfaction. In M. D. Dunnette (Ed.), *Handbook of industrial and organizational psychology* (pp. 1297–1349). Rand McNally.

Locke, E. A., Sirota, D., & Wolfson, A. D. (1976). An experimental case study of the successes and failures of job enrichment in a government agency. *Journal of Applied Psychology, 61*(6), 701–711. https://doi/10.1037/0021-9010.61.6.701

Maslow, A. H. (1943). A theory of human motivation. *Psychological Review, 50*, 370–396.

McGehee, W., & Tullar, W. L. (1979). Single-question measures of overall job satisfaction: A comment on Quinn, Staines, and McCullough. *Journal of Vocational Behavior, 14*(1), 112–117.

Meyer, J. P., Becker, T. E., & Vandenberghe, C. (2004). Employee commitment and motivation: A conceptual analysis and integrative model. *Journal of Applied Psychology, 89*(6), 991–1007.

Motowidlo, S. J., & Kell, H. J. (2013). Job performance. *Industrial and Organizational Psychology, 12*, 82–100.

Mujah, W., Ruziana, R., Sigh, H., & D'Cruz, O. T. (2011). Meaning of work and employee motivation. *Terengganu International Management and Business Journal, 1*(2), 18–26.

Panagiotis, G. P., & Petridou E. (2008). Employees' psychological empowerment via intrinsic and extrinsic rewards. *AHCMJ, 4*(1), 17–40.

Pattengale, N. D., Alipour, M., Bininda-Emonds, O. R., Moret, B. M., & Stamatakis, A. (2010). How many bootstrap replicates are necessary? *Journal of Computational Biology*, *17*(3), 337–354.

Porter, L., & Lawler, E. (1968). What job attitudes tell about motivation. Organizational development: Part 3. *Harvard Business Review*, *46*, 70–79.

Price, J. L., & Mueller, C. W. (1981). A causal model of turnover for nurses. *Academy of Management Journal*, *24*(3), 543–565.

Robbins, S. P., & Judge, T. A. (2013). *Organisational behavior* (15th ed.). Pearson.

Ryan, R. M., & Deci, E. L. (2000). Intrinsic and extrinsic motivations: Classic definitions and new directions. *Contemporary Educational Psychology*, *25*(1), 54–67.

Ryan, R. M., & Deci, E. L. (2008). From ego depletion to vitality: Theory and findings concerning the facilitation of energy available to the self. *Social and Personality Psychology Compass*, *2*(2), 702–717.

Ryan, R. M., & Deci, E. L. (2017). *Self-determination theory: Basic psychological needs in motivation, development, and wellness*. Guilford Publishing.

Ryan, R. M., & Deci, E. L. (2020). Intrinsic and extrinsic motivation from a self-determination theory perspective: Definitions, theory, practices, and future directions. *Contemporary Educational Psychology*, *25*(1), 1–11.

Scott, M., & Maclntyre, P. (1997). The generic job satisfaction scale: Scale development and its correlate. *Employee Assistance Quarterly*, *13*(2), 1–16.

Smith, P. C., Kendall, L., & Hulin, C. L. (1969). *The measurement of satisfaction in work and retirement: A strategy for the study of attitudes*. Rand Mcnally.

Spector, P. E. (1997). *Job satisfaction: Application, assessment, causes, and consequences*. Sage Publications, Inc.

Spreitzer, G., & Grant, A. M. (2005). A socially embedded model of thriving at work. *Organization Science*, *16*(5), 537–549.

Steiger, J. H. (1990). Structural model evaluation and modification: An interval estimation approach. *Multivariate Behavioral Research*, *25*(2), 173–180. https://doi.org/10.1207/s15327906mbr2502_4

Storey, M. A., Zimmermann, T., & Kalliamvakou, E. (2019). Towards a theory of software developer job satisfaction and perceived productivity. *IEEE Transactions on Software Engineering*, *47*(10), 1–18.

Timothy, A. J., Thoresen, C. J., Bono, E. J., & Patton, G. K. (2001). The job satisfaction–job performance relationship: A qualitative and quantitative review. *Psychological Bulletin*, *127*(3), 376–407.

Vallerand, R. J., & Blssonnette, R. (1992). Intrinsic, extrinsic, and amotivational styles as predictors of behavior: A prospective study. *Journal of Personality*, *60*(3), 599–620.

Van den Broeck, A., Lens, W., De Witte, H., & Van Coillie, H. (2013). Unraveling the importance of the quantity and the quality of workers' motivation for well-being: A person-centered perspective. *Journal of Vocational Behavior*, *82*(1), 69–78.

Warr, P., Cool, J., & Wall, T. (1979). Scales for the measurement of some work attitudes and aspects of psychological well-being. *Journal of Occupational Psychology*, *52*(2), 129–148.

Weibel, A., Rost, K., & Osterloh, M. (2010). Pay for performance in the public sector: Benefits and (hidden) costs. *Journal of Public Administration Research and Theory*, *20*(2), 387–412.

Weiss, D. J., Dawis, R. V., England, G. W., & Lofquist, L. H. (1967). *Manual for the Minnesota satisfaction questionnaire. Minnesota studies in vocational rehabilitation*. University of Minnesota, Industrial Relations Center.

Whang, P. A., & Hancock, G. R. (1994). Motivation and mathematics achievement: Comparisons between Asian-American and non-Asian students. *Contemporary Educational Psychology*, *19*(3), 302–322.

Wright, B. E., & Kim, S. (2004). Participation's influence on job satisfaction: The importance of job characteristics. *Power of Public Personnel Administration*, *24*(1), 18–40. https://doi.org/10.1177/0734371X03259860

Xie, B., Zhou, W., Huang, J. L., & Xia, M. (2017). Using goal facilitation theory to explain the relationships between calling and organization-directed citizenship behavior and job satisfaction. *Journal of Vocational Behavior*, *100*, 78–87.

CHAPTER 4

RETHINKING ORGANIZATIONAL HIERARCHY: A CRITICAL ANALYSIS OF STRATEGIC MANAGEMENT SCHOOLS

Mehmet Barca[a] and Semih Ceyhan[b]

[a]Department of Business Administration, Faculty of Political Science, Social Sciences University of Ankara, Türkiye
[b]Department of Business Administration, Business School, Ankara Yildirim Beyazit University, Türkiye

ABSTRACT

The purpose of this study is to find out the place of non-managerial workers, including blue- and gray-collar workers, through analyzing how different schools of thought in the strategic management (SM) literature approach strategy making from the viewpoint of an organizational hierarchy, especially top-level management team, or human competence, no matter whether they occupy any hierarchical position. There is a gap in the literature regarding the extent to which non-managerial workers engage in SM processes. While their role has been acknowledged by many scholars, there is a need for further explanation of how different schools of thought in SM hold varying assumptions about organizational actors in non-hierarchical positions. In this regard, this study aims to question the dominant hierarchy logics of different strategy schools. This will be done through analyzing the strategy literature with a "strategy-making skills & capability centered" lens, and conceptualization of the hierarchical positions' role in SM will be criticized.

By this way, the role of gray- and blue-collar workers in SM literature would be better understood.

Keywords: Strategic management; blue collar; gray collar; inclusion; participation

1. INTRODUCTION

It is a common finding that there is a lack of strategy participation of non-hierarchical workers in most organizations (Barca & Ceyhan, 2023). Scholars generally suggest that increasing the participation of workers from all levels in strategy formulation, implementation, and control would increase the quality of strategy (Brielmaier & Friesl, 2023; Splitter et al., 2023). The classical postulation of SM is that a responsibility of upper level managers (Hambrick & Mason, 1984) still has a predominance in the literature (Neely et al., 2020). However, there is a lack of scientific inquiry on questioning the blue- and gray-collar workers' role.

We challenge the generally accepted SM notion that treats the organization as a homogeneous phenomenon reacting to its competitive environment as a single entity. This turns the internal organizational factors and their variations into a black box, neglecting their impact on SM in different employee levels. When considering the human dimension of the organization, it is far from being homogeneous; on the contrary, it is heterogeneous. Our critique emphasizes that the strategic actors arise not only from the hierarchical positions but also from the employees at various non-managerial levels. We argue that SM capabilities (including formulation, implementation, control) should be based on individuals' competencies, rather than the position they hold in upper hierarchical levels. Our contribution here is to prioritize the skills and capabilities of organizational actors over their hierarchical positions. In clearer terms, the quality or level of contribution of an actor in the SM process is dependent on his/her individual skills and capabilities. It does not necessarily require holding an upper level managerial position within the organization.

Evaluating all these factors, in this study, we aim to comparatively explore the hierarchical perspectives of fundamental schools of SM. Through this, we seek to highlight the theoretical implications of the human role within organizations. We will assess how the roles of blue-collar and white-collar workers in SM are theoretically understood and contemplate on potential new perspectives. In this regard, this study questions the hierarchy perspectives of different strategy schools, in order to understand the theoretical visibility of non-managerial levels including blue- and gray-collar workers.

Borrowing the conceptualization of Barca (2022), in this study, we aim to analyze the hierarchical perspectives of the seminal works in four classifications of SM research. In this regard, process, content, context, and cognition schools will be examined regarding their emphasis on the roles of managers and lower level workers. Methodologically, we will conduct a literature review of significant works of the SM schools. While reviewing these foundational works, we will specifically aim to summarize their perspectives on organizational actors and their role in the SM process. This approach will enable us to conduct a critical assessment of the SM schools of thought, focusing on the position of blue-collar and gray-collar workers.

2. PROCESS LITERATURE – DESIGN AND LEARNING SCHOOLS

2.1. Design School

Chandler (1962) was among the first scholars who used the term of strategy in business context, highlighting that strategy is created by managerial decisions. Strategic objectives were believed to be formulated by top managers and then they align the other organizational actors to facilitate those predefined objectives. This perspective is later called design school by Mintzberg, pointing to the relation between strategy and structure in a way that top-level determined strategies are followed by the organizational structure (Mintzberg, 1990). There was no room for non-managerial actors in this classical "command and control" mentality (Hayes, 1985), which delegates all strategic decisions to the top executives who then enforce these decisions on the organization while monitoring them through intricate planning, budgeting, and control systems.

In classic management schools, there is an emphasis on strong hierarchies with at least three levels of management: top, middle, and lower (Teece, 2007, p. 1335). While claiming the structure must follow the strategy (Andrews, 1971), the design school was implicitly arguing that strategy is decided by top managers, and as a part of organizational structure, other organizational actors should follow the predefined strategy by chief executives. Quoting from Selznick (1957), "it is the function of the leader … to define the ends, … to design an enterprise distinctively adapted to these ends" (p. 37); Andrews considers chief executives as "architects of organizational purpose" (p. 19). Therefore, design school put a passive role to the non-managerial workers who need to follow and implement the strategy developed by top managers.

2.2. Planning School

Emerged in the 1960s and 1970s, scholars thought that firms need for a formal planning to respond to environmental complexity and competition (Ansoff, 1965). Strategic planning in this regard has been widely praised and has gained widespread application in practice. In this perspective, strategy is operationalized hierarchically; long-term visionary objectives sit on the top, followed by medium-term plans and then short-term operation plans. In parallel with this hierarchy of objectives, a corresponding hierarchy of budgets and action programs was also developed (Mintzberg et al., 2009). In this mechanical operationalization of SM, there were also a formalization in the division of SM labor among organizational actors.

Planning school appraised the formulation phase of the strategy as the most important phase. In the formulation, there is a need of harmonizing internal resources with the external requirements. In line with the traditional management approaches' endorsement of strong hierarchies (Teece, 2007), this school thought that only strategists who can do are top managers. As sitting at the top, they would have the necessary experience and perspective to set the visionary goals, develop master plans; middle- and low-level managers would then develop the shorter term strategies and action plans. While the strategic decisions were made by the top managers, low–middle levels would follow these strategies and operationalize the strategic perspective given by the top managers.

Another fallacy attributed to the planning school is its alleged detachment of planning from action. Despite claiming that decision-makers are top managers, the planning school separates them from the actual implementation of strategic planning. It positions top managers in a high, remote control place where they receive information from the implementers (Mintzberg et al., 2009). This division of labor in the strategy process implicitly argues that formulation is more important than other strategy processes. While the more "strategic" formulation is accepted as the duty of top managers, the steps of implementation and control are left to implementers in lower levels.

2.3. Learning School

Strategy is claimed to be about making choices (Porter, 1985); decision-makers' role as strategists is important here. While 1970s and 1980s research relied on the top managers' ability to plan good strategies, Mintzberg and Waters (1985) claimed that strategy emerges as a learning process in which contributions of middle-level managers matter for the quality. Parnell (2005), on the other hand, proposed that low-level managers and non-executors also play a crucial role in the strategy process. Bottom-up approaches became widespread in the 1990s and 2000s, highlighting the importance of workers and non-executives in formulating and implementing strategy (Floyd & Wooldridge, 2000). It is important to learn from the employee experiences from all levels (Noe et al., 2003).

We can see a clear distinction in the hierarchy perspective of learning school, by challenging the top-down structure of SM. Learning school seems to acknowledge the importance of non-managerial positions in the SM process. This school considers strategists as "learners," whether micro or macro, in every level of an organizational hierarchy, actors engage in learning activities. Due to the increasing environmental complexity and uncertainties, individuals need to learn how to respond to these requirements. Therefore, blue- and gray-collar workers could also take a strategist's role by learning within the limitation of their tasks and duties.

2.4. Strategy as Practice

Strategy as practice is one of the most important milestones which changes the level of analysis in SM into individual level rather than organization level (Jarzabkowski & Balogun, 2009; Jarzabkowski et al., 2007; Vaara & Whittington, 2012). In this perspective, rather than focusing on the effects of strategies on performance, scholars concentrated on how organizational actors (named as "practitioners") actually make, shape, and execute strategies over time (Whittington, 1996). Other than top managers, strategy as practice (SAP) research has highlighted the strategic role of middle managers, consultants, regulators, strategy teachers, and strategy gurus (Golsorkhi et al., 2015). They acknowledge the fact that strategy is not a top-down process, and there are strategy specialists who take responsibility in formulating, implementing, and controlling strategy (Paroutis & Pettigrew, 2007). SAP also focused on the role of middle-level managers in SM (Mantere, 2005).

By recognizing the humanistic nature of SM (Sminia & de Rond, 2012), and massifying strategy to low-level employees (Whittington, 2015), SAP seems to open up a much broader space for non-managerial workers in the strategy process. It provides a base to further discuss the roles of workers from lower hierarchical levels, including gray- and blue-collar workers (Barca & Ceyhan, 2023). According to SAP, anyone can be a strategist. It's a practice that encompasses every aspect of strategy, involving the development, monitoring, and reporting. The practice of strategizing extends beyond internal confines; consultants, state regulators, customers, and stakeholders actively participate in the strategizing process (Jarzabkowski & Spee, 2009). It opens up a broader space for the entire stakeholders. What the SAP adds to the learning school is the concept of "practice" where practitioners themselves become the strategists. Even monitoring and development are considered as integral practices, addressing every aspect comprehensively. This perspective certainly opens more place for gray- and blue-collar workers in strategy.

3. CONTENT LITERATURE – POSITIONING, RESOURCE-BASED VIEW, AND STRATEGY AS PRACTICE

3.1. Positioning School

While in positioning school, the main focus was on the external environment, and Porter does not say too much on the participation of non-managerial hierarchical levels in decision-making. Porter's framework has been extensively used to structure managers' perspectives (Campbell-Hunt, 2000). Explicitly his works consider top managers as focal points, and they are suggested to choose among generic strategies and position themselves considering the industrial competition factors (Porter, 1985, 1996). By doing so, Porter was trying to answer where to compete (which industry has more attractive characteristics; regarding dependence on buyer–supplier, rivalry, substitution, entry barriers) and how to compete (choosing one of the generic strategies: cost-leadership, differentiation, or focus).

However, there was an implicit assumption that top managers are the only strategists who are responsible for strategic thinking. The positioning school is also critiqued on the same grounds as design and planning schools, where top managers formulate and lower levels implement the strategy (Gavetti & Rivkin, 2007). Positioning schools consider a strategist as a "calculator" who collects hard data inside and outside of the company and calculates the best strategy for the firm (Mintzberg et al., 2009). In this perspective, the data are believed to be explicit and collectable, and lower level workers are expected to provide these data to top levels within the company. Based on these data, top-level management can create a fit between external environmental requirements and internal resources. While lower levels can only think within the boundaries of the firm, top managers are claimed to anticipate the external environmental competition factors. Competitive strategy is designed and planned by the top managers; by evaluating the external industry conditions, lower levels need to implement those strategies.

We observe a similar division in Porter's value-chain perspective. Despite recognizing the significance of aligning human resources with the strategies, the role of workers becomes meaningful only with a well-developed strategy from the top levels. The formulation–implementation division is evident in the value-chain conceptualization as well. Top managers anticipate competitive advantage in different activities of the value chain and enhance the competitiveness of a company by improving its structure (Simatupang et al., 2017), and the role of workers is to operationalize it. In each step of a value chain, we can only see blue- and gray-collar workers as the implementers. Moreover, it is claimed that Porter's value chain is a subordinate of resource-based analysis of organizational resources (Barney, 1991), highlighting a manager-centered perspective (Sheehan & Foss, 2017).

This perspective might be deficient due to the tendency of the positioning literature to focus on the "ideal" rather than what is precisely "realized." The potential deficiency in this perspective may stem from an emphasis on the "ideal" aspects of strategy rather than a comprehensive understanding of what is practically implemented in organizations. In attempting to explain sustainable competitive advantage, which means deviating from the norm (average performance) by definition, the emphasis on upper level hierarchies may inadvertently overlook the contributions of non-managerial "normal" workers. The focus on what sets companies apart in terms of leadership and strategic decisions might overshadow the critical roles played by the broader workforce in day-to-day operations, innovation, and the overall execution of strategies.

3.2. Resource-based View

According to the resource-based approach that emerged as the dominant perspective in the 1990s, competitive advantage began to be sought within the internal dynamics of companies (Barney, 1986, 1991; Rumelt, 1984; Wernerfelt, 1984). Internal resources, being specific to the business (such as patents, know-how, trained human resources, brand name, etc.), exhibited characteristics that were not easily imitable, purchasable, and even easily discernible. In this approach, the role of individuals naturally took a more prominent place compared to the classical perspectives. Contrary to Chandler's (1962) view of "structure follows strategy," it was claimed that structure of the firm primarily determines strategy. One of the most important elements of this "structure" was human resources.

Workers and managers in a company are considered as human capital (Becker, 1964), which could be an important determinant of competitive advantage as a strategic firm resource (Barney, 1991). Although resource-based view (RBV) is important in emphasizing the significance of the "human" as a strategic firm resource and opening a place for non-managers in the strategy process, it still lacks delving into the specific roles of non-manager workers. The main focus has still been on the managers and managerial teams as the sources of sustained competitive advantage (Barney, 1991).

Building on RBV, dynamic capabilities' perspective emphasized the importance of renewing the competencies to achieve fit with the changing requirements of the business environment (Gnizy, 2019; Helfat & Peteraf, 2009; Teece et al., 1997). Dynamic capabilities also overwhelmingly emphasize the role of managerial capabilities in coordinating, learning, and reconfiguring strategic resources (Adner & Helfat, 2003; Wilden et al., 2016). In this perspective, non-managerial workers are seen as factors of production in the classical sense, as Teece termed them as "unskilled labor" (Teece et al., 1997, p. 516). Dynamic capabilities are initially depicted as firm-level entities (Helfat & Winter, 2011); then, micro-foundational approaches have been developed, placing emphasis on the role of individuals (Winter, 2013). At the individual-level analysis, there is still a manager focus, for instance, dynamic managerial capabilities, an intriguing subject within the literature, have attracted considerable attention (Adner & Helfat, 2003; Helfat & Martin, 2015; Helfat & Peteraf, 2015). In recent studies, scholars also underlined the importance of lower level employees, by claiming that their contributions become aggregated into a firm-level capacity (Salvato & Vassolo, 2018, p. 1730).

Dynamic capabilities' perspective better apprehends the importance of individuals in the strategy process (Scheuer & Thaler, 2022; Salvato & Vassolo, 2018). It acknowledges workers as human capital which is not limited to top managers but a collective expertise and capabilities. Non-managerial workers often possess valuable tacit, intangible knowledge about operational processes, customer preferences, and other critical aspects of the business which can be a source of competitive advantage (Teece, 2007). Employees in lower level hierarchies are often the closest to the day-to-day operations of the business. Their ability to adapt to changes in the external environment and provide real-time feedback can enhance the firm's overall adaptability. When empowered and engaged, lower levels could be a rich source of strategic idea insights.

4. CONTEXT LITERATURE – DETERMINIST AND INDETERMINIST PERSPECTIVES

To gain a thorough understanding of the SM literature, it is crucial to consider the scholars' perspectives on the context in which the strategy is developed, implemented, and monitored. Barca (2022) claims that there are two context perspectives embedded in the previously mentioned strategy schools (planning/

positioning vs learning/RBV). Implicit in the design and positioning schools, the deterministic perspective considers the environment is objective and information is available to anyone (Mintzberg et al., 2009). This perspective underestimates the role of SM by simply narrowing it down to fitting the observable and objective environmental requirements. This deterministic perspective disregards the role of decision-makers, assuming that the right strategy is given by the environment and the only role of the decision-maker is to adapt to those conditions.

On the other hand, the indeterminist perspective considers that there is a mutual effect between a firm and its environment. While the environment requires some conditionality, decision-makers can also shape the environment through their strategic decisions (Hoskisson, 1999; Weick, 1987). This perspective gives more space for SM and decision-makers as a source of sustainable competitive advantage. Moreover, environmental conditions are often implicit and not easily observable; uncertainties prevail, and there is no singular objective way to comprehend them. The learning and resource-based schools align more closely with the co-evaluation and co-determination perspective of the indeterminist school.

In the indeterminist perspective, it is asserted that there exists a mutual interaction between the internal dynamics of a firm and its external environment, with both influencing each other. Unlike the deterministic viewpoint, which treats external conditions as given and objective, this perspective emphasizes the importance of decision-makers. Specifically, top managers, as key decision-makers, play a crucial role in this interactive process.

According to the deterministic perspective, the external environment's expectations from a firm are explicit, necessitating firms to conform accordingly. The strategist capable of achieving this is the top manager, responsible for establishing and monitoring the interaction with the external environment. In essence, the only organizational actor interpreting the external environment is the top manager (Andrews, 1971; Ansoff, 1965).

In contrast, the indeterminist perspective recognizes that external conditions are complex, uncertain, and not easily discernible (Rasche, 2008; Winsor, 1995). Consequently, identifying the right strategy demands a dynamic learning process. It is not limited to top-level management; every actor within their defined responsibilities can analyze external information. This analytical process is crucial for innovation, requiring the participation of all actors (Hutter et al., 2017; Mantere & Vaara, 2008). Unlike a mere planning or design exercise, strategy is fundamentally a learning process in which all participants can engage.

The indeterminist perspective, as signified by the RBV, emphasizes the alignment between the use of internal resources within a firm and its adaptation to the external environment. This notion underscores the importance of non-managerial employees in the overall strategic framework, recognizing their skills, knowledge, and experiences as potential sources of competitive advantage. In other words, even a non-managerial employee, in theory, holds the potential to influence the external environment. This perspective opens up the possibility that individuals across different hierarchical levels, including blue-collar and gray-collar workers, could contribute to shaping the firm's strategic outcomes.

5. COGNITIVE LITERATURE – RATIONAL/ANALYTIC AND BEHAVIORAL PERSPECTIVES

Research on the cognition of the decision-makers has been looking to answer the questions of who the strategists are and how their cognitions differ from each other. There are different answers to these questions in the SM literature: planner (Ansoff, 1965), designer (Andrews, 1971), learner (Mintzberg, 1979), positioner (Porter, 1980, 1985, 1996), and competence architect (Prahalad & Hamel, 2006). The motivation is to find out the cognitive antecedents of superior performance (Schmidt, 2015).

There are two schools mentioned by Barca (2022) here: rationalistic and behavioral. Both schools acknowledge that strategy exists at the individual level at the beginning and then move on to group and organization levels. SM in the first place is an individual cognitive process. Strategy was traditionally conceived as a rational deductive reasoning exercise (Calori, 1998). It has been discussed whether this reasoning is done in a deliberate or emergent way (Mintzberg & Waters, 1985). While rationalistic perspective thought that decision-makers are unboundedly rational actors, who can observe objective knowledge in the environment and plan and design strategy through deductive inferences, the latter acknowledge the fact that decision-makers are boundedly rational, and strategies are the results of their individual cognitive processes. This implies that there is no one best formal rational process in SM as rationalistic scholars suggest, but there are many different ways decision-makers develop their strategies. And these individual differences could be the source of performance differentials between organizations. It is claimed to be a necessity to comprehend the individual logics of executives as they navigate the challenges of a dynamically changing environment (Wright et al., 2013).

In the rationalistic perspective, cognitive acts of managers are claimed to be well-established (Garbuio et al., 2015). If a manager has necessary cognitive skills, he/she can generate innovative strategic options. However, from a behavioral perspective, there are not any identified codes of right or wrong cognitive processes that lead to strategies (Barca, 2022).

While the main focus is the top managers, when it comes to organizational or group-level cognitive processes (Ackermann & Eden, 2011), rationalistic perspectives ground on the neoclassical perspective of considering organizational actors as a collective mind (Akkerman et al., 2007) working together to one common goal of profit maximization. On the other hand, behavioral perspectives highlight the fact that each individual may have different interests within an organization, and rather than one common goal for everyone, this should be considered as a social process in which the collective cognitions are shaped.

In the discourse of the early 1980s, cognitive discussions on SM emerged, exemplified by Chaffe's seminal contribution that delineates distinct cognitive modes among decision-makers. Notably, Chaffe posited the existence of the linear mental mode, wherein strategy formulation and implementation are predominantly the purview of top managerial echelons. Conversely, the adaptive mode proposes a more decentralized SM paradigm, while the interpretive mode contends that strategy is a socially constructed phenomenon.

Within the interpretive mode, a noteworthy departure from the centrality of top management is observed. Here, the SM process is posited as an organization-wide endeavor, transcending the confines of exclusive top-level concern. Despite this departure, it is crucial to acknowledge that the discourse maintains a focal point on the pivotal role of top managers, who actively endeavor to influence and shape the conduct of other organizational participants in the strategic domain. Across all three modes, a shared understanding prevails, affirming that the crux of strategy formulation lies in the conceptual efforts undertaken by top management (Chaffee, 1985). However, it is also noted individuals from different hierarchies would have different cognitive representations of their strategic decision-making (Gavetti, 2005).

In the cognitive studies, the behavioral perspective opens more space to the non-managerial workers' role in SM. While not the primary focus in the literature until today, cognitive studies suggest the potential for analyzing the cognitive processes of lower level workers regarding strategy. This is a promising avenue for future exploration.

6. DISCUSSION

From the analysis, we can infer important implications. First, there is a tendency in the strategy theory advancement toward seeing strategy making as human competence rather than attributing to hierarchical positions. The latter schools emerged in the SM discipline are differing themselves from the earlier ones in terms of opening up an ample place for non-managerial workers in the process of strategy making. In clearer terms, in the earlier schools of SM, strategy work is bound to the hierarchical position rather than managerial action. However, the schools introduced later in all sub-areas SM, that is process, content, context, and cognition lean toward a wider perspective to encompass non-manager workers in strategy-making processes.

The reason behind this tendency is not just because of a theoretical advancement but also of a practical need. The nature of the economy changes from industrial to knowledge based. This means that the economy changes toward deeper and deeper expertise. New sectors, industries, and firms will emerge based on new/deeper expertise. The next generation of firms are going to be run by experts, rather than generalists. This will force them to act as an expert team, rather than one chief executive officer (CEO) or general. Most probably, the hierarchical organizations will be substituted by hierarchical-less, flat organizations. Organizational culture, language, relationship, and communication will change toward more language of expertise.

Another significant aspect is the changes in the structure of the labor market. In today's world, technologies like digitalization, artificial intelligence, and robotizing are taking over routine workloads in the workplace. In the future, labor demand will lean more toward non-routine, non-repetitive professions as a result. In this context, the workforce, defined as blue- and gray-collar, will see changes in routine job descriptions, shifting toward non-routine tasks. Consequently, the contribution of these workers to strategy will increase. They need to learn how to use these emerging technologies and how to adapt these to the organizational contexts they work in. This requires a shift from a routine job to more context-specific, technology-based competences. In simpler terms, in the future, blue- and gray-collar jobs will become more specialized rather than general, thereby increasing their strategic importance.

The evolution in SM thinking reflects a transformative shift from traditional planning-centric approaches to more adaptive and inclusive perspectives. This change is marked by a departure from rigid strategic plans toward a continuous learning process. Additionally, recognizing the importance of internal resources challenges the exclusive focus on industry positioning. Furthermore, the shift from a deterministic to an interactive understanding of the business context acknowledges the dynamic interplay between organizations and their environments. Importantly, the cognitive shift from unbounded rationality to bounded rationality challenges the assumption of perfect decision-making, recognizing the cognitive constraints of decision-makers. Throughout these transformations, there is a notable emphasis on the role and significance of lower level workers, as SM evolves to appreciate the diverse contributions of individuals at all organizational levels. Given all these changes, schools of thought in SM also need to be adapted and respond to these tendencies emerging in recent decades.

7. CONCLUSION

In this chapter, we aim to provide an alternative perspective on hierarchies while seeking to understand the role of organizational actors as the source of sustainable competitive advantage. When historical evolution of the SM field is analyzed, a clear perspective shift from a top-down approach to a more inclusive understanding of SM emerges, recognizing the critical role of lower level and non-managerial workers. We can see that rather than the classical understanding of top managers planning the strategy, it has been accepted as a learning process in which the dominance of top managers is questioned. In addition to viewing SM as a positioning choice of top managers, the RBV recognizes the strategic role of non-managerial workers. While neoclassical management maintains a deterministic outlook, recent studies adopt a perspective that perceives the context as indeterminist and interactive. These studies assert that organizational actors at all levels influence the boundaries of SM. Lastly, the cognitive perspective extends its focus beyond top managers to include the cognitive processes of lower level workers.

In conclusion, the evolving landscape of SM calls for a paradigm shift that accommodates the active involvement of non-managerial workers, including blue- and gray-collar workers, in the strategic decision-making process. In essence, the future of SM hinges on its capacity to propel advancements within each sub-area of the discipline, particularly with regard to the comprehensive inclusion of all organizational actors from all levels.

REFERENCES

Ackermann, F., & Eden, C. (2011). Negotiation in strategy making teams: Group support systems and the process of cognitive change. *Group Decision and Negotiation, 20*(3), 293–314. https://doi.org/10.1007/s10726-008-9133-y

Adner, R., & Helfat, C. E. (2003). Corporate effects and dynamic managerial capabilities. *Strategic Management Journal, 24*(10), 1011–1025. https://doi.org/10.1002/smj.331

Akkerman, S., Van den Bossche, P., Admiraal, W., Gijselaers, W., Segers, M., Simons, R.-J., & Kirschner, P. (2007). Reconsidering group cognition: From conceptual confusion to a boundary area between cognitive and socio-cultural perspectives? *Educational Research Review, 2*(1), 39–63. https://doi.org/10.1016/j.edurev.2007.02.001

Andrews, K. (1971). *The concept of corporate strategy*. Dow-Jones-Irwin.

Ansoff, H. I. (1965). *Corporate strategy*. McGraw-Hill.

Barca, M. (2022). Bilim Alanı Olarak Stratejik Yönetimin Değerlendirilmesi. In M. Barca & M. S. Döven (Eds.), *Stratejik Yönetim Araştırmaları* (1st ed., pp. 25–98). Efe Akademi Yayınları.

Barca, M., & Ceyhan, S. (2023). Silent heroes of strategy: Neglected role of blue and gray collar workers. In J. Paliszkiewicz & D. Varoğlu (Eds.), *Management and organizational studies on blue- and gray-collar workers: Diversity of collars (international perspectives on equality, diversity and inclusion)* (1st ed., Vol. 8, pp. 197–210). Emerald Publishing Limited. https://doi.org/10.1108/s2051-233320230000008018

Barney, J. B. (1986). Organizational culture: Can it be a source of sustained competitive advantage? *Academy of Management Review, 11*(3), 656–665.

Barney, J. B. (1991). Firm resources and sustained competitive advantage. *Journal of Management, 17*(1), 99–120. https://doi.org/10.1177/014920639101700108

Becker, G. S. (1964). *Human capital*. Columbia.

Brielmaier, C., & Friesl, M. (2023). Pulled in all directions: Open strategy participation as an attention contest. *Strategic Organization, 21*(3), 709–720. https://doi.org/10.1177/14761270211034515

Calori, R. (1998). Essai: Philosophizing on strategic management models. *Organization Studies, 19*(2), 281–307.

Campbell-Hunt, C. (2000). What have we learned about generic competitive strategy? A meta-analysis. *Strategic Management Journal, 21*(2), 127–154.

Chaffee, E. E. (1985). Three models of strategy. *The Academy of Management Review, 10*(1), 89–98. https://www.jstor.org/stable/258215?seq=1&cid=pdf-

Chandler, A. D. (1962). *Strategy and structure – Chapters in the history of the industrial enterprise*. MIT Press.

Floyd, S. W., & Wooldridge, B. (2000). *Building strategy from the middle: Reconceptualizing strategy process*. Sage Publications.

Garbuio, M., Lovallo, D., Porac, J., & Dong, A. (2015). A design cognition perspective on strategic option generation. In G. Gavetti & W. Ocasio (Eds.), *Cognition and Strategy (Advances in Strategic Management)* (Vol. 32, pp. 437–465). Emerald Group Publishing Ltd. https://doi.org/10.1108/S0742-332220150000032014

Gavetti, G. (2005). Cognition and hierarchy: Rethinking the microfoundations of capabilities' development. *Organization Science, 16*(6), 599–617. https://doi.org/10.1287/orsc.1050.0140

Gavetti, G., & Rivkin, J. W. (2007). On the origin of strategy: Action and cognition over time. *Organization Science, 18*(3), 420–439. https://doi.org/10.1287/orsc.1070.0282

Gnizy, I. (2019). The role of inter-firm dispersion of international marketing capabilities in marketing strategy and business outcomes. *Journal of Business Research, 105*(December), 214–226. https://doi.org/10.1016/j.jbusres.2019.08.015

Golsorkhi, D., Rouleau, L., Seidl, D., & Vaara, E. (2015). Introduction: What is strategy as practice? In D. Golsorkhi, L. Rouleau, D. Seidl & E. Vaara (Eds.), *Cambridge handbook of strategy as practice* (2nd ed., pp. 1–30). Cambridge University Press. https://doi.org/10.1017/CBO9781139681032

Hambrick, D. C., & Mason, P. A. (1984). Upper echelons: The organization as a reflection of its top managers. *The Academy of Management Review, 9*(2), 193–206.

Hayes, R. H. (1985). Strategic planning forward in reverse? *Harvard Business Review, 63*(6), 111–119.

Helfat, C. E., & Martin, J. A. (2015). Dynamic managerial capabilities: Review and assessment of managerial impact on strategic change. *Journal of Management, 41*(5), 1281–1312. https://doi.org/10.1177/0149206314561301

Helfat, C. E., & Peteraf, M. A. (2009). Understanding dynamic capabilities: Progress along a developmental path. *Strategic Organization, 7*(1), 91–102. https://doi.org/10.1177/1476127008100133

Helfat, C. E., & Peteraf, M. A. (2015). Managerial cognitive capabilities and the microfoundations of dynamic capabilities. *Strategic Management Journal, 36*(6), 831–850. https://doi.org/10.1002/smj.2247

Helfat, C. E., & Winter, S. G. (2011). Untangling dynamic and operational capabilities: Strategy for the (n)ever-changing world. *Strategic Management Journal, 32*(11), 1243–1250. https://doi.org/10.1002/smj.955

Hoskisson, R. E. (1999). Theory and research in strategic management: Swings of a pendulum. *Journal of Management, 25*(3), 417–456. https://doi.org/10.1177/014920639902500307

Hutter, K., Nketia, B. A., & Füller, J. (2017). Falling short with participation – Different effects of ideation, commenting, and evaluating behavior on open strategizing. *Long Range Planning, 50*(3), 355–370. https://doi.org/10.1016/j.lrp.2016.08.005

Jarzabkowski, P., & Balogun, J. (2009). The practice and process of delivering integration through strategic planning. *Journal of Management Studies, 46*(8), 1255–1288. https://doi.org/10.1111/j.1467-6486.2009.00853.x

Jarzabkowski, P., Balogun, J., & Seidl, D. (2007). Strategizing: The challenges of a practice perspective. *Human Relations, 60*(1), 5–27. https://doi.org/10.1177/0018726707075703

Jarzabkowski, P., & Spee, A. P. (2009). Strategy-as-practice: A review and future directions for the field. *International Journal of Management Reviews, 11*(1), 69–95. https://doi.org/10.1111/j.1468-2370.2008.00250.x

Mantere, S. (2005). Strategic practices as enablers and disablers of championing activity. *Strategic Organization, 3*(2), 157–184. https://doi.org/10.1177/1476127005052208

Mantere, S., & Vaara, E. (2008). On the problem of participation in strategy: A critical discursive perspective. *Organization Science, 19*(2), 341–358. https://doi.org/10.1287/orsc.1070.0296

Mintzberg, H. (1979). An emerging strategy of "direct" research. *Administrative Science Quarterly, 24*(4), 582–589. http://www.jstor.org/stable/2392364

Mintzberg, H. (1990). The design school: Reconsidering the basic premises of strategic management. *Strategic Management Journal, 11*(3), 171–195. https://doi.org/10.1002/smj.4250110302

Mintzberg, H., Ahlstrand, B., & Lampel, J. (2009). *Strategy safari – The complete guide through the wilds of strategic management* (2nd ed.). Pearson Education Limited.

Mintzberg, H., & Waters, J. A. (1985). Of strategies, deliberate and emergent. *Strategic Management Journal, 6*(3), 257–272. https://doi.org/10.1002/smj.4250060306

Neely, B. H., Lovelace, J. B., Cowen, A. P., & Hiller, N. J. (2020). Metacritiques of upper echelons theory: Verdicts and recommendations for future research. *Journal of Management, 46*(6), 1029–1062. https://doi.org/10.1177/0149206320908640

Noe, R. A., Hollenbeck, J. R., Gerhart, B., & Wright, P. M. (2003). *Human resource management: Gaining a competitive advantage*. McGraw-Hill.

Parnell, J. A. (2005). Strategic philosophy and management level. *Management Decision, 43*(2), 157–170. https://doi.org/10.1108/00251740510581894

Paroutis, S., & Pettigrew, A. (2007). Strategizing in the multi-business firm: Strategy teams at multiple levels and over time. *Human Relations, 60*(1), 99–135. https://doi.org/10.1177/0018726707075285

Porter, M. E. (1980). *Competitive strategy: Techniques for analyzing industries and competitors*. Free Press.

Porter, M. E. (1985). *Competitive advantage* (Vol. 15). Free Press.

Porter, M. E. (1996). What is strategy? *Harvard Business Review*, November–December, 37–55.

Prahalad, C. K., Hamel, G. (2006). The Core Competence of the Corporation. In D. Hahn & B. Taylor (Eds.), *Strategische Unternehmungsplanung — Strategische Unternehmungsführung*. Springer. https://doi.org/10.1007/3-540-30763-X_14

Rasche, A. (2008). *The paradoxical foundation of strategic management*. Springer. https://doi.org/10.1007/978-3-7908-1976-2

Rumelt, R. P. (1984). Towards a strategic theory of the firm. In R. B. Lamb (Ed.), *Competitive strategic management* (3rd ed., Vol. 26, pp. 556–570). Prentice Hall.

Salvato, C., & Vassolo, R. (2018). The sources of dynamism in dynamic capabilities. *Strategic Management Journal, 39*(6), 1728–1752. https://doi.org/10.1002/smj.2703

Scheuer, L. J., & Thaler, J. (2022). How do dynamic capabilities affect performance? A systematic review of mediators. *European Management Journal*, *41*(6), 914–931. https://doi.org/10.1016/j.emj.2022.12.006

Schmidt, J. (2015). Cognition, resources, and opportunities: Managerial judgment, theories of success and the origin of novel strategies. In G. Gavetti & W. Ocasio (Eds.), *Cognition and strategy* (Advances in Strategic Management, Vol. 32, pp. 549–575). Emerald Group Publishing Limited. https://doi.org/10.1108/S0742-332220150000032017

Selznick, P. (1957). *Leadership in administration: A sociological interpretation* (Vol. 62, pp. 67–68). Harper & Row.

Sheehan, N. T., & Foss, N. J. (2017). Using Porterian activity analysis to understand organizational capabilities. *Journal of General Management*, *42*(3), 41–51. https://doi.org/10.1177/0306307017690518

Simatupang, T. M., Piboonrungroj, P., & Williams, S. J. (2017). The emergence of value chain thinking. *International Journal of Value Chain Management*, *8*(1), 40. https://doi.org/10.1504/IJVCM.2017.082685

Sminia, H., & de Rond, M. (2012). Context and action in the transformation of strategy scholarship. *Journal of Management Studies*, *49*(7), 1329–1349. https://doi.org/10.1111/j.1467-6486.2012.01059.x

Splitter, V., Jarzabkowski, P., & Seidl, D. (2023). Middle managers' struggle over their subject position in open strategy processes. *Journal of Management Studies*, *60*(7), 1884–1923. https://doi.org/10.1111/joms.12776

Teece, D. J. (2007). Explicating dynamic capabilities: The nature and microfoundations of (sustainable) enterprise performance. *Strategic Management Journal*, *28*(13), 1319–1350. https://doi.org/10.1002/smj.640

Teece, D. J., Pisano, G., & Shuen, A. (1997). Dynamic capabilities and strategic management. *Strategic Management Journal*, *18*(7), 509–533. https://doi.org/10.1002/(SICI)1097-0266(199708)18:7<509::AID-SMJ882>3.0.CO;2-Z

Vaara, E., & Whittington, R. (2012). Strategy-as-practice: Taking social practices seriously. *Academy of Management Annals*, *6*(1), 285–336.

Weick, K. E. (1987). Substitutes for strategy. In D. J. Teece (Ed.), *The competitive challenge – Strategies for industrial innovation and renewal* (pp. 221–233). Ballinger.

Wernerfelt, B. (1984). A resource-based view of the firm. *Strategic Management Journal*, *5*(2), 171–180.

Whittington, R. (1996). Strategy as practice. *Long Range Planning*, *29*(5), 731–735. https://doi.org/10.1016/0024-6301(96)00068-4

Whittington, R. (2015). The massification of strategy. *British Journal of Management*, *26*, S13–S16. https://doi.org/10.1111/1467-8551.12078

Wilden, R., Devinney, T. M., & Dowling, G. R. (2016). The architecture of dynamic capability research identifying the building blocks of a configurational approach. *Academy of Management Annals*, *10*(1), 997–1076. https://doi.org/10.1080/19416520.2016.1161966

Winsor, R. D. (1995). Marketing under conditions of chaos. *Journal of Business Research*, *34*(3), 181–189. https://doi.org/10.1016/0148-2963(94)00115-U

Winter, S. G. (2013). Habit, deliberation, and action: Strengthening the microfoundations of routines and capabilities. *Academy of Management Perspectives*, *27*, 120–137. https://doi.org/10.5465/amp.2012.0124

Wright, R. P., Paroutis, S. E., & Blettner, D. P. (2013). How useful are the strategic tools we teach in business schools? *Journal of Management Studies*, *50*(1), 92–125. https://doi.org/10.1111/j.1467-6486.2012.01082.x

CHAPTER 5

PLACING NON-MANAGERIAL EMPLOYEES IN THE MANAGEMENT THEORIES: TOWARD A THEORETICAL ADVANCEMENT

Mehmet Barca

Department of Business Administration, Faculty of Political Sciences, Social Sciences University of Ankara, Türkiye

ABSTRACT

This chapter responds to recent calls for a more in-depth examination of the crucial role played by non-managerial employees, including those in various strata such as blue and gray collars, from an alternative neo-human relations perspective. By exploring recent initiatives aimed at developing a new theory of management or extending existing ones, the goal is to broaden the conceptualization of management to include non-managerial perspectives, thereby contributing to the advancement of management theory. From this, the recent efforts in management theory—universalistic, strategic/contingent, and value-based—are evaluated for their potential. Utilizing the method of synthesizing, the aim is to introduce a significantly reconceptualizing of existing efforts toward a candidate explanation that leads to default theory enabling to generate and solve problems concerning the phenomenon of non-managerial employees in management processes. Toward this end, two arguments are put forward.

First, the constrictions inherent in current management theories devalue and underestimate the significance of blue- and gray-collar employees in the overarching management processes. Second, the future trajectory of management will involve three integral dimensions: the universal dimension of cooperation and coordination inherent in management, the strategic responses to continuously evolving environmental changes as the management of contingencies, and the normative dimension of value-creation to address the specific needs of blue- and gray-collar employees. By synthesizing these three dimensions, we provide insightful signposts for the prospective evolution of management theories.

Keywords: Theories of management; universalistic management perspective; strategic management perspective; neo-human relations management perspective; blue and gray collars

INTRODUCTION

In the realm of management studies, there exists a widely acknowledged understanding of the pivotal role that management theories play in both attracting scholarly interest and fostering research endeavors. However, a notable lacuna exists within the academic discourse as management scholars often overlook the imperative task of cultivating new theories or expanding existing ones to elucidate and prognosticate phenomena pertinent to blue- and gray-collar employees. The profound influence wielded by management theories remains underestimated, resulting in a dearth of scholarly endeavors dedicated to re-evaluating, developing, or extending these theories to enhance the comprehension and prediction of phenomena associated with these non-managerial employees.

Numerous efforts have been undertaken to critically examine existing management theories and either generate new frameworks or enhance current paradigms from diverse perspectives. A recent trend in management theory has emerged, characterized by a humanistic critique and extension of prevailing theories (Bhattacharyya, 2020). A notable example is a European initiative led by Koslowski (2010) from Vrije Universiteit Amsterdam, culminating in the publication of a promising work titled *Elements of a Philosophy of Management and Organization*. Esteemed scholars, including Stephen Ackroyd from Lancaster University Business School and Christoph Luetge from the University of Technology, Braunschweig, contributed to this volume, representing the United Kingdom, Germany, Netherlands, and Denmark.

Similarly, an insightful contribution from Italy is Vittorio Coda's (2010) work, *Entrepreneurial Values and Strategic Management: Essays in Management Theory*, featuring a compelling introduction by Robert Grant (2010) from Bocconi University. Another notable editorial initiative reflecting a humanistic perspective on the philosophy of management and organization is *General Management in Latin and Ibero-American Organizations: A Humanistic Perspective*, edited by Adrian A. Caldart from IESE Business School, Joan E. Ricart, and Alejandro A. Carrera, published by Routledge in 2020. These endeavors exemplify a noteworthy shift toward incorporating humanistic viewpoints into the discourse of management theories.

Such endeavors share a common focus on the notable progression of management theory and the exploration of novel frontiers by challenging the extant knowledge foundation. These efforts frequently gravitate toward fostering organizational orientations that are more attuned to human welfare, social responsibility, or market dynamics. However, a conspicuous dearth exists in substantial efforts directed toward the augmentation of existing theories or the formulation of novel ones specifically tailored to address the intricacies pertinent to blue- and gray-collar employees. It is imperative to underscore that the quest for a non-managerial worker-centric enterprise, one that is explicitly cantered on blue- and gray-collar employees, transcends the realm of mere idealistic aspirations; rather, it is an imperious requisite.

In contrast to the limited instances wherein pioneering endeavors "challenge the established knowledge base" from a "humanistic critique" viewpoint, a majority of studies endeavor to "fill gaps" in the management literature from a "human factor" perspective. This prevalent approach frequently compels researchers toward the iterative and expansive extension of existing knowledge, rather than fostering a departure from established paradigms. Rather than embarking on the development or extension of management theories, researchers in this orientation exhibit a proclivity for adopting atheoretical or weak theoretical initiatives. These initiatives merely superficially engage with problems such as personnel motivation, participation, communication, and performance, instead of delving into the intricate intricacies of management theories. While instrumental in elucidating the internal dynamics of organizations from a human factor standpoint, these frameworks fall short in facilitating an examination of the essential contributions made by blue- and gray-collar employees as substantial entities within the domain of management processes.

Also, in recent years, scholars such as Daft and Lewin (1990, 1993), Hamel and Breen (2007), and Hamel (2009) have raised concerns about the relevance and effectiveness of the current management paradigm. They argue that it may be outdated or at least insufficient in addressing the complex nature of management in today's rapidly changing business landscape. For instance, Hamel suggests that traditional management principles, rooted in mechanistic approaches from the early 20th century, are ill-equipped to handle the challenges posed by modern technology and global competition. He advocates for a shift toward decentralized innovation, participatory decision-making, and market-driven mechanisms. In contrast, Grant (2008) takes a more universalistic view, suggesting that contemporary management theories have emerged as responses to the enduring challenges of cooperation and coordination. He argues that despite changes in organizational structures, fundamental principles of management remain relevant.

The research objective of this study is to critically evaluate the recent endeavors within the management discipline that ostensibly advocate opposing theoretical frameworks, namely value-based, strategic/contingent, and universalistic approaches. Through the methodological framework of synthesis, our aim is to propose a substantial reconceptualization of these disparate efforts, culminating in the development of a candidate explanatory framework. This proposed framework seeks to establish a default theory capable of addressing and resolving issues pertaining to the involvement of non-managerial employees within management processes.

To achieve this objective, three interconnected questions are posited:

1. What is the role or impact of the availability of relevant theoretical foundations in examining management problems specific to blue- and gray-collar employees?
2. Do contemporary management theories furnish theoretical foundations capable of explaining and predicting various management problems encountered by blue- and gray-collar employees?
3. What dimensions must a management theory possess to effectively explicate and predict the management problems encountered by blue- and gray-collar employees?

In addressing these questions, three principal arguments are advanced: First, we contend that the impetus behind scientific progress lies not solely in empirical contributions but fundamentally in theoretical advancements. Theory precedes empirical contributions, and the absence of theoretical progress precludes empirical advancements. Consequently, the absence of relevant theories impedes focused inquiry and research endeavors. Our second argument posits that existing management theories, owing to their paradigmatic stance, inadequately facilitate the examination of issues related to blue- and gray-collar employees within their existing framework. We argue that these theories perceive the phenomena associated with blue- and gray-collar employees as trivial, thereby restricting the potential for in-depth and warranted inquiry. The constrictions inherent in current management theories devalue and underestimate the significance of blue- and gray-collar employees in the overarching management processes. Third, we posit that the future trajectory of management will involve three integral dimensions: the universal dimension of cooperation and coordination inherent in management, the strategic responses to continuously evolving environmental changes as the management of contingencies, and the normative dimension of value-creation to address the specific needs of blue- and gray-collar employees. By synthesizing these three dimensions, we provide insightful signposts for the prospective evolution of management theories.

METHOD FOR THEORETICAL ADVANCEMENT

In the pursuit of advancing scientific understanding regarding the involvement of non-management employees in management processes, it is imperative to assess the foundational underpinnings of existing management theories. According to Kuhn (1962, 1993), the determination of whether management theories offer inherent explanations for observed phenomena, delineate pertinent questions, prescribe question structuring, and provide guidelines for interpreting inquiry results is pivotal. A paradigmatic framework, characterized by a shared set of beliefs within the scientific community, is essential for attracting researchers to explore the identified phenomenon. Should current management theories lack default base explanations for the specified phenomenon, the imperative arises to formulate a paradigm tailored to facilitate the generation and resolution of issues surrounding non-management employees' roles in management processes. Notably, as underscored by Eckberg and Hills (1979), the paradigm need not be all-encompassing but rather should establish a subdiscipline for investigating the phenomenon. The emphasis lies in fostering a focused avenue for inquiry rather than developing a discipline-wide theory of management.

The process of developing or extending theory within the realm of management research encompasses a myriad of approaches, as elucidated by Cornelissen and Durand (2014). Their investigation delves into the reasoning and methodology employed by management researchers in the pursuit of novel theoretical frameworks. The identified methodologies span diverse avenues, encompassing "disciplined imagination" (Weick, 1989), "thickening thin abstractions" (Folger & Turillo, 1999), "contrastive explanations" (Tsang & Elsaesser, 2001), "problematizing assumptions" (Alvesson & Sandberg, 2011), the "bricolage of concepts" (Boxenbaum & Rouleau, 2011), the "combination of scientific logics" (Kilduff et al., 2011), and the "borrowing" and "blending" of theory and fragments thereof (Whetten et al., 2009), culminating in "top-down inductive theorizing" (Shepherd & Sutcliffe, 2011). Cornelissen and Durand's (2014) comprehensive analysis of 24 recognized theories, acknowledged for their pioneering contributions to management and organizational development, illustrates a divergence in the paths pursued by different management researchers in their quest for original theoretical contributions. Their findings emphasize that various management researchers adopt distinct trajectories, leading to diverse outcomes in theory development. Consequently, the absence of a singular or predefined approach to theory development is posited. Instead, Cornelissen and Durand (2014) posit that theory development is inherently a creative process, underscoring that "not every approach towards theory development generates the same returns" (p. 996). It is inferred that the variability in paths undertaken by researchers stimulates disparate results in the realm of theory development.

In light of the aforementioned arguments, Cornelissen and Durand's (2014) delineation of various systematic and creative avenues for management researchers to develop theoretical contributions highlights synthesis as a particularly efficacious method. This approach is deemed optimal for establishing connections between conceptual frameworks and comprehending the involvement of non-managers in management processes. Synthesis, in this context, entails the bridging of seemingly divergent perspectives such as universalistic, contingent, and value-based paradigms. The primary objective of synthesis is to introduce a substantial reconceptualization of extant efforts in theory development within the field of management.

While this chapter does not aspire to propose an exhaustive management theory, as the creation of such a theory demands a protracted temporal orientation with ramifications extending across a broad time horizon, the objective is, through synthesis, to indicate the potential of an alternative framing. Consequently, the focus is not to present an entirely novel theoretical framework but to underscore the importance of elaborating alternative causal dynamics, paving the way for a prospective explanation that forms the basis of a default theory. Synthesis facilitates a directed exploration of the implications inherent in existing endeavors, articulated in the form of alternative theories. The anticipated outcome, in the long term, is the gradual evolution and expansion of this synthesized candidate explanation into a comprehensive theory of management, or at the very least, an indication of the trajectory that the default theory may follow.

It should also be pointed out that to evolve into a paradigm, the subdiscipline necessitates not only the presence of default theoretical base beliefs but also the cultivation of a cohesive community of researchers unified by shared bodies of belief. This unified community, utilizing the established paradigm as a guiding framework, becomes instrumental in steering the generation and resolution of problems pertaining to the phenomenon. Over time, with a substantial body of research, the subdiscipline can mature into a recognizable and enduring research tradition.

THE ROLE OF THEORY FOR EMPIRICAL INQUIRY AND ADVANCEMENT

As with any scientific discipline, management theories are driven by an agenda reflecting proponents' shared sense of tractable, significant, and interesting problems. The chosen paradigm, problem dependency, and ontological standpoint influence the problems set for resolution and presuppose core assumptions or heuristics. Consequently, within their paradigmatic settings, it is pertinent to question whether blue- and gray-collar employees' management problems are recognized, ignored, or partially acknowledged.

In the absence of theories, our efforts in management research lack direction and coherence (Alvesson & Sandberg, 2011). Emphasizing the significance of theories in guiding research, Popper (1959) asserted that the primary goal of academic research output should be to contribute to theory within the field of study. He defined theory as conceptual frameworks designed to comprehend, elucidate, and navigate the complexities of the world. Popper underscored the continuous refinement of these theoretical "nets" to enhance their ability to rationalize, explain, and master the intricacies of the world.

The presence of scientific inquiry is contingent upon the availability of theoretical frameworks to illuminate phenomena. In the context of blue- and gray-collar employees, the absence of a management theory guiding the examination of these phenomena may result in a lack of research attention. Consequently, to attract scientific inquiry toward the issues surrounding blue- and gray-collar workers, a requisite is the establishment of robust theoretical foundations. The correlation between the depth of theory and the level of scientific attention suggests that a relevant theoretical framework leads to increased systematic and sustained inquiry into these phenomena.

In essence, the absence of theory impedes scientific progress, as theory plays a pivotal role in shaping both thinking and behavior. Recognizing the substantial impact of management theories on the research concerning blue- and gray-collar employees is crucial, highlighting the need for relevant theoretical frameworks that can guide both research and real-world management practices.

The imperative for theory arises not only from a research standpoint but also from pragmatic necessities. A notable observation underscores the comparatively sluggish evolution of management theories over the past half-century, particularly when contrasted with the rapid transformations in technology, lifestyle, geopolitics, and other realms (Agoston, 2009). Reflecting on this temporal misalignment, it becomes apparent that contemporary management principles have not kept pace with societal, technological, and political shifts. While hierarchical structures have become less rigid, they persist, and though ordinary employees are more educated, they continue to adhere to managerial decisions. The overarching question emerges: Have modern management theories reached a zenith, or is there an impending need for a revolutionary paradigm shift to align with technological and social progress? (Agoston, 2009; Hamel, 2009; Hamel & Breen, 2007).

In nutshell, theory is akin to a compass; it indicates the direction to be taken. The absence of theory equates to a lack of direction; it signifies an undefined path. Existing theories exhibit a disregard for blue- and gray-collar workers, overlooking their presence. In other words, current theories fail to provide a research orientation or shed light on investigations concerning blue- and gray-collar workers. Consequently, there is a need for new theories, new compasses that will point toward and illuminate research on blue- and gray-collar workers.

In pursuit of this objective, our initial endeavor involves an examination of the positioning of blue- and gray-collar employees within contemporary management theories. Subsequently, we endeavor to articulate a comprehensive management theory that accords rightful consideration to blue- and gray-collar employees. Finally, we seek to reposition extant management theories through the synthesis of disparate elements into a coherent framework. In scrutinizing management theories, the central question emerges: Do these theories possess relevant theoretical structures and governing logic to address the management problems of blue- and gray-collar employees, or, if not readily so, do they have the potential to be extended in that direction?

A BRIEF ASSESSMENT OF THE EXTANT MANAGEMENT THEORIES FOR THEIR RELEVANCE TO INQUIRY INTO THE ISSUES OF NON-MANAGER EMPLOYEES

Now we turn our attention to the second inquiry: "Do contemporary management theories furnish theoretical underpinnings upon which diverse management challenges pertinent to blue and grey collar employees can be elucidated, examined, and prognosticated?"

This query implies the existence of manifold and potentially conflicting conceptualizations of managerial phenomena, thereby prompting an assessment of their applicability to research issues pertaining to blue- and gray-collar employees. Presently, we encounter diverse conceptualizations of managerial phenomena, encompassing paradigms such as Taylorist Scientific Management, system and contingency theories of management, and strategic management, among others. In light of these theoretical frameworks, the initial question may be reformulated as follows: "Can diverse conceptualizations of managerial phenomena be effectively employed to generate deductive propositions, assumptions, or hypotheses concerning the phenomena specific to blue and grey collar employees?"

Management science currently lacks a comprehensive grand theory that encompasses all sub-theories within its domain. While numerous management theories exist, each addressing specific facets of the discipline, they are not in competition but rather complement each other. In essence, these theories contribute collectively by illuminating diverse dimensions of management phenomena.

The predominant discourse within the realm of management theory has predominantly focused on managerial prerogatives and strategic considerations, often overlooking the nuanced challenges faced by the workforce engaged in non-managerial roles. The significance of this lacuna cannot be overstated, particularly in light of the pervasive influence that blue- and gray-collar employees wield in organizational functionality.

Within Taylorist Scientific Management theoretical framework, blue- and gray-collar employees are relegated to a status akin to other operational factors, such as technology. Their potential for innovation, intellectual input, and managerial contributions is largely overlooked. This perspective discounts the significance of factors such as consent, participation, and motivation among those subject to managerial influence. Furthermore, it fails to acknowledge the embedded nature of an organization within its internal and external social milieu. In the same vein, Fayolist division of departments' theoretical framework associates enhancing efficiency in management with factors such as specialization, formalization, routinization, fragmentation, and division of labor. However, the existing Fayolian theory does not adequately account for the inclusion of blue- and gray-collar non-managerial workers. Notably, Fayol's paradigm lacks provisions for structures that prioritize individuals, facilitating active participation in decision-making processes.

However, rooted in the traditions of human relations (Mayo, 1924), Douglas McGregor's "Theory Y" underscores the significance of understanding and integrating humanistic principles within organizational frameworks. McGregor's seminal work, particularly "Theory X" and "Theory Y," delineates from an epistemic standpoint two sets of assumptions about human nature that shape managerial behavior toward subordinates (McGregor, 1957, 1969a, 1969b, 2000a, 2000b). The adoption of Theory Y assumptions, emphasizing employee self-actualization and organizational objectives, is posited as a catalyst for promoting organizational success. Nevertheless, the place and role of non-managers in management processes are yet obscure in human relations theories of management. Though they open an ample place for humanistic considerations, they lack providing relevant theoretical foundations for the inquiry of non-manager workers in management processes.

Systems theory, in particular, presupposes a unidirectional causation, contending that the organizational structure is primarily shaped by the environment, as opposed to the alternative proposition wherein organizations may exert influence on and even control the environment through direct interventions. The system and its subsystems, according to systems theory, necessitate a diverse array of internal regulatory mechanisms that are appropriately integrated to align with the complexity of the external environment upon which they are contingent. Notably, systems theory places considerable emphasis on environmental determinism as a pivotal determinant influencing the organizational system. Within this theoretical paradigm, the role of blue- and gray-collar employees is construed as integral to the organizational adaptation to its environment. Blue- and gray-collar employees are regarded as reflexive agents of their environment, assuming a significant role in the adaptive processes of the firm. However, this perspective tends to understate the significance of the internal environment, particularly the degree of discretion accorded to power-holders, including blue- and gray-collar employees. As a result, there exists an oversight in acknowledging and incorporating the unique contributions of blue- and gray-collar workers as a crucial working subsystem within the organizational context. Grounded in system theory, the Contingency Theory of Management asserts that adept managers can influence organizational outcomes by identifying optimal adaptations to environmental contingencies. However, it tends to overlook the pivotal role of blue- and gray-collar employees, treating them merely as passive subjects of management rather than integral components influencing organizational adaptation. Systems and contingency theories lack substantive solutions for the management challenges associated with blue- and gray-collar employees.

The stakeholder management theory departs from mainstream theories, emphasizing a distinct perspective on a company's nature, purpose, and human aspects. It advocates engagement with stakeholders with both utility and mindfulness, aligning with humanistic principles. Firms are urged to treat stakeholders with humane considerations for harmonious coexistence in society and the environment. The stakeholder theory of management centers on human beings, emphasizing humanity, ethical behavior, and contextual needs. This approach evaluates how employees perceive ethical acknowledgment, management's concern for ethical practices, and managers' ethical conduct within the firm. Incorporating humanistic considerations into technology-based interactions enhances stakeholder satisfaction. The theory builds on humanism and management works by scholars, recognizing human constituents in firms and society. It addresses concerns about the company's purpose, highlighting the confusion between long-term goals and short-term financial performance objectives. This underscores the need for senior managers, often lacking in long-term articulation compatible with short-term performance delivery, to develop a clear company purpose.

Strategic management provides an avenue for investigating management challenges related to blue- and gray-collar employees. More crucially, postmodernism, a movement in contemporary philosophy, plays a significant role in shaping management theories with a human-centric perspective.

While two theories, namely Upper Echelon Theory and Strategy as Practice (SAP), may offer avenues for researching blue- and gray-collar employees, they do not inherently provide theoretical perspectives or foundations for such endeavors. Nevertheless, these theories exhibit potential for extension in that direction.

As previously posited, theories serve as cognitive lenses, shaping not only the identification of problem areas for research but also influencing the perceived nuances within those areas. Evidently, the existing management theories carry a "too narrow a focus" in relation to a management phenomenon, which provide a basis for upper echelon as a formal managerial stratum rather than a large and comprehensive base for including non-managerial ranks and contributions in explanation or understanding of a management phenomenon. In clearer terms, existing management theories fall short in facilitating an insightful examination of the role of blue- and gray-collar employees within management processes as a significant problem area in the broader landscape of management phenomena. Instead, these theories afford visibility to a spectrum of colors, ranging from white to golden, from pink to yellow, yet conspicuously omitting the hues associated with blue and gray. When subjected to rigorous scrutiny, these theories may reluctantly permit the consideration of blue- and gray-collar employees as a peripheral subject matter, relegated to the margins of scholarly attention.

The positioning and significance of blue- and gray-collar employees within management theories are either non-existent or, at best, insufficient to provide comprehensive insights into relevant phenomena. A prevailing characteristic across management sciences is the passive treatment of blue- and gray-collar workers throughout various managerial processes, often rooted in a rigid dichotomy between those in managerial roles and those being managed. This prompts critical questions about the current state of affairs: Is this paradigm genuinely reflective of reality, and is it conducive to effective management practices? Moreover, is this dichotomy likely to persist, or should there be a reconsideration of the roles blue- and gray-collar workers play in management processes? Is the scope of management confined solely to the actions of those within managerial hierarchies, or does it extend beyond, encompassing both managers and those managed in predetermined positions?

Several challenges persist in adequately addressing certain research problems within the existing landscape of management theories. The limitations become particularly pronounced when attempting to comprehensively explore issues related to blue- and gray-collar employees and other stakeholders. Here are notable examples of problems that remain inadequately addressed within the existing management theories:

1. *Inadequate exploration of blue- and gray-collar employees' roles*: The current management theories fall short in elucidating the intricate involvement of blue- and gray-collar employees and other stakeholders in the management process. These theories neglect to portray blue- and gray-collar employees as active decision-makers and practitioners whose actions significantly influence

the outcomes of the management process. The failure to recognize the agency of these employees obstructs a nuanced understanding of their impact on organizational management.
2. *Insufficient examination of interactions among organizational layers*: The existing theories lack explanatory power concerning the interactions and actions of blue and gray actors within the middle and lower organizational layers. This extends to their engagements with the upper management team and the overall organizational structure. To address this deficiency, it becomes imperative to focus on the intricate relationships between the top management team and the organizational structure they represent. Adopting the Social Action Perspective (SAP) becomes essential for understanding the characteristic structure and processes of managing within the organizational context. Notably, existing theories fail to account for the impact of the organizational setting on practitioners, how they utilize their information, and the consequential effects on organizational outcomes. Furthermore, the efficacy of non-managerial players in the management process remains inadequately explicated.
3. *Neglect of the informal character of management by non-managerial employees*: The prevailing management theories do not provide a framework for examining management as an informal characteristic structure and process enacted by blue- and gray-collar employees. This oversight neglects the crucial acts and contributions of non-managerial employees in shaping the informal dimensions of organizational management. Consequently, a comprehensive understanding of the informal aspects of managing, as carried out by non-managerial practitioners, remains conspicuously absent from current management discourse.

In light of these deficiencies, there is an urgent need for a paradigm shift in management theories. This shift should involve a more inclusive consideration of the roles and impacts of blue- and gray-collar employees, the exploration of complex interactions among organizational layers, and a recognition of the informal dimensions of management practices carried out by non-managerial actors. Such a transformative approach is crucial for advancing the field of management and fostering a more holistic understanding of organizational dynamics.

The current discourse highlights a notable oversight in management theory and research, particularly concerning blue- and gray-collar employees. While industrial relations extensively address these concerns in an adversarial manner, industrial organization predominantly examines them through a sociological lens rather than a managerial perspective. The prevalent research themes within this context encompass wages, motivations, power relations, job loss, stress, mobbing, productivity, ethnicity, gender, and worker class, primarily scrutinized from a sociological standpoint.

The ideological nature of management and industrial relations theories is evident, with the former aligning with capitalist interests and focusing on management phenomena through the lens of capital and profit, while the latter advocates for workers and views employee phenomena through their interests. This antagonistic or dialectic perspective, deeply embedded in the culture of the Western world, has significantly shaped scientific theories since the inception of scientific inquiry.

Recognizing the damage caused by behaviors rooted in capitalist and unionist antagonistic approaches, there is a growing awareness of the necessity for a paradigm shift. The transition from an adversarial view of firms and labor relations to a collaborative one requires not only a cultural revolution but also a philosophical and scientific transformation. Recent developments in both management and industrial disciplines underscore the imperative to shift from this antagonist perspective, particularly as knowledge economies replace the industrial era.

In essence, the marginalization or downplaying of blue- and gray-collar employees in management theorizing and research is not a consequence of their mere existence, but rather a manifestation of the absence of adequate epistemological lenses through which their presence can be comprehensively perceived, theorized, and studied as research phenomena. This initiative, in simpler terms, seeks to rectify this oversight by placing blue- and gray-collar employees within the framework of a general theory of management. The advantage of such an undertaking lies in transcending the limitations of superficial, temporal analyses of business phenomena and avoiding reliance on transient rhetoric.

CRITICAL APPROACHES TO THE EXTANT MANAGEMENT THEORIES

The prevailing discourse on management has faced scrutiny with regard to its principles and underlying theories, prompting assertions that the existing management paradigm is either obsolete or, at the very least, insufficient in comprehensively addressing the myriad facets of management phenomena. This has led to a compelling argument in favor of the development of new or extended theories of management, primarily anchored in three broad categories of reasoning: the imperative of radical change and challenges in the contemporary business environment, non-contingent universalistic conceptions, and value-based philosophical considerations. Scholars in the first category base their reasoning on the changing business landscape and required changes in management theories out of necessity. On the other hand, those in the second group take a non-contingent position and argue how to extend the extant management theories toward universalistic conceptions and assumptions. Scholars in the third category develop arguments out of virtue rather than necessity.

In the context of radical change and challenges in the business environment, influential management scholars such as Arie Lewin, Richard Daft, and Gary Hamel posit that the evolving business landscape has rendered existing management theories and practices obsolete. They contend that conventional management paradigms are ill-equipped to contend with the fundamental requirements of contemporary firms amid a rapidly changing business environment characterized by globalization, turbulence, technological advancements, and hypercompetition.

Against this backdrop, out of necessity rather than virtue, Hamel, for instance, traces the roots of current management principles to mechanistic thinking originating from Frederick Taylor's scientific management and Max Weber's bureaucratic principles of the early 20th century. Despite subsequent developments, Hamel argues that contemporary management is still entrenched in outdated paradigms, emphasizing efficiency at the expense of other critical objectives. He advocates for a paradigm shift toward distributed innovation, participative decision-making, and market-based mechanisms to meet the challenges posed by technological advancements and the rise of global competitors.

Contrary to Hamel's call for a new management paradigm, Grant adopts a universalistic perspective, positing that modern management theories are responses to the enduring challenges of cooperation and coordination inherent in the management process. Grant contends that the recent evolution of hierarchical structures, such as delayering and self-organization, does not negate the continued efficacy of basic organizational principles. In contrast to Hamel's proposition, Grant argues against the necessity for entirely new management theories, advocating instead for the extension of existing theories to accommodate higher levels of complexity, emphasizing multidimensional integration and informal structures. According to Grant, this evolution may involve changes in leadership styles and decision-making approaches but does not warrant the wholesale dismantling of existing management practices.

As to philosophical considerations, another group of scholars contends that the theoretical underpinnings of current management fall short in addressing the inherent challenges of managing, particularly from various philosophical perspectives that are likely to shape the future of management. The evolution of management perspectives from the largely mechanistic, economically driven views of the early 20th century to the human relations and professionalism-oriented approach of the 1930s has paved the way for the contemporary consensus that distinguishes companies based on "people matters," as articulated by professor and author Dave Ulrich. This progression highlights the increasing prominence of human beings in corporate settings, marking a significant shift in the understanding and valuation of individuals within organizational contexts. One of the contributors worth mentioning in this respect is Vittorio Coda (2010). His examination of the objectives and raison d'être of the business enterprise sheds light on the enduring discourse surrounding the firm's goals. His conceptual framework for the firm and its societal interconnections surpasses stagnant debates cantered on shareholders versus stakeholders. Rather than perceiving the firm solely as an agent serving individual interests, Coda envisions it as a catalyst for social advancement, harmonizing the diverse interests of various participants. By formulating a model of the entrepreneurial firm intricately integrated into a social system and grounded in a set of values, he moves beyond conventional dichotomies to offer a nuanced perspective on the firm's role in broader societal development. Coda explores contemporary challenges in management theories, specifically focusing on circular entrepreneurial views in Western businesses, categorized as Type A and Type B. Type A emphasizes profitability and competitiveness, while Type B connects workers' well-being, stakeholder satisfaction, and long-term organizational prosperity. The scarcity of Type B adoption in the West is attributed to common antagonistic or paternalistic views. He challenges the antagonistic model in labor relations, proposing a shift to a collaborative perspective for long-term company growth aligned with economic and ethical needs. He advocates for owners and management to embrace a shared circular view, addressing challenges posed by antagonistic perspectives. He emphasizes the creative integration of social needs and market demands in entrepreneurial visions, promoting a synergistic approach to reconcile economic and social concerns. Coda calls for the evolution of management theories toward a collaborative model, critiquing simplistic profit and ethics discourse and highlighting the need for a comprehensive entrepreneurial ideology. He underscores the reciprocal functionality of economic demands and humanistic concerns in shaping the future of firms and society.

The humanistic perspective in management theory, notably absent from contemporary discourse, offers a vital lens through which to examine firm–stakeholder interactions (Melé, 2012; Ricart & Llopis, 2020). Management, within the realm of social science, serves as a lens through which we comprehend the ways in which individuals and societies navigate their existence, influenced by both philosophical conceptions and material circumstances. Scholars increasingly contend that the conceptualization of individuals within organizations extends beyond universalistic imperatives, encompassing ontological considerations, to incorporate epistemic perspectives.

The assertion is made that a company's robust performance is intricately linked to its dedication to the quality of life experienced by its members and their holistic development. Here, the interpretation of quality of life transcends mere access to superior material goods. It is underscored as a profound commitment to "the respect for human beings and their dignity, as well as the attention to their higher endeavours: the advancement of knowledge and the effective use of freedom" (Llano, 2000, 2010; cited by Carrera, 2020). This nuanced perspective implies a departure from conventional paradigms that solely emphasize material outcomes, urging a shift toward a more comprehensive understanding that encompasses the dignified treatment of individuals and the fostering of their intellectual and creative pursuits.

Out of virtue rather than necessity, the humanistic perspective, against the backdrop exemplified by McGregor's "Theory Y" and complemented by Pirson's advocacy for the inclusion of dignity in management theories, and Koslowski (2010) presents a compelling avenue for advancing contemporary management theories. Pirson (2019) introduces the neglected concept of dignity into the management theory landscape, emphasizing its intrinsic value despite its historical oversight in economics and management. The paper contends that the inclusion of dignity in management theory can enhance its overall robustness, align it more closely with the public interest, and strengthen its ties to social welfare creation. Proposing a framework based on two dimensions – unconditional or conditional understanding of human dignity and wealth creation or well-being creation as the basis for social welfare – the author introduces alternative management theory archetypes. These archetypes, the paper argues, hold theoretical implications for management research and offer a pathway for realigning management theory toward direct contributions to social welfare creation.

Koslowski (2010) contends that existing management theories must seek human-centered solutions to preserve human autonomy, dignity, integrity, and mitigate increasing vulnerability in contemporary organizations. He argues that the unpredictable and open nature of humans cannot be adequately captured by traditional bureaucratic representations of organizational reality. Consequently, a shift must occur from the bureaucratic vocabulary of efficiency and organizational imperatives to a softer language of values. In the context of change processes, values-driven management calls for a transcendent approach, emphasizing characteristics such as radicalism and creativity to propose ethics and social responsibility as alternatives to conventional organizational governance. Applying existentialist philosophy to management, Koslowski (2010) underscores the existential requirement to respect individuals as "goals in themselves," with dignity and humanity. This ethical responsibility extends beyond individual concerns, highlighting the broader challenge faced by organizations. From a theoretical perspective, agency is deemed central to organizational change, emphasizing that management's role is to realize the overall interests of the organization. The manager's fiduciary duty extends beyond shareholders to encompass the entire corporation, with each organization possessing a unique common interest. The obligation to prioritize the common interest becomes more pronounced with the impact and power of decision-makers, considering the potential positive and negative side effects of their actions. He suggests that the complexity of contemporary organizational challenges cannot be reduced to simplistic notions like profit maximization. He asserts that the contemporary business paradigm necessitates the incorporation of corporate social responsibility (CSR), business ethics, and corporate citizenship as essential elements for legitimizing corporations in society. This involves institutionalizing reflective practices and employing public relations as a ceremonial means of legitimation. In the context of the so-called poly-contextual society, he envisions the emergence of new patterns of societal adjustment for corporations. The discussion refers to Susanne's new business paradigm, contrasting it with the outdated Friedman paradigm that prioritized profit maximization. The new paradigm emphasizes the triple bottom line of sustainable development, focusing on "people, planet, [and] profit." In this poly-cantered society, characterized by diverse communication contexts, managers are obligated to fulfill their duties, prioritizing the well-being of the entire corporation over individual or shareholder interests. Shareholders entrust managers with their positions to advance the collective good of the corporation rather than solely pursuing their own or shareholders' interests.

Given these recent attempts to develop an alternative theory of management and growing influence of these attempts, we can say that "a minor revolution" has been witnessed in management discipline. What I am going to do in the following section is to give a voice to these recent developments and thus open a tract for inquiry into non-manager workers, encompassing the blue- and gray-collar employees as significant phenomena in the management processes.

DIMENSIONS OF NEW MANAGEMENT THEORIES

Each critique of existing management theories reflects a particular conception of what an organization represents, its core characteristics, its purpose, and an implicit or explicit notion of human beings. Despite the divergence in perspectives, these critiques do not necessarily contradict each other. For instance, Koslowski (2010) acknowledges the challenge of cooperation in management theory but expands its meaning. He posits that a corporation serves as a means to enhance wealth creation through a higher degree of cooperation than the market can offer. The corporation establishes cultural and social capital, fostering increased cooperation among its members. The justification for engaging with corporations, with their hierarchies and regulations, rather than participating in market transactions, lies in the corporation's ability to provide higher returns to its employees and shareholders. This surplus is the cultural value generated by the organization's corporate culture, enabling a greater degree of cooperation within the corporation compared to market transactions.

CSR aligns with a common good theory of the firm, emphasizing the responsibility of managers to consider the effects of commercial activities on the common good of both internal and external stakeholders. Every organization, whether a business corporation, university, or school, is characterized not only by individual interests but also by a common interest shared by all participants.

Another example in case is Grant's (2008) position. Grant, acknowledging the need for management theory evolution in response to changing circumstances, advocates not only adapting existing theories but also considers the possibility of a comprehensive overhaul. He views environmental evolution as prompting alterations in leadership styles, decision-making approaches, and the restructuring of hierarchies, such as delayering and self-organization, as responses to environmental changes. Grant perceives the persistent challenges of cooperation and coordination in the management process as foundational aspects, emphasizing their significance from a dynamic management theory perspective.

Given the increasing influence of such initiatives, it is apparent that a subtle revolution has occurred within the management discipline. However, despite acknowledging the necessity of a dynamic view of management, the discipline has, until now, only partially and disjointedly developed this perspective. These developments lack integration, and there is a need to rearrange them into a cohesive set of interdependent theories. The call is for theory to adapt to the complexity of the phenomena it seeks to address – specifically, the reality of management phenomena. The proposition is to realign management theories within a renewed and concurrent framework that unifies non-manager workers with managers, presenting a comprehensive approach to better explain management phenomena.

In light of the harmonious nature of these critiques, each undertaking contributes a crucial facet to management: organizational, strategic, and cultural dimensions. These dimensions, far from being in competition, are complementary. The organizational dimension highlights the universalistic aspect, the strategic aspect underscores the dynamic nature, and the cultural aspect embodies the normative dimension of management. Collectively, they constitute the intricate phenomena of management. Consequently, in the context of recent efforts to formulate alternative or extended management theories, the development of a new theory or extensions of existing ones should seek to integrate and synthesize these three perspectives:

- Extension of Management Theories Toward the Universalistic-based View: Focusing on the centrality of "organization" in management theory.
- Extension of Management Theories Toward the Environmental Changes-based View: Focusing on the centrality of "strategy" in management theory.
- Extension of Management Theories Toward the Value-based View: Focusing on the centrality of "value-based" in management theory.

The purpose of this synthesis is to amalgamate these recent developments into a cohesive framework, thereby laying the foundation for an exploration of the pivotal role played by blue- and gray-collar employees as significant phenomena in the domain of management processes.

These elucidations underscore the requirement for in-depth refinement. Subsequent endeavors will be channeled toward the exploration and development of this integrative approach.

Extension of Management Theories Toward the Universalistic-based View: Focusing on the Centrality of "Organization (Organizing)" in Management Theory

From a universalistic viewpoint, it can be theorized that the emergence of organizations is rooted in their capacity to enhance wealth creation through a heightened level of cooperation and coordination, surpassing what the market can offer. However, achieving this objective is not a mechanical process. Organizations can excel in this realm by managing strategic contingencies as well as cultivating corporate cultural or social capital, fostering increased cooperation and coordination among their members. This perspective extends beyond the conventional argument presented by transaction cost theory, asserting that organizations or hierarchies governed by contracts are more efficient than the market. Efficiency in this context is contingent on the creation and management of strategies, in particular innovation of management, and corporate cultural or social capital to elevate collaboration and coordination among organizational members. The effective management of strategic contingencies and organizational values is pivotal in realizing this efficiency, challenging the notion that cooperation and coordination automatically follow organizational structures. Effective management necessitates a comprehensive approach, addressing both strategic contingencies and humanistic value-based essentials. Consequently, a novel management theory must transcend universal assumptions about coordination and cooperation, integrating strategic contingencies and normative values into the management paradigm.

The dynamic nature of cooperation and coordination necessitates an adaptive approach to respond to both internal and external shifts. Integrating a strategic dimension alongside universal aspects is imperative to effectively manage these processes. Rather than reacting passively, organizations should adopt proactive and transformative strategies to stay ahead of changes, aiming to outperform competitors. Thus, managing cooperation and coordination with a competitive mindset represents the strategic dimension of management's universal facet.

Achieving cooperation and coordination within organizations is not inherent; they require active management as organizations are not homogeneous entities. Conflicts of interest among individuals, groups, hierarchies, and stakeholders pose significant challenges to efficient cooperation and coordination. Managing these conflicts is vital for enhancing efficiency, and value-based approaches offer effective solutions. Additionally, organizations encounter differences in perspectives, even when not directly conflicting, which further complicates the process. Enriching cooperation and coordination with organizational values is crucial as they are integral components of human capital, necessitating motivation, respect, and ideal contribution for effectiveness.

The strategic dimension of organizational management pertains to the manipulation and adaptation of the external environment surrounding workers. Organizations engage in strategic positioning and repositioning maneuvers to navigate interactions both within and outside the organizational boundaries, affecting individuals and group dynamics. Conversely, the value dimension of management focuses on shaping the internal environment of workers. This involves cultivating paradigms and worldviews regarding work, the environment, colleagues, hierarchies, and products, as well as managing the psychological aspects of workers. Essentially, while the strategic dimension deals with external environmental factors, the value dimension concentrates on shaping the internal perceptions and attitudes of workers.

Extension of Management Theories Toward the Environmental Changes-based View: Focusing on the Centrality of "Strategy (Strategizing)" in Management Theory

Despite the progress in strategic management, the incorporation of strategic considerations into contemporary management theories is an insufficiently explored area. Theoretically, there is a crucial need to foster research streams aimed at determining the trajectory that the management discipline should follow in terms of evolving cooperation and coordination over time, particularly in response to environmental changes. This aligns with the aspirations of strategy-oriented endeavors to contribute to the understanding and development of management theories.

Cooperation and coordination, as highlighted earlier, are dynamic rather than static concepts. While their essence remains unchanged, they are susceptible to adaptations that respond to the evolving environmental landscape more effectively. According to Hamel, the most potent approach to enhance cooperation and coordination in response to environmental changes is through developments, inventions, or innovations in management itself. Management innovation not only positions organizations for improved competition and advantage over rivals but also ensures the sustainability of that advantage over time. It's crucial to note that these innovative variations in cooperation and coordination do not signify a fundamental change in the essence of management. Cooperation and coordination persist as indispensable fundamentals of effective management.

The argument suggests that the anticipated shift in organizational structures from traditional hierarchical frameworks to flatter, hierarchical-less structures does not diminish the significance of cooperation and coordination in management practice and theory. Additionally, this structural evolution is expected to trigger corresponding transformations in organizational culture, language, relationships, and communication. Leadership paradigms are foreseen to undergo changes, emphasizing expertise as the foundation of effective leadership. The conventional model of a single charismatic leader is predicted to be replaced by a distributed leadership approach, where multiple leaders concurrently guide their respective expert groups. However, the changes in cooperation and coordination encompassing structures, leadership, management styles, organizational culture, and communication do not render classical considerations unnecessary or invalid. On the contrary, cooperation and coordination, as essential components of management practice and theory, retain significance in managing global companies today, much like their importance in Ancient Egypt during the construction of pyramids.

Management stands as the paramount core competency within any organization, significantly influencing its success trajectory. This influence is not uniform across organizations, as they exhibit varying levels of management prowess. Disparities in management capabilities translate directly into disparities in success, with organizations falling below industry average facing competitive disadvantages and those exceeding industry averages gaining competitive advantages. Mere adaptation to industry norms results in average success, while misadaptation leads to below-average outcomes. However, organizations that strategically innovate their management practices can reshape industry dynamics in their favor, securing and maintaining competitive advantages. Notably, management innovation emerges as a crucial driver of sustainable competitive advantage, as highlighted by Prahalad. Nevertheless, at its fundamental core, management innovation invariably revolves around fostering effective cooperation and coordination within organizations.

Given recent advancements and the prevalent resource-based approach in strategic management, a firm is conceptualized as a strategic entity, representing a reservoir of resources, capabilities, and competencies. Within this framework, management assumes three core responsibilities: exploiting, exploring, and expanding human resources. The primary managerial duty involves maximizing the potential of employees, operating through two essential modes: exploitation and exploration (discovery and invention). Exploitation leverages existing capabilities, professionalism, and competencies, while exploration entails investment in building capabilities and professionalism, subsequently harnessing their enhanced contributions.

In light of these discussions, it is posited that the greater the competence of blue- and gray-collar employees, the more they actively participate in decision-making processes, thereby contributing significantly to the formulation and sustainability of the competitive advantage pursued by the organization.

Extension of Management Theories Toward the Value-based View: Focusing on the Centrality of "Value-based (Valuing)" in Management Theory

In the pursuit of formulating a new management theory or extending existing ones, a reliance on intuitive comprehension of strategic contingencies and inherent management challenges, such as cooperation and coordination, is insufficient. A comprehensive understanding must also encompass the philosophical and normative foundations of business management.

In a value-based approach, it is imperative to recognize the human aspect of workers rather than treating them as mere robots as order-takers. By acknowledging and respecting their inherent worth and potential, organizations can unlock benefits commensurate with human capabilities. This emphasis on valuing individuals adds a crucial dimension to cooperation and coordination within the organizational framework. It aligns with the philosophy of management, wherein cooperation and coordination are founded on principles of respect and appreciation for employees. Implementing a value-based management strategy establishes a solid foundation for robust cooperation and coordination. Conversely, neglecting to value individuals results in a fragile and vulnerable foundation, hindering the realization of universal and strategic organizational objectives.

This perspective is rooted in humanistic principles, as it advocates for the realization of human potential across various domains: individual, team, organizational, and societal. It rejects the notion of exploiting humans as mere tools for generating shareholder profit. Performance is understood to operate on multiple levels, encompassing the self, team, organization, and broader stakeholder community. At each level, the fulfillment of human potential is intricately linked to the overall performance of the firm or organization. Central to this conception is the recognition that inefficiencies, in economic terms, represent squandered human potential, regardless of whether it pertains to individuals, teams, organizations, or society as a whole. Consequently, this framework accommodates blue- and gray-collar employees within its theoretical framework, free from hierarchical constraints.

Koslowski (2010) advocates for a realist perspective in management, emphasizing the influence of structures on non-manager employees. In this view, these workers are both constrained and enabled by their circumstances, with structures possessing distinct real properties beyond discourse. Emphasizing a people-centric approach, Koslowski underscores the importance of democratic organizational structures and employee participation.

In light of these principles, management is urged to create relevant structures that grant autonomy, delegate decision-making, and actively involve non-manager workers in the decision-making process. This shift, essential for adapting to the knowledge economy, aligns with both strategic and normative perspectives. Granting more freedom to non-manager workers becomes a key driver for the innovation necessary in today's business landscape. Management theories, moving away from the notion of an organization as a "uni-brain," should integrate the autonomy of non-manager workers, extending the argument for the human dimension. Such theoretical development not only reflects the changing environmental trends but also challenges the hegemony of organizational elites in management structures and activities.

Traditionally, blue- and gray-collar employees have been conceptualized in current management theories as communities of practice, analogous to technology within an organization. Much like technology, their role is typically directive, where decisions are made without soliciting their perspectives, and they are subsequently instructed on what to do. However, there is a crucial need not only to integrate these workers into the decision-making processes but also to impart meaning to their organizational roles. Therefore, the normative aspect of management theories is as crucial as the strategic and inherent universal dimensions. The normative dimension extends beyond merely adding meaning to management practices; it serves as a cohesive force, binding together the intertwined strands of strategic and universalistic orientation literature, emphasizing social responsibility, humanity, morality, and ethics while operationalizing these concepts. This normative conception avoids falling into impractical romantic ideals, applying argumentative logic to systematically construct a value-based theory of management (Aktouf, 1992).

The significance of this corporate religion lies in its ability to foster emotional engagement among employees and customers, providing insights into bridging the internal and external environments. Additionally, corporate religion, characterized by a robust and charismatic leadership style, democratic organizational structures, and ethical considerations, emerges as a pivotal element in effectively managing organizations within competitive, dynamic, and technology-driven landscapes over the long term.

DISCUSSION

Each perspective – organization (organizing), strategy (strategizing), and human-centric (valuing) – provides valuable insights into management's multifaceted dimensions. The universalistic viewpoint posits that organizations thrive by optimizing wealth creation through enhanced cooperation and coordination, surpassing market capabilities. However, this achievement is not mechanistic but relies on adept management of strategic contingencies and the cultivation of corporate cultural or social capital, fostering collaboration among members. This perspective challenges transaction cost theory, emphasizing that organizational efficiency hinges on strategic management, innovation, and the development of cultural capital for heightened collaboration. The argument refutes the notion that cooperation and coordination are automatic outcomes of organizational structures. Effective management demands a holistic approach, integrating both strategic contingencies and humanistic, value-based essentials. A forward-looking management theory should transcend universal assumptions, incorporating strategic contingencies and normative values to enrich the management paradigm.

Yet, the current critiques of the extant management theories also have some significant shortcomings. In the initial analysis, critiques across various management theories portray non-managerial workers as inherently passive and determined, irrespective of whether the theoretical framework is classical, strategic, or value-based. Notwithstanding certain exceptions, the foundational tenets of classical, strategic, and value-based theories continue to underpin the notion that non-managerial workers are subject to determination by managerial figures. This prevailing perspective characterizing non-workers as passive persists across the spectrum of classic, strategic, and value-based management theories.

Second, the exclusive attribution of cooperation/coordination, strategy, and value development to managers is a prevailing paradigm. However, management is inherently a collaborative endeavor involving both managerial and non-managerial actors. The scope of management should transcend the confines of managerial roles. By extending the perspective of non-workers within the domain of management, management theory can encompass the entirety of an organization, rather than a restricted segment. While acknowledging the distinct roles of managers and non-managers, particularly concerning hierarchical power dynamics, it is essential to recognize that power within an organization is not solely hierarchical or positional. Various forms of power emanate from individual attributes, group dynamics, expertise, and situational factors. These diverse sources of power empower non-managers to play a substantive role in all facets of management, including planning, coordination, and execution.

Third, except for strategic-oriented theorizing, the critiques of management theories tend to depict cooperation and coordination as static phenomena. Nevertheless, the dynamic nature of cooperation and coordination becomes apparent when considering organizational strategies and culture. A more accurate portrayal involves recognizing a reciprocal relationship: alterations in cooperation and coordination influence organizational strategies and values, while concurrently being influenced by them.

In the subsequent discussion, we will identify the limitations inherent in existing management theories and propose strategies for their mitigation.

1. *A holistic approach involving diverse organizational actors*: Instead of top-level centric management theorizing, reconceptualizing management as the business of a broader spectrum of organizational actors. As discussed above, one primary constraint lies in the prevalent top-level centric management theorizing, which disproportionately emphasizes the smallest organizational stratum, namely top management. The preoccupation with this diminutive layer often results in a generalized interpretation of management activities across all organizational tiers. Consequently, issues pertinent to the cooperation and coordination of blue- and gray-collar workers assume a marginal and secondary status within this paradigm, overshadowed by the primacy accorded to the upper echelon.

    Existing management theories predominantly elucidate the involvement of top management as individuals (leaders, entrepreneurs, chief executive officers (CEOs), directors) or teams (boards, teams of executives, etc.) in the management process. This narrow focus on the managerial level precludes a holistic examination of organizational-wide management issues, thereby impeding a nuanced exploration of concerns specific to blue- and gray-collar employees.

To address this limitation, it becomes imperative to challenge the conventional confinement of management discourse to the managerial level and advocate for a shift toward an organizational-level perspective.

This concentration on the top management stratum is predicated on the assumption that, despite their numerical scarcity, managers wield decisive power. Thus, the prevailing power-centric reasoning posits that a comprehensive understanding of this central and influential layer would inherently encompass management issues at large. However, such a perspective obscures the broader reality that management is not solely the purview of a select group but rather an encompassing function spanning the entire organizational populace and its diverse layers.

A novel management theory should transcend the traditional tenets of Taylorian efficiency, Fayolian organizational divisional structure, and Mayo's psychological insights, evolving toward a practice-centric understanding of management. Under such a paradigm, management is reconceptualized not merely as the prerogative of managers but as the collective everyday practice, routines, norms, and plans enacted by a broader spectrum of organizational actors. This encompasses deliberate, undeliberate, or emergent actions constituting the manifold facets of management work.

In this revised conceptualization, management involves not only planning, giving orders, delegating, and coordinating but also encompasses participation, sense-making, communication, implementation, monitoring, and review at various organizational levels and across different teams. Management is thus portrayed as an organizational collective understanding and interaction that transcends hierarchical boundaries and engages with both formal and informal structures within the organization.

This approach acknowledges practitioners not only as senior management but also includes intermediate and lower-level managers, as well as non-managerial participants contributing to the management processes. Consequently, the perspective broadens the definition of the management team to encompass formal and informal actors, mechanisms, and processes, thereby facilitating an inquiry into the activities and potential roles of blue- and gray-collar workers.

In essence, this approach posits that management permeates every facet of organizational functioning, involving the everyday operations of individuals who may not conventionally be classified as managers. These practitioners, regardless of their managerial designation, are influenced by the organizational structure and the management they encounter, while concurrently exerting a direct impact on organizational structures and outcomes through the application of their knowledge and the establishment of their own managerial practices.

2. *Shifting from positional conceptions to practice-based perspectives*: Instead of conceptualizing management as a position occupied, reconceptualizing management as a practice. The conceptualization of management as a practice extends beyond the confines of top-level functions, such as planning and development, to encompass active engagement at middle and lower organizational levels. This holistic approach incorporates various facets of management

practice, including participation, sense-making, communication, implementation, monitoring, and review across different organizational levels and within and between diverse teams.

It is imperative to underscore that the conceptualization of management as a practice holds greater significance, comprehensiveness, authenticity, and reflexivity compared to its portrayal merely as a position within a hierarchical structure. This perspective contends that management is inherently tied to the actions and practices undertaken, rather than being contingent on specific managerial positions.

In particular, the "management-as-practice" approach is posited as a valuable lens for generating novel insights into the decision-making, implementation, and enactment of people-related initiatives within organizations. This perspective proves instrumental in understanding how blue- and gray-collar employees, along with other organizational stakeholders, interpret and engage with management processes. Further, it sheds light on how individuals in these roles become more effective and influential agents within the organizational framework, and it discerns the short-term and long-term effects of these actions and activities.

Consequently, management, when viewed through the lens of everyday actions, settings, processes, and content, emerges as a multifaceted and dynamic phenomenon that transcends specific hierarchical positions. This paradigm shift offers a more nuanced understanding of managing organizations, emphasizing the diverse practices that collectively contribute to the intricate tapestry of managerial actions and interactions.

3. *Embracing the dual nature of formal and informal management as collective work and structure*: Instead of conceptualizing management as a formal work and structure, reconceptualizing management as both formal and informal collective work and structure. Prevailing management theories predominantly emphasize management as the formal characteristic structure and processes associated with organizational control. However, in recognizing management as the intrinsic work of the organization, it becomes evident that the management process operates within a framework of both formal and informal collective understanding and interaction across all organizational levels (top, middle, and low) and among teams. The inclination to confine management within the formal structures of an organization often overlooks the equally significant informal facets of management, characterized by unplanned and unformalized power relations and competence-based interactions.

This alternative perspective posits that management should be apprehended as the interplay of both formal and informal dynamics within the organizational behavioral context. This inclusive approach enables the integration of individual and group behaviors of blue- and gray-collar employees into the broader network of social practices, thereby highlighting the nuanced links and interactions between social structures and individuals in the interpretation of actions (Iasbech & Lavarda, 2018; Vaara & Whittington, 2012).

Central to the managing process is the interaction mechanism, with formal organizational structures facilitating relatively straightforward relationship establishment, while informal social structures present a more complex challenge due to localized meanings. These social structures play a pivotal role in establishing management order and ensuring the continuity of the management practice/action flow. The embedded nature of implicit knowledge sharing within both organizational and social structures underscores the importance of localized methods within the organizational context.

This conceptualization implies that the managing process initiates with intention and mediates the relationship between the organizational context and practitioners' thoughts and behaviors. The recognition that intention and action are embedded in the organizational context rejects the notion that the strategy process operates solely through formal procedures. Instead, the managing process is socially embedded, necessitating an understanding of the concept of management within the broader context of social practice and formation, encompassing both formal and informal interactions among practitioners.

For instance, informal meetings emerge as crucial platforms for information processing, sharing, the integration of activities, and the dynamics of interaction. The contention that the same institutionalized strategic practices can manifest in diverse ways across contexts or by different actors further underscores the intricate nature of management dynamics.

In this holistic perspective, the implicit social practices ingrained in the actions of the top management team and other groups or teams of actors, including blue- and gray-collar employees, constitute a vital component of the collective understanding of management. This acknowledgment emphasizes the need for a comprehensive examination that goes beyond the formal organizational structures, incorporating the intricacies of informal interactions that shape the broader landscape of organizational management.

4. *Toward a multifaceted understanding of organizational purpose*: Instead of conceptualizing management limited to profit-maximizing purpose, reconceptualizing management as multifaceted purposes. Contemporary management theories are largely characterized by a conceptualization of management that is circumscribed within the confines of a profit-maximizing purpose. This prevalent perspective tends to consolidate diverse organizational purposes into a singular objective – profit maximization. While ostensibly promoting organizational unity under a common goal, this reductionist approach not only presents an unrealistic portrayal of organizational dynamics, presuming a homogeneity of individuals uniformly aligned with the singular goal of organizational prosperity, but it also poses significant constraints on the exploration and understanding of issues pertinent to non-managerial workers.

The homogenization of organizational actors around the singular aim of profit maximization oversimplifies the complex and multifaceted nature of individuals within an organizational context. It overlooks the inherent diversity of motivations, values, and perspectives that individuals, both managerial and non-managerial, bring to the workplace. This oversimplification hampers a nuanced understanding of the intricacies of organizational behavior, stifling the potential for exploring the varied and legitimate purposes that different stakeholders within the organization may have.

An alternative dimension within this management paradigm posits practitioners as dynamic social entities actively engaged in the decision-making processes inherent to organizational management (Vaara & Whittington, 2012). Unlike a mechanistic portrayal solely focused on profit maximization, practitioners are acknowledged not merely as instrumental entities but as individuals with multifaceted purposes. This conceptualization perceives practitioners as socially embedded beings, actively participating in decision-making while considering their socio-political perspectives, skills, gender, national cultures, and other distinguishing attributes (Vaara & Whittington, 2012). They assume a pivotal role in decision formulation, shaping, and execution (Splitter & Whittington, 2019; Whittington, 2003), thereby attributing a primary responsibility to humans, or the implementers, in the decision-making process. Consequently, a comprehensive consideration of a diverse array of practitioner traits becomes imperative.

Within this framework, blue- and gray-collar employees are not relegated to the status of organizational property; rather, they are regarded as integral contributors to the intricate web of organizational interactions.

These social practices, infused with the diverse purposes and perspectives of practitioners, contribute to the articulation of organizational objectives, the delineation of strategic goals, and the molding of the implementation process. The outcomes of these practices extend beyond a narrow focus on profit maximization, fostering mutual benefits that align with both the organization's overarching purpose and the diverse interests of stakeholders. Importantly, this perspective emphasizes the inclusive consideration of all practitioners and stakeholders, transcending the traditional emphasis on shareholders and top management.

In essence, this alternative viewpoint contends that management is not solely beholden to a profit-centric purpose but encompasses a broader spectrum of organizational and stakeholder objectives. This nuanced understanding underscores the interconnectedness of social practices with organizational goals, thereby fostering a more inclusive and socially responsible approach to management.

5. *Transitioning from hierarchy to competence as the foundation of authority*: Instead of conceptualizing management as hierarchical power, reconceptualizing management as a power based on expertise and competence. Contemporary management theories frequently characterize management within the framework of hierarchical power structures, emphasizing positional authority rather than acknowledging power grounded in expertise and competence. This prevailing perspective often overtly or implicitly aligns with a Weberian conceptualization of management, wherein authority is derived from organizational positions and formal structures. However, a more nuanced and forward-looking approach is imperative – one that shifts the paradigm toward a conceptualization of management rooted in the power emanating from individuals' expertise and competence.

The conventional hierarchical view of management, influenced by Weberian principles, tends to prioritize authority derived from organizational positions.

This emphasis on formalized power structures can inadvertently foster a rigid and potentially outdated approach to leadership, overlooking the dynamic nature of contemporary organizational challenges and the evolving requirements of a knowledge-based economy.

To address this limitation, there is a compelling need to reorient management theories toward a framework that places expertise and competence at the forefront. This entails recognizing that effective management is not solely contingent on one's hierarchical position but is profoundly influenced by the depth of knowledge, skills, and proficiency that individuals bring to their roles.

A transformative perspective on management would involve a departure from traditional notions of authority tied solely to rank and position, toward an emphasis on the power of expertise. This approach highlights the significance of cultivating and leveraging specialized knowledge, skills, and competencies as essential sources of influence and leadership effectiveness.

Moreover, a power-based-on-expertise paradigm encourages a more inclusive and collaborative organizational culture. It fosters an environment where individuals are valued for their unique competencies, irrespective of hierarchical levels, and where decision-making is informed by a diversity of perspectives grounded in specialized knowledge.

This conceptual shift not only aligns with the demands of a rapidly changing business landscape but also promotes a more adaptive and resilient organizational structure. It acknowledges that expertise and competence are dynamic assets that can transcend traditional power structures, empowering individuals at various levels to contribute meaningfully to organizational success.

Redefining management through the lens of expertise-based power represents a crucial evolution in management thinking. This approach not only aligns with contemporary organizational realities but also paves the way for a more agile, adaptive, and knowledge-centric model of leadership that is better suited to meet the multifaceted challenges of the modern business environment.

CONCLUSIONS

The foundational premise underpinning this study lies in the contention that endeavors aimed at theory construction or extension serve as pivotal mechanisms for advancing both theoretical and empirical understanding within the realm of non-managerial involvement in management processes. In light of the criticisms directed toward existing management theories and the ongoing endeavors to cultivate novel frameworks or augment existing ones, it becomes apparent that a comprehensive theory of management comprises three distinct dimensions: organizational, strategic, and value based. The organizational dimension, characterized by coordination and cooperation, is posited in essence as a non-contingent universalistic facet, though it is dynamic. In contrast, the strategic dimension encapsulates contingent elements, notably innovations in management aimed at navigating the imperative of radical change and addressing challenges inherent in the contemporary business landscape. Furthermore, the value-based dimension denotes a paradigm wherein organizational ethos and principles are deeply entrenched, akin to an organizational religion. These dimensions, while discrete, are intricately intertwined and interdependent. Neglecting any one dimension serves to undermine the holistic comprehension of organizational management. Indeed, within organizational contexts, all three dimensions concurrently manifest to varying extents. The equilibrium and distribution among these dimensions profoundly shape an organization's management philosophy, comprehension, and ultimately, its trajectory toward success.

Implicit in the foundational dimensions of a management theory is the imperative to elucidate the role of non-managerial personnel in various organizational functions. This necessitates a thorough examination of their involvement in organizing, strategizing, and valuing within the organizational framework. In the domain of organizing, non-managerial employees play a crucial role in facilitating coordination and cooperation. This entails their engagement in decision-making and implementation processes in value-chain activities, intra-departmental collaborations, as well as inter-departmental and hierarchical interactions within the organizational social networks. Strategizing involves a multifaceted approach wherein non-managerial personnel are instrumental in sensing, seizing, and reconfiguring contingencies. Additionally, they contribute to the strategic positioning and repositioning of the organization in response to external environmental dynamics. Furthermore, non-managerial employees participate in architecting organizational capabilities and competences, thereby influencing the organization's strategic trajectory. In the realm of valuing, non-managerial employees contribute significantly to the formation of organizational culture, vision, and mission. They also play a pivotal role in shaping the philosophy of work and working practices within the organization. Moreover, their involvement is integral to the development and enactment of organizational principles that underpin the organizational ethos. Thus, a comprehensive understanding of the dimensions of management theory necessitates a detailed exploration of the roles and contributions of non-managerial employees in organizing, strategizing, and valuing within the organizational context.

Similar to scholars operating within the framework of SAP, who inquire into the context of strategy activity, we can expand our focus to encompass the question of how management is enacted within organizations, thereby contextualizing decision-making processes. Within this scope, the category of practitioners extends beyond a select few within managerial hierarchies to encompass all employees exerting influence on decision-making processes to varying degrees. In this reconceptualization, formal management ceases to occupy an unquestioned "heroic" default position but rather emerges as one among several groups of actors. Indeed, management is not an abstracted activity solely attributable to formal management figures; rather, it emerges as a product of collective efforts within a network of management interactions shaped by organizational, environmental, and psychological factors. Recognizing this dynamic nature of management prompts a re-evaluation of its boundaries: management is co-constructed by both managerial and non-managerial practitioners. This inclusive perspective affords a more comprehensive and realistic portrayal of management, aligning with the notion that historical narratives should not solely focus on heroic figures but also consider grassroots perspectives, as history is not solely dictated by heroic actions.

In pursuit of this direction, there is a need to develop theories that explore the processes, content, cognition, and context factors influencing management from the perspectives of both managerial and non-managerial employees. This approach promises to enrich our understanding of management practices by integrating insights from diverse actors involved in decision-making processes within organizations.

REFERENCES

Agoston, S. (2009). New management theories – An alternative to current crisis? *Review of International Comparative Management*, 2, 1299–1305.

Aktouf, O. (1992). Management and theories of organizations in the 1990s: Toward a critical radical humanism? *Academy of Management Review*, 17(3), 407–431.

Alvesson, M., & Sandberg, J. (2011). Generating research questions through problematization. *Academy of Management Review*, 36, 247–271.

Bhattacharyya, S. S. (2020). Humanistic orientation in firm–stakeholder technology-based interaction and its impact on stakeholder satisfaction. *Emerging Economy Studies*, 6(1), 86–105.

Boxenbaum, E., & Rouleau, L. (2011). New knowledge products as bricolage: Metaphors and scripts in organizational theory. *Academy of Management Review*, 36, 272–296.

Caldart, A. A., Ricart, J. E., & Carrera, A. A. (2020). *General management in Latin and Ibero-American organizations: A humanistic perspective* (Edited by A. A. Caldart, J. E. Ricart, & A. A. Carrera). Routledge.

Carrera, A. A. (2020). The organization centred on its people. In A. A. Caldart, J. E. Ricart, & A. A. Carrera (Eds.), *General management in Latin and Ibero-American organizations: A humanistic perspective* (pp. 37–61). Routledge.

Coda, V. (2010). *Entrepreneurial values and strategic management: Essays in management theory*. Palgrave Macmillan.

Cornelissen, J. P., & Durand, R. (2014). Moving forward: Developing theoretical contributions in management studies. *Journal of Management Studies*, 51(6), 995–1022.

Daft, R. L., & Lewin, A. Y. (1990). Can Organization studies begin to break out of the normal science straitjacket? An editorial essay. *Organization Science*, 1(1), 1–9.

Daft, R. L., & Lewin, A. Y. (1993). Where are the theories for the "new" organizational forms? An editorial essay. *Organization Science*, 4(4), i–vi.

Eckberg, D. L., & Hills, L., Jr. (1979). The paradigm concept and sociology: A critical review. *American Sociological Review*, 44(6), 925–937.

Folger, R., & Turillo, C. J. (1999). Theorizing as the thickness of thin abstraction. *Academy of Management Review*, 24, 742–758.

Grant, R. M. (2008). The future of management: Where is Gary Hamel leading us? *Long Range Planning*, 4, 469–482.

Grant, R. M. (2010). Introduction: Some thoughts on Vittorio Coda's contributions to strategic management. In V. Coda (Ed.), *Entrepreneurial values and strategic management essays in management theory* (pp. 1–14). Palgrave Macmillan.

Hamel, G. (2009). Moonshots for management. *Harvard Business Review*, 87(2), 91–98.

Hamel, G., & Breen, B. (2007). *The future of management*. Harvard Business School Press.

Iasbech, P., & Lavarda, R. A. B. (2018). Strategy as practice and the role of middle manager in organizations: The future of the field. *Revista de Administração da UFSM*, 11(4), 1125–1145.

Kilduff, M., Mehra, A., & Dunn, M. B. (2011). From blue sky research to problem solving: A philosophy of science theory of new knowledge production. *Academy of Management Review*, 36, 297–317.

Koslowski, P. (2010). The philosophy of management: Philosophy as a challenge to business, management as a challenge to philosophy. In P. Koslowski (Ed.), *Elements of a philosophy of management and organization* (pp. 3–18). Springer-Verlag Heidelberger.

Kuhn, T. S. (1962). *The structure of scientific revolutions*. University of Chicago Press.

Kuhn, T. S. (1993). Metaphor in science. In A. Ortony (Ed.), *Metaphor and thought* (pp. 553–542). Cambridge University Press.

Llano, C. (2000). *Sistemas versus persona*. McGraw Hill.

Llano, C. (2010). *Viaje al centro del hombre*. Rialp.

Mayo, E. (1924). The basis of industrial psychology. *Bulletin of the Taylor Society, 9*, 249–259.

McGregor, D. (1957). The human side of enterprise. *Management Review, 46*(11), 166–171.

McGregor, D. (1969a). Theory X: The traditional view of direction and control. In R. A. Sutermeister (Ed.), *People and productivity* (2nd ed., pp. 186–193). McGraw Hill.

McGregor, D. (1969b). Theory Y: The integration of individual and organizational goals. In R. A. Sutermeister (Ed.), *People and productivity* (2nd ed., pp. 194–202). McGraw Hill.

McGregor, D. (2000a). New concepts of management. In G. Heil, W. Bennis, & D. C. Stephens (Eds.), *Revisited: Managing the human side of the enterprise* (pp. 145–153). John Wiley.

McGregor, D. (2000b). The human side of enterprise. In G. Heil, W. Bennis, & D. C. Stephens (Eds.), *Revisited: Managing the human side of the enterprise* (pp. 130–144). John Wiley.

Melé, D. (2012). *Management ethics: Placing ethics at the core of good management*. Palgrave MacMillan.

Pirson, M. A. (2019). A humanistic perspective for management theory: Protecting dignity and promoting well-being. *Journal of Business Ethics, 159*(3), 1013–1036.

Popper, K. R. (1959). *The logic of scientific discovery*. Routledge.

Ricart, J. E., & Llopis, J. (2020). A general manager's agenda: What good managers do? In A. A. Caldart, J. E. Ricart, & A. A. Carrera (Eds.), *General management in Latin and Ibero-American organizations: A humanistic perspective* (pp. 7–18). Routledge.

Shepherd, D. A., & Sutcliffe, K. M. (2011). Inductive top down theorizing: A source of new theories of organization. *Academy of Management Review, 36*, 361–380.

Splitter, V., & Whittington, R. (2019). Employee participation in strategy making over time: Discursive competence and influence. *Academy of Management Annual Meeting Proceedings, 2019*(1), 11040. https://doi.org/10.5465/AMBPP.2019.11040abstract.

Tsang, E. W. K., & Elsaesser, F. (2001). How contrastive explanation facilitates theory building. *Academy of Management Review, 36*, 404–419.

Vaara, E., & Whittington, R. (2012). Strategy-as-practice: Taking social practices seriously. *The Academy of Management Annals, 6*(1), 1–52.

Weick, K. E. (1989). Theory construction as disciplined imagination. *Academy of Management Review, 14*, 516–531.

Whetten, D., Felin, T., & King, B. G. (2009). The practice of theory borrowing in organizational studies: Current issues and future directions. *Journal of Management, 35*, 537–563.

Whittington, R. (2003). The work of strategizing and organizing: For a practice perspective. *Strategic Organization, 1*(1), 117–112.

SECTION II

INNOVATIONS AND BUSINESS PRACTICES

CHAPTER 6

A STUDY ON ENVIRONMENT, SOCIAL AND GOVERNANCE DISCLOSURE IN THE CASE OF THE PACKAGING SECTOR IN ROMANIA

Anca Draghici[a], Gabriela Banaduc[a],
Roxana Mihaela Sirbu[a,b] and Tamas-Szora Attila[b]

[a]*Politehnica University of Timisoara, Timisoara, Romania*
[b]*"1 Decembrie 1918" University of Alba Iulia, Alba Iulia, Romania*

ABSTRACT

This study is based on actual legal requirements in Europe on disclosure of nonfinancial information and the principle of the United Nations Principles of Responsible Investment (UNPRI), reflecting environmental, social, and governance (ESG) commitment behavior from companies. Given that plastic pollution is the world's biggest source of climate change, stakeholders want sustainable packaging and an ESG disclosure approach that creates value over the long run. The research aims to identify the critical factors that influence ESG reporting and contribute to Romanian packaging firms' long-term financial success. Using the ideas of value creation process theory, a content analysis was done in the first research stage to examine sustainability/ESG reports from the five companies on their long-term value development process and the techniques they used. Second, the findings were verified for validity (credibility and reliability) using semi-structured interviews with Romanian ESG professionals. The research results, aligned with the literature, indicate that a strong business strategy integrated with ESG across the value chain, along with a multistakeholder and commitment-driven approach, is critical in creating long-term business value. Lastly, it is highly advised that reporting practitioners, sustainability leaders and policymakers of consumer goods packaging companies implement all the key determinants of ESG reporting as identified in this study to create long-term business value through ESG reporting by moving beyond compliance-driven strategy.

Keywords: Environment, social, and governance; sustainability; value creation; nonfinancial disclosure; content analysis; semi-structured interviews

1. INTRODUCTION

The most dynamic sustainability concerns that currently affect the financial performance and competitiveness of businesses include the effects of climate change, (micro)plastic waste, new and emerging job forms, and widening inequities. In this context, reporting of nonfinancial disclosure has become of huge interest and concern not only for companies but also for their investors and stakeholders; nonfinancial reporting disclosure is discussed and correlated together with the financial reports by detailing organization's performance, operations, and responsibilities, together with the legal compliance. Consequently, this study is based on the actual legal framework in Europe on disclosure of nonfinancial information and the UNPRI, reflecting ESG commitment behavior from companies (WBCSD, 2019).

These efforts were recently demonstrated by the 2023 Report of the Governance and Accountability Institute, Inc. (G&A, https://www.ga-institute.com/research/ga-research-directory/sustainability-reporting-trends/2023-sustainability-reporting-in-focus.html). G&A's research analyzes the content of sustainability reports providing detailed breakdowns of the reporting frameworks and standards used (such as the Global Reporting Initiative (GRI), the Sustainability Accounting Standards Board (SASB), the Task Force on Climate-related Financial Disclosures (TCFD)), alignment with initiatives such as the United Nations (UN) sustainable development goals (SDGs), trends in external assurance, and the carbon disclosure project (CDP) reporting.

By assessing their effects on the economy, society, and the environment, businesses help to achieve SDGs. ESG measures are becoming more and more ingrained in investor research, helping investors make smarter decisions and lower long-term risks while increasing profits (MacNeil & Esser, 2022). Thus, corporate sustainability reporting (CSR) is the process by which companies communicate their ESG performance to their stakeholders, including investors, customers, employees, and the public. It is the current business trend to switch from the classical corporate social responsibility (CSR) approach to the more comprehensive ESG approach; the importance of ESG reporting is backed by the Corporate Sustainability Reporting Directive (CSRD), which will impact around

50,000 companies in the European Union (EU) in the future most because of introducing the Directive 2014/95/EU (nonfinancial reporting directive, NFRD). Consequently, top management of companies is trying to meet the requirements of stakeholders with priority, and shareholders agree with this shift (Mio et al., 2020). In a recent study, Arvidsson and Dumay (2022) support the idea that "regulatory requirements around the world are one of the key driving forces for companies to continuously measure, improve, and report on ESG performance."

According to the NFRD, "all companies are required to report their ESG information." In addition, other organizations introduce smoothly different frameworks or/and guidelines or so-called standards to improve the ESG reporting, such as UNPRI, the UN Global Compact, and GRI. ESG reporting, while primarily voluntary, faces a growing number of global regulations mandating adherence to and disclosure on ESG issues, with the European Green Deal (EGD) standing out as one of the most ambitious of these initiatives. The EU has set ambitious 2030 goals for greenhouse gas (GHG) emission reductions, renewable energy, and energy efficiency to create a low-carbon and climate-resilient economy. The EU Taxonomy, CSRD, CDP framework, and the Sustainable Finance Disclosure Regulation (SFDR) are part of the EGD and are designed to direct financial support to sustainable activities. The taxonomy requires certain entities to disclose information about the extent to which their activities comply with the taxonomy, as it amends the disclosure requirements in the CSRD and SFDR. The aim is to provide investors with a clearer understanding of the sustainability characteristics and objectives of different investment funds. Companies covered by CSRD must disclose to what extent their activities are linked to activities considered environmentally sustainable.

It is relevant to take into consideration the debate in the gray literature (reports and studies of consulting companies and policymakers positions) where companies' long-term value creation is not completely explained in their sustainability or annual reports. A long-term value creation process through ESG disclosure and sustainable packaging is demanded by stakeholders because (micro)plastic is the primary worldwide issue risk in the packaging industry, as it is increasing due to the climate change (Beghetto et al., 2023; Pasonen, 2023). Many information gaps have been discovered that will be filled by the presented research, which is based on preliminary investigations on ESG disclosure, in general, and its specifics in the packaging industry.

Specifically, in the case of Romania, although certain companies are starting to pay more attention to ESG factors, in general, domestic companies have a reluctant approach to this concept. A recent study by the Global ESG Monitor (GEM), which also analyzed the main companies in the BET20 index, shows that Romanian companies are significantly behind companies around the world in terms of ESG reporting. According to the study, unfortunately for stakeholders, investors, and managers, transparency in reporting on sustainable development has not yet been a priority for Romanian companies. Collectively, Romania's index ranked last in the global GEM ranking, with an average of only 41 points out of a possible 100, far behind the top indices in the United States, Asia, Australia, and other parts of Europe.

Furthermore, it can be noted that in Romania, steps are being taken to implement a clear and articulated legal framework regarding ESG:

- The Ministry of Finance issued two official orders transposing the provisions of Directive 2014/95.
- The Body of Expert and Licenced Accountants of Romania (CECCAR) has developed a guide on nonfinancial reporting and reporting for management in the context of the crisis generated by the coronavirus pandemic (CECCAR, 2020).
- The Bucharest Stock Exchange (operate using index constituents – BET) has published (April 2022) a guide for the ESG reporting process as a manual for companies (BET, 2022).

In this context, this research focuses on providing a knowledge base related to ESG reporting to companies active in the Romanian market, specifically those operating in the packing industry. The purpose of this study is to identify how long-term corporate value may be strategically generated and how it can be communicated through an ESG reporting activity. In the case of the present study, five packaging companies with ESG reporting practices were considered for characterizing the main aspects of the ESG-adopting process and that has been followed by the validation research with a group of ESG practitioners in Romania.

2. BRIEF LITERATURE REVIEW

2.1. Some Considerations on ESG Disclosure

CSR is the process by which companies communicate their ESG performance to their stakeholders, including investors, customers, employees, and the public. Studies on ESG ratings demonstrate the impact and evolution of the reporting process and relevant critical aspects (Khan, 2022; Khandelwal et al., 2023; WBCSD, 2019). Recently, it has been realized that due to "the lack of reporting guidelines and the low degree of comparability across ESG information provided by companies, it is crucial to investigate the potential credibility-enhancing mechanism of such disclosures using either internal or external mechanisms" (Tsang et al., 2023).

Khan (2022) developed a meta-literature analysis that encompasses content and bibliometric analysis along with meta-regression on corporate finance through the lens of ESG ratings from 2012 to 2022. According to this study, three categories can be used to classify the literature on corporate sustainability: (1) the financial consequences of nonfinancial information disclosure, (2) corporate governance as a predictor of nonfinancial information disclosure, and (3) business characteristics that affect sustainability performance. The main consequences of the Khan (2022) study are as follows: first, most of the ESG studies presented in the literature are slanted toward larger companies, which suggests the need for future orientation to small- and medium-sized enterprise (SME)'s behavior. Second, market capitalization has an impact on ESG risk. Because they face greater social pressure, are more visible when engaging in unsustainable activity, and see a stronger response from the market, larger companies typically maintain higher ESG performance.

Furthermore, the literature supports the idea that "ESG disclosure and integrating reporting, compliance provide incentives for companies in terms of lower cost of debt, allowing them to time the debt markets" (Gerwanski, 2020; Khan, 2022; Tsang et al., 2023). Global investors and other stakeholders are giving more weight to nonfinancial ESG information provided by enterprises or nonfinancial rating agencies because of the increased understanding of the significance of ESG activities to corporate sustainability in recent decades. Although

> the role of these data for issuing companies is somewhat understood, given the lack of reporting guidelines and the low degree of comparability between ESG information provided by firms, it is crucial to investigate potential mechanisms that could improve the credibility of such disclosures through internal or external mechanisms. (Tsang et al., 2023)

According to Xie et al.'s (2019) findings, there is a moderate (i.e., neither high nor low) effect of ESG disclosure on business performance. However, social and environmental disclosure comes after governance disclosure, which has more advantageous effects. For instance, if environmental regulations are not adequately managed, noncompliance with them may result in a decline in the value of the company. To mitigate these negative effects, companies are encouraged to use green practices such as reducing, reuse, and recycling throughout their value chain. Capability upgrades and commitment of the management are critical factors for business growth in terms of social and governance components. Furthermore, the study's findings indicate that there is little correlation between under- or over-reporting and an organization's performance.

In the synthesis of Daugaard and Ding (2022) on the factors that influence ESG performance (and impact), they conclude that approaches are very dispersed. Numerous solitary study contributions have demonstrated that a multitude of factors impact ESG performance such as firm size, auditing, strategic decisions, board composition, stock exchange innovation, investors, and if the company is in a sector that is more sensitive to ESG issues. However, the findings in the literature are not well organized, making it difficult to draw logical conclusions about how to improve ESG outcomes.

In addition, according to the reviewed literature, financial gains from ESG reporting benefit investors and enterprises alike, and reporting on the governance aspect is essential to generate long-term corporate value. In fact, maintaining a solid relationship between companies and investors is necessary for long-term value.

2.2. Brief Overview of the Sustainable Business Value Creation (SBVC)

The research of Manda et al. (2016) describes sustainable value creation by integrating environmental sustainability through life cycle assessment (LCA) in business. Thus, sustainable value creation identifies strategies and practices that help create a more sustainable company and society and uses those strategies and practices to maximize shareholder value. From Manda et al. (2016) research, "a contribution to sustainable development is possible when companies implement an integrated value creation process within their business strategy that includes ESG factors, risk assessments and reporting, governance and strategy, stakeholder engagement, etc." (also supported by Pryshlakivsky & Searcy, 2021; Sazdovski et al., 2021).

The study by Lüdeke-Freund et al. (2020) underlined that

> value creation is typically associated with how companies create and offer products and services for which customers are willing to pay and how they try to capture a share of the total value that is created in the corresponding economic exchange processes.

They extended assumptions and research on SBVC based on the "People-Planet-Profit" (3P) or "triple bottom line" (TBL) models and stakeholder theory perspectives (these are the most accepted approaches in the sustainable business model domain as mentioned by Prakash, 2020).

In addition, the scientific debate on SBVC has evolved in the context of circular economy development. Relevant study of Ranta et al. (2020) illustrates how B2B suppliers can use customer value propositions to facilitate a systematic transition toward the circular economy. Additionally, the sustainable value creation business model required strong involvement from all stakeholders and particularly consumers (Aarikka-Stenroos et al., 2022; Hankammer et al., 2019). Furthermore, Laukkanen and Tura (2020) examine the sustainable value creation potential of different types of sharing economy business models. Thus, the authors introduce a taxonomy of 13 different sharing economy business models that also demonstrate the variety of B2B SBVC.

From the different approaches present in the literature, evolution contribution to the SBVC model is possible when companies integrate ESG factors and reporting, risk assessments, strategy, governance, stakeholder management, etc. in the value creation process. Visser and Kymal (2015) developed a relevant model of the integrated value creation (IVC) process to support "companies in achieving their goals and stakeholders' expectations, thus contributing to long-term value creation by tackling global environmental and social challenges" (also supported by Samans & Nelson, 2022; Zaccone & Pedrini, 2020). The Visser and Kymal (2015) framework has inspired the approach of the theoretical framework development of the present study (Fig. 6.1).

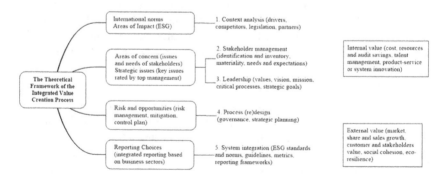

Fig. 6.1. The Theoretical Framework of the IVC Process.

First, businesses need to be aware of the most recent changes that have an impact on their sector, such as legal changes, risks or hazards, technology advancements or disruptions, best practices, etc. The organization's second stage involves identifying every stakeholder in their value chain, prioritizing the most crucial stakeholders, ascertaining their expectations, and completing the materialistic mapping, also known as the materiality matrix, in compliance with the guidelines for GRI sustainability reporting. The third phase, the leadership review, calls for senior management to assess the company's vision and mission and, if necessary, make changes to bring it into compliance with regulations. Based on the material challenges that have been recognized, leaders should create strategic goals and targets. Then, they should periodically assess the progress made toward these targets.

In the subsequent phase of process (re)design, businesses should use integrated risk assessment to identify business risks and opportunities in addition to the material hazards that have been identified. Firms can adjust strategic goals considering the risks and possibilities discovered and can adapt their business process based on all processes to meet stakeholder expectations. The final phase, system integration, involves integrating strategic goals and business-relevant standards with the needs of the management system (e.g., ISO 45001, ISO 14001, etc.). Integrating your business processes, which also include planning, budgeting, auditing, management reviews, and reporting, is essential and required for businesses.

The research employs qualitative methodologies to constructively use this comprehensive framework (Table 6.1) and to provide advice to Romanian packaging companies to produce long-term value through disclosure of ESG.

This chapter concludes by identifying the present gap in the development of long-term value through disclosure of ESG. Given that stakeholders assert that corporations are failing to provide the necessary information, there appears to be a knowledge gap regarding the idea of value generation. Additionally, the literature indicates that investors' primary requirement, the application of governance factors, remains a difficulty for enterprises. These challenges include those related to data quality, transparency, priority, and the selection of reporting frameworks and ESG ratings. This research contributes value by assessing the value creation tactics employed by multinational consumer goods packaging manufacturers and bridging the information gaps regarding ESG reporting standards currently utilized in the worldwide market. Based on the research findings and data analysis, suggestions are given for implementing a sustainable business strategy. The following section goes into the methodology used to carry out this investigation.

3. RESEARCH METHODOLOGY

3.1. Description of the Research Scenario

The object of the present study is the ESG reporting process in the case of packaging companies operating in Romania. From a methodological point of view, this study combines theory (bibliographic research) and practice-orientated research (based on content analysis and interpretations) with reference to the ESG reporting process implications, in the case of packing companies. A synthesis of the research methodology is presented in Fig. 6.2.

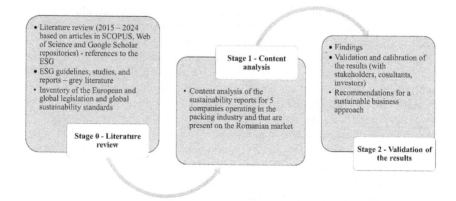

Fig. 6.2. Study Stages.

In the preliminary stage, a literature review of relevant concepts and theories was developed to know the specifics and trends in the reporting of ESG. Furthermore, references to the ESG, guidelines, studies, and reports have been collected (European and global legislation) and most important global sustainability standards from the knowledge repository created within the Erasmus + project "Smart Education for Corporate Sustainability Reporting" (https://csr-secure.eu/).

Next, the conceptual model design has been developed as presented in Fig. 6.3. The elements of the theory of SBVC discussed earlier (see Table 6.1) were considered to define the three groups: (1) drivers, (2) strategic management, and (3) metrics; this approach has been adopted for a deeper analysis:

- The drivers (Group 1) of the ESG reporting process are associated with motivations and reasons for companies to be transparent in reporting.
- To define the factors in Group 2, the relevant aspects of the business strategy were considered: mitigation of material risks related to packaging, formulation of objectives considering the expectations of various stakeholders and investors' expectations, and description of the internal governance mechanism of governance.
- Group 3 has been considered to better characterize the value creation process of the business and to demonstrate how competitive advantage is achieved.

3.2. Data Collection

For the research purpose of this study (first stage), five large packaging companies were considered because of their ESG performance in 2021 and 2022 (large companies listed on the BET and the preliminary information provided by the GEM study in 2022). Companies need to meet two of the three criteria: (a) on average more than 250 employees, (b) balance sheet of more than 20 M€, and (c) turnover of more than 40 M€ (Table 6.1).

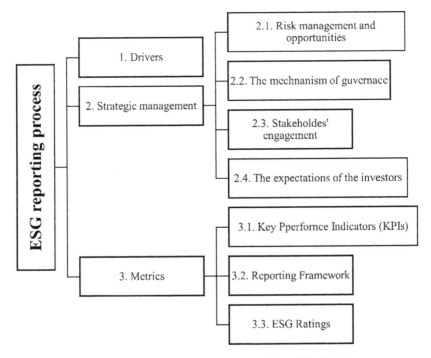

Fig. 6.3. The Conceptual Model Design of the Study.

Table 6.1. Synthesis of the Data on ESG and/or Sustainability Reports of the Packaging Companies Considered in the Research.

Organization	Reporting Period	Report Length (Pages)	Compliance to Sustainability Reporting Frameworks
A	2020–2021	62	GRI Adopting the nonfinancial reporting guidelines of the CECCAR
B	January 2021–December 2022	54	GRI Adopting the nonfinancial reporting guidelines of the CECCAR
C	2021	46	Sustainability report Adopting the nonfinancial reporting guidelines of the CECCAR
D	January 2021–December 2021	32	GRI. AA1000APS[a] Communication on progress of the UN global compact
E	July 2021–June 2022	45	GRI Extended report by adopting ESG guidelines from the BET (2022)

[a]Accountability's AA1000 Series of Standards, https://www.accountability.org/standards/aa1000-assurance-standard/ (accessed December 6, 2023).

For the second stage of the investigation, validation of the results and findings (using semi-structured interviews based on open questionnaire), there have been considered a small group of ESG professionals ($n = 4$): two managers from two different packaging companies not included in the study (Man 1, Man 2), a consultant specialized in the ESG reporting process (Cons), and an investor from investment firms (Inv). The selected practitioners are professionals with extensive experience (managers) and expertise in the field of CSR and sustainable development.

From the perspective of the data collection method, sustainability reports and annual reports of selected companies were identified and collected (e.g., from their websites or directly from company representatives) together with other additional reports on specific issues such as resource efficiency and cleaner production, energy, waste or water management, risk management plans, materiality analysis reports, or other articles directly or indirectly related to ESG reporting issues. These documents have been studied and follow a content analysis process.

In the research results validation (second) stage, a series of four semi-structured interviews (45–60 minutes each, recorded for data analysis) using open-ended questionnaires have been developed (based on the designed theoretical framework described in Figs. 6.1 and 6.3). The objective of this qualitative research stage was to collect and understand the opinion of respondents on the ESG reporting process and value creation (as suggested by Hennik et al., 2020 and as described by Prakash, 2020):

- For certain participants, a contextualized knowledge of behavior, beliefs, etc.
- Comprehensive auto-reporting that provides an understanding of the impacts and the process.
- Interpretative analysis of mainly textual data.
- Identify perceptions and compare them to the theoretical model.

3.3. The Approach of Data Analysis

The analysis of each sustainability report has been developed based on the theoretical framework (Figs. 6.1 and 6.3). It is important to point out that the research methodology is a mix, considering the mix of qualitative and quantitative data occurring in the different stages of the scenario. The author uses the word "legitimation" rather than "validity" in reference to mixed ways of legitimation. Indeed, the model of Collins et al. (2012) "proposes a process-orientated legitimation which allows a step-by-step validation, and this throughout the entire research process; the present research is concerned with two aspects of legitimation: weakness minimisation and multiple validities" (supported also by Perez et al., 2023; Rusnac, 2021). "Qualitative data analysis can be achieved by using several computer-assisted qualitative data analysis software, CAQDAS" (also tested and confirmed by the research of Rusnac, 2021).

> CAQDAS propose a diverse range of analytical functions that can be used according to the construction of the research process and methods. Therefore, the analysis of three considered software (Atlast.ti, MAXQDA, and Nvivo) aims at identifying strong points and limitations for each one, while keeping in mind that the central feature of CAQDAS is the assignment of codes to data, independently of format.

Finally, MAXQDA software was selected for the content analysis technique because it fits best to the purpose and objectives of the research (arguments considered have been provided by the study of (Rusnac, 2021)).

It is accepted that MAXQDA has an intuitive user interface, as well as coding features (such as segment retrieval and color assignment or drag-and-drop). Lastly, it is acknowledged for its ability to do sophisticated analysis, even with enormous data sets, and for its generous customer assistance program. Data conversion may be used to get quantitative data, which can then be conveniently transmitted for further mining in quantitative software like SPSS (Rusnac, 2021). This approach should be the subject of future studies.

4. RESEARCH RESULTS: DEBATES AND IMPLICATIONS

4.1. Content Analysis

In this study, the content analysis objective was to compare dimensions of the theoretical framework (as presented in Figs. 6.1 and 6.3, dimensions used for the coding process) with current organizational practices by identifying important points of view in the ESG disclosures of the packaging companies considered. Therefore, in the case of the packing companies under consideration, the goal is to analyze the content of sustainability reports in order to comprehend the relationships and applications that organizations have with respect to the critical factors of ESG disclosure in the creation of long-term business value. The research objective is to uncover relationships that are not immediately apparent in the provided textual data. As such, based on the works of Krippendorff (2018) and Lindgren et al. (2020), content analysis is considered "an appropriate research technique; indeed, the research aims at unearthing relations that are not readily discussed within the data set and for which there is no direct source of data. Consequently, the questions asked are those of the researcher and not those of the owner (packing companies) of the data set, while the answers will emerge from legitimate inferences based on the data set" (similar research approach done by Rusnac, 2021).

4.1.1. Coding Process

The sustainability reports content was analyzed based on predefined codes (and using MAXQDA functionalities): "drivers," "implications," "long-term value creation," "stakeholders," "engagement process," "materiality," "investors expect," "reporting framework," "ratings," "strategy," "governance." These codes are in accordance with the research framework and supported the study by condensing the data. The list of variables considered in the theoretical model yields the codes that may be assigned to each coding unit. The coding process was carried out as follows: first, the available sustainability reports were read and the code unit was determined based on the subject matter only for codes "implications," "drivers," "long-term value creation," and "stakeholders." A second reading of each sustainability report was performed to determine the coding units and attribute the remaining codes. To guarantee coding consistency across the range of business models, regional settings, organizational practices, and reporting systems, several loops were carried out on the units of analysis as the coding process progressed. This methodology guaranteed adaptability in the examination. There were 2,885 coded units in total because of the coding procedure. Details of the code frequencies within the code system are shown in Table 6.2.

4.1.2. The Portrait of the Documents (ESG Considered Reports)

An illustration of the coded and uncoded material of each analysis unit is provided by the document picture. The mathematical representation of the document's picture is a matrix made up of squares, the quantity of which may be altered. In the current study, all the coded regions are grouped together based on the assigned code and scaled to a consistent size in a 1,200-square matrix (30 rows of 40 squares). From there, they are dispersed proportionately to their relative use in the coded text. Furthermore, each document's visual representation may make use of the color that was previously allocated to each code in the coding system. The MAXQDA document portrait feature may be used to create document portraits. The arrangement, scope, and duration of each coded segment are made easier to understand by the document picture. There are two types of displays available: code frequency and code order. Two document portraits were created for the current study for every analysis unit:

1. A 30 row by 40 square matrix was used to create the document portrait, which was then displayed according to code frequency to enable easy comprehension and comparison of the documents (see Graph Set 1 from the Annex presented in the digital repository of Politehnica University of Timisoara, Romania, https://dspace.upt.ro/jspui/handle/123456789/6253).
2. A document portrait that shows coded and uncoded segments in the order that they occur, based on the 30 rows by 40 squares matrix. This representation allows for a more in-depth visualization, as it allows to situate codes more easily relative to one another and to view the proportion of coded segments relative to uncoded segments, too. This representation allows for a visualization

Table 6.2. Total Code Units Over the Data Set (Code System).

Code System	Frequency	Color Code
Drivers (of ESG/sustainability reporting)	764	Green
Implications (of ESG/sustainability reporting)	369	Magenta
Long-term value creation	287	Red
Stakeholders	266	Light blue
Engagement process	237	Lila
Materiality	227	Black
Reporting framework	217	Khaki
Investors expect	201	Brown
Rating	123	Blue
Strategy	110	Orange
Governance	84	Yellow
Total coded segments	2,885	

of the structure of each unit of analysis (see Graph Set 2 from the Annex presented in the digital repository of Politehnica University of Timisoara, Romania, https://dspace.upt.ro/jspui/handle/123456789/6253).

In the present cases, the limitations of the document portrait are that they do not account for simultaneous coding. In fact, several portions received multiple codes since the coding followed the developed notion. It is evident that the majority of the uncoded sections appear at the start and finish of each analysis unit due to the natural structure of sustainability reports. In fact, unless there was a clear textual growth, neither the concluding sections – glossaries or appendices – nor the starting sections – table of contents or introductory lines – were coded. A centralized hierarchy perspective for each packing company is presented in Table 6.3, based on the analysis presented in Graph Set 2 from the Annex presented in the digital repository of Politehnica University of Timisoara, Romania, https://dspace.upt.ro/jspui/handle/123456789/6253.

4.1.3. In Deep Analysis Based on Codeline Function
As was previously said, coded segments might be concurrently assigned to many codes because of the coding process. The document portrait is a suitable representation for observing the distribution and size of codes inside the analysis unit, but it is not appropriate for several codes to occur at the same time.

The sustainability/ESG reports' content was thoroughly understood with the usage of the MAXQDA Codeline function. The result is a table with the page numbers of the chosen document (a non-configurable option of MAXQDA) as column headings, and a list of the considered column codes in the leftmost column. Each code's existence on a page is indicated by a horizontal stripe that is of the same color as the codes. The length of the stripe is determined according to the number of coded characters (see the Graph Set 3 from the Annex presented in the digital repository of Politehnica University of Timisoara, Romania, https://dspace.upt.ro/jspui/handle/123456789/6253). The MAXQDA Codeline representations give a summary of each organization's contribution to each aspect or phenomenon under study, since all reports contain paragraphs pertaining to every issue that was taken into consideration (a variable of the research framework). Since each unit of analysis's data is freely arranged by its creator – packaging companies – a depiction of the simultaneous coding in many documents was not acceptable nor pertinent to the subject of the current investigation.

Regarding the application of the codeline function, this raises a structural problem, because the ESG reports which were analyzed do not have the same structure, fonts, or pages nor the same structure. So, topics are addressed in different orders within each unit of analysis (document and groups of pages analyzed). The application of the MAXQDA Codeline functionality for the sustainability/ESG reports analyzed highlighted the same mode of operation of the authors and their developers. From the analysis of the representations of the research results presented by the Graph Set 2 from the Annex presented in the digital repository

Table 6.3. Total Code Units in the Data Set Sorted by Descending Frequency Per Each Company.

Code System	Frequency	Color Code
Company A		
Drivers (of ESG/sustainability reporting)	168	Green
Long-term value creation	125	Red
Materiality	68	Black
Implications (of ESG/sustainability reporting)	67	Magenta
Engagement process	34	Lila

The document started with an important part dedicated to the implications and importance of ESG and then the drivers are presented and analyzed. In the final part, the materiality analysis is conducted and implications for stakeholders and investors are pointed, most for long-term value creation.

Company B		
Implications (of ESG/sustainability reporting)	186	Magenta
Drivers (of ESG/sustainability reporting)	102	Green
Long-term value creation	78	Red
Strategy	74	Orange
Rating	37	Blue

The document is dominated by arguments and statements on ESG reporting implication and importance. The ESG drivers are described in the first half of the document, presented, and analyzed. In the final part, there is a focus on strategic aspects, long-term value creation, and investors' expectations.

Company C		
Drivers (of ESG/sustainability reporting)	204	Green
Implications (of ESG/sustainability reporting)	145	Magenta
Long-term value creation	121	Red
Stakeholders	67	Light blue
Engagement process	31	Lila

The first half of the document offers arguments for the implication and importance of ESG, by recognizing the ESG drivers for business and its stakeholders. The next half of the document is dominated by explanations of ESG driver drivers.

Company D		
Drivers (of ESG/sustainability reporting)	104	Green
Long-term value creation	98	Red
Implications (of ESG/sustainability reporting)	78	Magenta
Stakeholders	28	Light blue
Engagement process	18	Lila

The first half of the document offers arguments for the implication and importance of ESG, based on strategic vision, good governance. The next half of the document is dominated by explanations on the drivers of ESG reporting considering long-term value creation.

Company E		
Drivers (of ESG/sustainability reporting)	162	Green
Long-term value creation	134	Red
Implications (of ESG/sustainability reporting)	68	Magenta
Stakeholders	62	Light blue
Engagement process	32	Lila

The document stands out for its homogeneity with respect to the arguments for long-term value creation and ESG drivers.

Note: Based on the research results shown in Graph Set 2 from the Annex presented in the digital repository of Politehnica University of Timisoara, Romania (https://dspace.upt.ro/jspui/handle/123456789/6253).

of Politehnica University of Timisoara, Romania (https://dspace.upt.ro/jspui/handle/123456789/6253), it is noted that for each group of analyzed pages and for all companies there is a uniformity of presentation/use of keywords/codes: "Long-term value creation" is in the first place, followed by "stakeholders" and then by "drivers." This stage of the content analysis demonstrates the orientation and concern of packing companies' management on ESG drivers and stakeholders' management, in a vision that generates long-term value creation.

4.2. Conclusions of the Content Analysis

4.2.1. Drivers for ESG Reporting

In terms of what motivates ESG reporting, the analysis reveals that key drivers are investor demands and stakeholder awareness of climate change, as well as regulations and legal compliance (e.g., UN SDG, EGD, GRI, or other ESG frameworks supported by different national guidelines). Packaging companies are compelled to report ESG disclosures. It has been noted that companies view sustainability management as essential to their operations (having implication in their logistic chain and value chain) and have based their business strategies on these drivers. Furthermore, all the companies included in the study attach great importance to ESG drivers (Table 6.4, frequency of appearance of this word/code).

The gray literature on the current market trend for ESG reporting (in Europe and Romania, too) shows that social and environmental factors were more studied and investigated that governance factors. Considering this fact, we were curious to find out how these multinational corporations implement governance principles within their businesses. According to the data study, each of these packaging companies has a specific agile group or department working on sustainability and ESG and which are directed by the top management. By extension, the group or department works closely with all operational departments' managers, including those from the value-chain operations.

4.2.2. Management of Stakeholders

According to the analysis, each firm determined its material themes after consulting with important stakeholders and considering the nature of their businesses. As a general conclusion, businesses believe that evaluating the possibilities and risks throughout their value chain is crucial for creating long-term value. It has been seen that the content analysis highlighted a special concern that packing companies have for investor expectations and investor requirements. In this context, materiality analysis is shown to be the primary component of SBVC through reporting in both the literature and findings, considering stakeholder participation and investor requirements.

4.2.3. Long-term Value Creation and Sustainable Business Strategy

The study verifies that there are variations in the structures used by the companies in the data set to convey their influence and value in relation to business strategy and value generation. However, important elements that include their goal (vision and commitment), significant concerns, current state, influence along their governance, and value chain are found to be included in their disclosure; it demonstrates that each organization has a unique perspective on aspects that adds long-term value to its operations.

4.2.4. Implications on Business

Regarding the analysis's business implications, the findings generally support the ideas discovered by the literature review: investing in innovation boosts output and talent retention and considering the needs of customers and other stakeholders raises stakeholder and market value. Furthermore, content analysis demonstrates that in terms of value creation, the most carefully thought-out option is the ethical, management-regulated source of materials and technology resources. Furthermore, the findings of the study demonstrate how these companies create long-term value for themselves and their stakeholders by being transparent on their reporting, operational procedures, business strategies and contributions to the SDGs, etc. All things considered, these findings suggest that all elements of ESG reporting need to be evaluated for potential risks and possibilities and included in business strategy.

4.2.5. ESG Reporting Framework

Sustainability/ESG reporting frameworks have been adopted by packing companies for at least two years (once with the increase in concerns for the SDGs and the introduction of EGD measures, as well as supporting implementation guidelines of ESG). However, companies do not cover all topics of ESG interest and face challenges in selecting the right reporting framework to communicate their value creation. The present study confirms that the GRI reporting framework is widely used by the analyzed companies.

In addition, each company chooses where to distribute the report; organizations prefer keeping their data as yearly reports. Companies A, D, and E present both financial and nonfinancial data in a single report. The external attestation of third-party ensuring for data reliability was applied to all company sustainability reports.

Based on the formulated conclusions on content analysis, the results are grouped according to the sub-research question and summarized in Table 6.4.

The content analysis findings show that external factors are an important one in encouraging businesses to transparently disclose their ESG data. All the components should be considered for a coherent organization's value creation narrative to be revealed through reporting to reap long-term benefits on the financial, social, and environmental areas. To verify the credibility of the gathered results, the next section discusses and validates them from the perspectives of internal and external stakeholders, namely employees and investors.

ESG Disclosure in the Packaging Sector in Romania

Table 6.4. Synthesis of the Research Findings From the Content Analysis.

Dimensions of the Research Framework	Implications/Subgroups
Drivers for ESG/sustainability reporting process	- Customer awareness - Investor requirements - Legal compliance - Climate Change
Implications of the ESG/sustainability reporting process	- Competitive advantage - Increase productivity through innovation (open and collaborative) - Talent management (acquisition and retention) - Sustainability governance
Stakeholder engagement investor expectations	- Double-materiality analysis - Fair and transparent reporting - Assessment of risks and opportunities
Reporting frameworks	- Adequacy of the reporting framework to business
Long-term value creation and sustainable business strategy	- External partnerships - Open and collaborative innovation (with partners in the logistic chain) - LCA - Circularity across the value chain - Leadership review - Performance management (with relevant key performance indicators, KPIs)

4.3. Validation and Implications

At this stage of the research, a limited number of ESG professionals were consulted to validate the findings, as well as to obtain more information on how ESG reporting can be strategically addressed to produce long-term value and to assess the validity of the findings of the previous section. Based on the conclusions formulated in the validation stage of the research (using semi-structured interviews based on an open questionnaire), the results are grouped according to the sub-research question and summarized in Table 6.5 (research questionnaire adapted from Prakash, 2020).

Table 6.5. Synthesis of the Research Findings From the Validation Stage.

Question in the Interviews/Dimensions of the Research Framework	Implications/Subgroups
Drivers for the ESG/sustainability reporting process: What drivers motivate ESG reporting?	- Customer demand, investor demand, regulatory compliance, climate change, and internal company incentives are the main forces behind ESG reporting. - The market trend for ESG reporting shows that, in addition to E factors, more attention is paid to S and G factors. - Multistakeholder partnerships and global difficulties are integral components of company strategy, helping to address the problems

(Continued)

Table 6.5. (*Continued*)

Question in the Interviews/Dimensions of the Research Framework	Implications/Subgroups
Implications of the ESG/sustainability reporting process: What effects and implications can ESG reporting have on companies? Stakeholder engagement investor expectations: What are the perspectives and expectations of stakeholders/investors from the ESG reporting?	- Benefits include a competitive edge, an increase in financial worth, the ability to retain personnel, improved investor relations in the long term, and increased stakeholder value - ESG reporting is seen by investors and employees as adding value to the company. - Stakeholders include nongovernmental organizations (NGOs), external partners, suppliers, workers, investors, and customers. - Investors expect a systematic approach to climate change, as well as open reporting on all aspects of ESG
Reporting frameworks: What reporting frameworks are available and how important are ESG ratings?	- There are several reporting frameworks available, including GRI, SASB, CDP, TCFD, etc. - Businesses are allowed to select a framework that best suits the interests of their stakeholders. - Investors consider multi-ESG ratings to be significant and use them when making investment selections
Long-term value creation and sustainable business strategy: How can this be strategically addressed at the organizational level in accordance with the main drivers?	- To increase the value of the company and its stakeholders, an integrated business strategy that is well defined and has goals and goals that are in line with its commitment is essential. This kind of approach is known as commitment driven. - Integration of ESG throughout the value chain to ensure circularity, partnerships and precise waste management metrics, a strong risk management procedure, an innovative strategy, high performance in stakeholder management, effective social and governance mechanisms, the appropriate skill sets are important factors that determine ESG reporting

5. CONCLUSIONS

With an emphasis on long-term value generation, this study highlights the critical factors influencing packaging businesses' ESG disclosure. Improving stakeholder and business value requires disclosure of value generation. This study used two qualitative techniques to validate its findings: semi-structured interviews with Romanian ESG professionals and content analysis of the value creation processes utilized by five packaging companies. The research results were validated based on the opinions of a small group of ESG professionals who know the specifics of the packaging industry, also.

The results of the key determinant analysis show that a strong business strategy integrating measures to face the global challenge of climate change can lead to long-term value creation through sustainability/ESG reporting. In addition, when companies are addressing ESG-related concerns, a multistakeholder viewpoint via partnerships was discovered to be a competitive advantage. This study reveals that the following factors contribute to long-term business value and stakeholder value: business strategy alignment with SDGs, tracking waste footprint, materiality analysis, innovation practices for stakeholder engagement and in governance management, education about ESG, monitoring the quality and transparency of data through third-party assurance, communication, and participation in multi-ESG ratings as part of sustainability strategy. The research results underline that the implementation (consideration and characterization) of these crucial elements in the sustainability/ESG reports of companies (reflecting their way of acting at the operational level) has provided a knowledge base that has bridged the gap in the literature regarding the idea of value creation through ESG reporting. In summary, strong commitment is needed to drive all determinants to create long-term commercial value.

According to previous studies in the literature (Patil et al., 2021; Prakash, 2020; Słoński & Ilbasmis, 2020), packaging businesses use a compliance-oriented strategy to their business practices, a fact that was also confirmed by the present study. As a recommendation, a commitment-driven approach must replace the actual compliance-oriented approach to provide long-term business value through ESG reporting. To support this change in practice, some recommendations have been provided referring to the packaging companies' ESG reporting process, based on the knowledge achieved from this study.

A few suggestions are provided below to help practitioners use a commitment-driven strategy to disclose ESG to all stakeholders to generate long-term economic value:

- Companies must integrate into the corporate value chain and match their objectives and strategy with global commitments regarding ESG. A complete LCA of the entire value chain is needed to find opportunities for circularity at every stage of the process and search for other approaches in terms of technology, materials, or product design to minimize environmental effects and boost output. All activities that begin with sustainable sourcing, procurement, production, logistics, as well as human resources and supplier relations will fall under this category. This demonstrates that businesses are committed to acting ethically as they work to meet their sustainability objectives.
- Special attention should be paid to waste management by tracking and disclosing not only the amount of waste generated–recycled annually but also the quantity of different categories of waste produced (as those highly polluted, toxic, etc.) in the value chain; of great interest are the disposal techniques used. Companies should provide a clearer picture of their efforts to reduce waste generation and adopt circular practices.
- Combine risk mitigation along the value chain with participation and commitment of stakeholders. Businesses must pledge to mitigate all material risks, including those related to climate change (to support a resilient business), and declare the steps they are taking to address these challenges going forward, as well as the current state of execution. It is recommended that a comprehensive description of the risk management technique followed by the organization be provided to stakeholders for them to comprehend the company's value development.

- Develop an innovative strategy, which is a comprehensive approach to problem-solving that details the work being done on process or design improvements to satisfy stakeholders' needs and support the SDGs. This study has shown that open and collaborative innovation practices create a positive impact at the operational level of sustainability management, providing long-term sustainability value.
- Establish a sustainability agenda and form a distinct sustainability committee (the packing companies involved in the study do not have a sustainability/ESG reporting department or a clear organizational unit). This committee will consist of individual representatives from each department along the value chain, as well as top management representatives who should report directly to the board management. This committee should define an inventory of the requirements of all stakeholders to be included in the materiality analysis. Furthermore, the ESG report should disclose key stakeholders and how their requirements have been addressed.
- Build a coherent communication strategy to support stakeholder participation and internal communication (support change processes at the operational level). This strategy should generate a strong commitment to transparent reporting and data assurance of ESGs.

The research limitations are related to the sample of packing companies considered in the study and the available data provided for the content analysis and validation.

Future research will approach the operational level of the company to identify and characterize the requirements of key stakeholders and how they have been addressed. Furthermore, another direction of research is to explore the vale creation of ESG reporting through digital innovation (operationalization of ESG reporting using an information system could be a valuable tool for practitioners).

ACKNOWLEDGMENTS

This chapter is related to the "Education for Plastic in a Circular and Climate Neutral Economy Preventing Waste From Ending Up in the Environment" (Erasmus+ 2023-1-RO01-KA220- HED-000166242), founded with the support of the European Commission. This chapter and the communication reflect the views only of the authors, and the Commission cannot be held responsible for any use which may be made of the information contained therein.

The authors acknowledge Dr Eng Aida Szilagy and Dr Eng Gabriela Fistis for including us in the training program: "Smart Education for Corporate Sustainability Reporting" developed via the Erasmus+ project, https://csr-secure.eu/. This has facilitated a structured understanding of the ESG terminology and the actual legal framework.

REFERENCES

Aarikka-Stenroos, L., Chiaroni, D., Kaipainen, J., & Urbinati, A. (2022). Companies' circular business models enabled by supply chain collaborations: An empirical-based framework, synthesis, and research agenda. *Industrial Marketing Management, 105*, 322–339.

Arvidsson, S., & Dumay, J. (2022). Corporate ESG reporting quantity, quality and performance: Where to now for environmental policy and practice? *Business Strategy and the Environment, 31*(3), 1091–1110.

Beghetto, V., Gatto, V., Samiolo, R., Scolaro, C., Brahimi, S., Facchin, M., & Visco, A. (2023). Plastics today: Key challenges and EU strategies towards carbon neutrality: A review. *Environmental Pollution, 334*, 122102. https://doi.org/10.1016/j.envpol.2023.122102

Bucharest Stock Exchange. (2022). *ESG reporting guidelines*. Retrieved January 8, 2024, from https://bvb.ro/info/Rapoarte/Ghiduri/ESG_Reporting_Guidelines.pdf

CECCAR. (2020). *A guide on nonfinancial reporting and reporting for management in the context of the crisis generated by the coronavirus pandemic*. Retrieved January 9, 2024, from https://ceccar.ro/ro/?p=18037

Collins, K. M., Onwuegbuzie, A. J., & Johnson, R. B. (2012). Securing a place at the table: A review and extension of legitimation criteria for the conduct of mixed research. *American Behavioral Scientist, 56*(6), 849–865.

Daugaard, D., & Ding, A. (2022). Global drivers for ESG performance: The body of knowledge. *Sustainability, 14*(4), 2322.

Gerwanski, J. (2020). Does it pay off? Integrated reporting and cost of debt: European evidence. *Corporate Social Responsibility and Environmental Management, 27*(5), 2299–2319.

Hankammer, S., Brenk, S., Fabry, H., Nordemann, A., & Piller, F. T. (2019). Towards circular business models: Identifying consumer needs based on the jobs-to-be-done theory. *Journal of Cleaner Production, 231*, 341–358.

Hennik, M., Hutter, I., & Bailey, A. (2020). *Qualitative research methods* (2nd ed) SAGE Publications Ltd. ISBN 978-1-4739-0390-6

Khan, M. A. (2022). ESG disclosure and firm performance: A bibliometric and meta-analysis. *Research in International Business and Finance, 61*, 101668.

Khandelwal, V., Sharma, P., & Chotia, V. (2023). ESG disclosure and firm performance: An asset-pricing approach. *Risks, 11*(6), 112.

Krippendorff, K. (2018). *Content analysis: An introduction to its methodology*. Sage Publications.

Laukkanen, M., & Tura, N. (2020). The potential of sharing economy business models for sustainable value creation. *Journal of Cleaner Production, 253*, 120004.

Lindgren, B. M., Lundman, B., & Graneheim, U. H. (2020). Abstraction and interpretation during the qualitative content analysis process. *International Journal of Nursing Studies, 108*, 103632.

Lüdeke-Freund, F., Rauter, R., Pedersen, E. R. G., & Nielsen, C. (2020). Sustainable value creation through business models: The what, the who and the how. *Journal of Business Models, 8*(3), 62–90.

MacNeil, I., & Esser, I. M. (2022). From a financial to an entity model of ESG. *European Business Organization Law Review, 23*(1), 9–45.

Manda, B. K., Bosch, H., Karanam, S., Beers, H., Bosman, H., Rietveld, E., Worrell, E., & Patel, M. K. (2016). Value creation with life cycle assessment: An approach to contextualize the application of life cycle assessment in chemical companies to create sustainable value. *Journal of Cleaner Production, 126*, 337–351.

Mio, C., Fasan, M., & Costantini, A. (2020). Materiality in integrated and sustainability reporting: A paradigm shift?. *Business Strategy and the Environment, 29*(1), 306–320.

Pasonen, J. (2023). *Promoting sustainable development as a packaging manufacturer in the EU and the US regulatory environments*. Retrieved February 27, 2024, from https://lutpub.lut.fi/bitstream/handle/10024/165564/Pasonen_Jarno_Publication_ready_thesis.pdf?sequence=1&isAllowed=y

Patil, R. A., Ghisellini, P., & Ramakrishna, S. (2021). Towards sustainable business strategies for a circular economy: Environmental, social and governance (ESG) performance and evaluation. In L. Liu & S. Ramakrishna (Eds.), *An introduction to circular economy* (pp. 527–554). Springer Singapore.

Perez, A., Howell Smith, M. C., Babchuk, W. A., & Lynch-O'Brien, L. I. (2023). Advancing quality standards in mixed methods research: Extending the legitimation typology. *Journal of Mixed Methods Research, 17*(1), 29–50.

Prakash, B. (2020). *Environment, social and governance (ESG) reporting: Shift from compliance to commitment* [Master's thesis, University of Twente].

Pryshlakivsky, J., & Searcy, C. (2021). Life cycle assessment as a decision-making tool: Practitioner and managerial considerations. *Journal of Cleaner Production, 309*, 127344.

Ranta, V., Keränen, J., & Aarikka-Stenroos, L. (2020). How B2B suppliers articulate customer value propositions in the circular economy: Four innovation-driven value creation logics. *Industrial Marketing Management, 87*, 291–305.

Rusnac (Dufour), C. (2021). *A proposed occupational health and safety infrastructure as enabler for sustainability-oriented innovation* [PhD thesis, Politehnica University of Timisoara].

Samans, R., & Nelson, J. (2022). *Sustainable enterprise value creation: Implementing stakeholder capitalism through full ESG integration* (p. 289). Springer Nature.

Sazdovski, I., Bala, A., & Fullana-i-Palmer, P. (2021). Linking LCA literature with circular economy value creation: A review on beverage packaging. *Science of the Total Environment, 771*, 145322.

Słoński, T., & Ilbasmis, G. (2020). Corporate social responsibility activities and the firm's value: The case of containers and packaging industry sector. In K. Daszyńska-Żygadło, A. Bem, B. Ryszawska, E. Jaki, & T. Hajdíková (Eds.), *Finance and sustainability: Proceedings from the 2nd finance and sustainability conference, Wroclaw 2018* (pp. 335–347). Springer International Publishing.

Tsang, A., Frost, T., & Cao, H. (2023). Environmental, social, and governance (ESG) disclosure: A literature review. *The British Accounting Review, 55*(1), 101149.

Visser, W., & Kymal, C. (2015). Integrated value creation (IVC): Beyond corporate social responsibility (CSR) and creating shared value (CSV). *Journal of International Business Ethics, 8*(1), 29–43.

WBCSD. (2019). *ESG disclosure handbook*. World Business Council for Sustainable Development. Retrieved January 9, 2024, from https://www.wbcsd.org/Programs/Redefining-Value/External-Disclosure/Purpose-driven-disclosure/Resources/ESG-Disclosure-Handbook

Xie, J., Nozawa, W., Yagi, M., Fujii, H., & Managi, S. (2019). Do environmental, social, and governance activities improve corporate financial performance? *Business Strategy and the Environment, 28*(2), 286–300.

Zaccone, M. C., & Pedrini, M. (2020). ESG factor integration into private equity. *Sustainability, 12*(14), 5725.

CHAPTER 7

IS DIGITALIZATION BAD FOR TRADE UNION DENSITY IN OECD COUNTRIES IN THE AGE OF GLOBALIZATION?*

Orhan Cengiz[a] and Ömer Demir[b]

[a]*Department of Accounting and Taxation, Pozanti Vocational School, Çukurova University, Türkiye*
[b]*Department of Management and Organization, Silopi Vocational School, Şırnak University, Türkiye*

ABSTRACT

Nowadays, digital transformation, which is an integral part of globalization, has a substantial effect on the labor market. Along with globalization and digitalization, the nature of work and the structure of the labor market have changed, resulting in a transformation in the relationship between employees and employers. This chapter aims to investigate the impact of digitalization on trade unions in 25 Organisation for Economic Co-operation and Development (OECD) countries over the period 2000–2019. The panel quantile regression results indicate that digitalization negatively affects trade unions in OECD countries in all quantiles. In other words, digitalization reduces trade union density. The labor force hurts trade union density in all quantiles. Wage positively affects trade union density in all quantiles except the Q09 quantile.

---

*This chapter is an extended version of the abstract titled "Is Digitalization Bad for Trade Union Density in OECD Countries in the Age of Globalization?" presented at the 2nd International Congress on Blue & Grey Collar Workers, An Alternative Neo-Human Relations Perspective, held in Warsaw, Poland, on May 8–11, 2024.

Future Workscapes: Emerging Business Trends and Innovations
International Perspectives on Equality, Diversity and Inclusion, Volume 11B, 113–128
Copyright © 2025 by Orhan Cengiz and Ömer Demir
Published under exclusive licence by Emerald Publishing Limited
ISSN: 2051-2333/doi:10.1108/S2051-23332025000011B007

Institutional quality negatively affects trade union density in the Q01–Q07 quantiles. Globalization has a positive effect in the Q01 and Q09 quantiles and a negative effect in the Q05 and Q06 quantiles. Economic growth positively impacts trade unions in the Q03–Q09 quantiles. Our empirical findings prove that since digitalization transforms the economic structure and nature of work, it causes a reduction in the importance of being a member of a trade union for the labor force. Hence, as digital technologies replace the labor force, it is inevitable that the protection and representation of unskilled labor by trade unions will decrease. Therefore, despite several contributions of digitalization in the sphere of life, it is crucial to keep the labor force's rights in the age of globalization for policymakers.

Keywords: Digitalization; trade union; globalization; labor market; worker; OECD

1. INTRODUCTION

Digitalization has become a transformative phenomenon that significantly impacts the global economy in the era of globalization (Demir et al., 2023; Raj-Reichert et al., 2021) and rapidly changes all aspects of the world of work in the global economy. Due to the widespread adoption of new technologies such as big data, machine learning, the Internet of Things, and artificial intelligence (AI), the work structure and employment relations have transformed (Voss & Bertossa, 2022). Over the past two decades, the world economy has experienced significant digital transformation. With the rapid digitalization process, digital tools have become the primary drivers of economic activities. E-commerce, e-marketing, digital financial activities, and digital content production have been identified as key factors in the new economic structure (Xia et al., 2024). It appears that digitalization will become one of the primary sources of the economy. According to the McKinsey Global Institute's (2019) estimation, the global gross domestic product (GDP) could increase by an additional $13 trillion by 2030 due to digitalization, automation, and AI, which create new investment and business opportunities and increase productivity. The advancement of globalization and digital transformation has made it easier to spread knowledge and technology, resulting in reduced costs and simplified complex economic activities. As a result, long-distance coordination has become more cost-effective, leading to the fragmentation of productive processes. This has increased dependence on multinational companies (MNCs) in the global economy and exacerbated competition among workers (Moreno et al., 2024). However, the impact of digitalization on jobs still needs to be clarified. Because adopting new digital tools is closely tied to the labor market and employment relations, one claims that digitalization provides individuals with several job opportunities through digital tools (Øvretveit, 2020). More importantly, it changes the dependence on traditional work and shifts the employment structure from full-time to non-traditional jobs, including different job arrangements. The new form of work based on digital tools is widespread worldwide. For example, gig work or short-term work is spreading day by day in the world. The World Bank (2023) report pointed out that the share of online gig work over the global labor force has risen from 4.4% to 12.5%, and it is estimated that the number of gig workers ranges from 154 million to 435 million. It is estimated that 20% of dependent employees were temporarily employed in 2018 (Charles et al., 2022).

In contrast, some argue that digitalization hampers working conditions and negatively affects employment as it changes the power dynamic between capital and labor. According to Basualdo et al. (2021), the increase in automation and digitalization leads to reduced employment, resulting in higher unemployment rates and insecure working conditions. This shift also weakens collective bargaining and trade union density. As the economy becomes more automated, there are fewer members in trade unions, negatively affecting their ability to represent workers. Additionally, low-union density sectors such as information and communication technologies (ICTs) challenge employee rights, as remote workers are not well-represented by collective organizations (Dittmar, 2022). Since employees become freelancers or gig workers, it is not surprising that they have challenges acting collectively (Charles et al., 2022). However, digital labor platforms provide job opportunities for young people, women, people with disabilities, and migrants, which inevitably leads to limited freedom of association, collective bargaining, and representation of workers and reduces social protection (ILO, 2021). An increase in non-standard employment erodes trade unions' organizational power to protect workers' rights. Considering the mission of trade unions, non-standard employment causes them to be reluctant in order to struggle for workers (Jolly, 2018).

The transformation of the world of work results in the erosion of labor protection. Because with the emergence of digital tools, the traditional tasks executed by trade unions are now digital tools to perform them. Hard devices, networking software, and informational software are used to organize the labor force and interact with trade union members (Mwamadzingo et al., 2021).

In the new era of digitalization, digital tools have become a prevailing trend both in developed and developing countries. Simultaneously, digitalization transforms the production methods and economic models (Lei et al., 2024). Over recent years, the digitalization process in the OECD countries has accelerated.

According to the IMD World Competitiveness Center (2024) ranking, the 20 countries with the highest digital competitiveness index mainly consist of OECD countries. Fig. 7.1 shows that 15 of the 20 countries with the highest digital competitiveness index are OECD members. As an important member of the OECD, the United States has the highest digital competitiveness with a 100 index score, followed by the Netherlands, Singapore, Denmark, and Switzerland.

It is widely accepted that trade unions are vital in promoting labor standards, improving working conditions, ensuring social justice, protecting purchasing power, and providing healthy and safe work environments (Qehaja & Zhushi, 2021). However, due to globalization and digitalization, the transformation in the world of work has weakened the trade unions and collective bargaining in OECD countries, as in many countries around the globe. According to the OECD (2019)

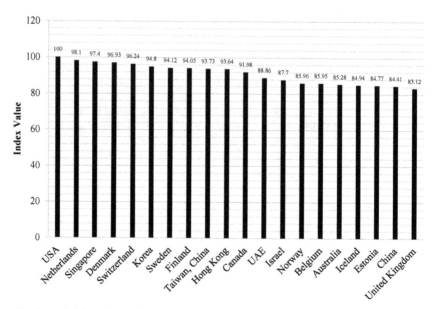

Fig. 7.1. Digital Competitiveness Ranking 2023. *Source*: Authors' own work based on the IMD World Competitiveness Center (2024) data.

report, *Employment Outlook: the Future of Work*, automation will lead to the disappearance of 14% of current jobs within the next 15–20 years. Moreover, 32% of other jobs may change significantly as more tasks become automated. In addition, according to a recent study, the OECD (2023) reported that construction and extraction, farming, fishing, forestry, production, transportation and material moving, installation, maintenance, and repair sectors are mostly at risk due to AI and other automation technologies.

The impact of digitalization on the labor market has affected trade union density in OECD countries over the last two decades. With job structures changing rapidly due to digitalization and globalization, the trade union density[1] has been challenged. As shown in Fig. 7.2, trade union density has decreased from 20.9% to 15.8% in the OECD total since 2000. This decline has been observed in all countries except Chile, Costa Rica, and Iceland. Iceland has the highest trade union density among OECD countries, with 90.7%, while Estonia has the lowest density at 6% as of 2019. The largest decline in trade union density has been observed in Sweden, where it has decreased from 81% to 65.2%. Finland and Ireland follow with 15.4% and 10.8% decline, respectively. On the other hand, the smallest drop in trade union density has been observed in Korea and New Zealand, with only 1% and 1.9%, respectively.

Given the burgeoning studies in the literature investigating the determinants of trade unions for different samples, as discussed above, the impact of digitalization on trade union density is still required to be clarified in the age of

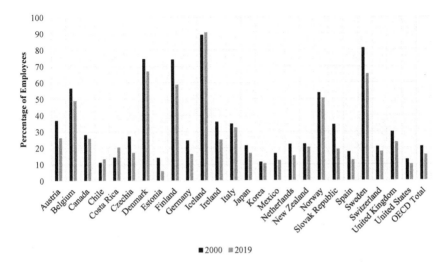

Fig. 7.2. Trade Union Density: Percentage of Employees in OECD Countries. *Source*: Authors' own work based on the OECD (2024) data.

globalization. Therefore, this chapter uses the panel quantile regression method to investigate the effect of digitalization on trade union density for a panel sample of 25 OECD member countries during the 2000–2019 period. There are three expected contributions of the current study to existing literature: (i) To the best of our knowledge, this is the first study analyzing the effect of digitalization on trade unions for the OECD countries. (ii) We used the information ICTs index as a proxy for digitalization instead of a single digitalization indicator. This comprehensive ICTs index comprised fixed line and mobile phone users, internet accessibility, and server security. (iii) We utilize the panel quantile regression estimation technique to reveal the relationship among variables by quantiles.

The remainder of this chapter is organized as follows: Section 2 briefly presents a literature review. Section 3 describes data, model, and methodology. Section 4 reports and discusses empirical findings. Finally, Section 5 concludes and recommends policy implications.

2. LITERATURE REVIEW

In the age of digitalization and globalization, the concepts of digitalization in the labor market have attracted attention and been discussed in the relevant literature and among scholars. It is a fact that it requires much research to deepen our understanding in terms of the nexus between digitalization and the labor market. Table 7.1 summarizes the relevant literature investigating digitalization and the labor market.

Table 7.1. Summary of Literature Review.

Study	Sample	Period	Findings
Meyer (2019)	21 OECD countries	1970–2010	Financial development has a negative effect on unions' institutional structures, and routine-biased technology also negatively affects trade union density
Meyer and Biegert (2019)	21 OECD countries and German firms and industry level	1970–2010 and 1993–2007	A negative relationship exists between technological change and collective bargaining coverage in OECD countries that do not adopt or slightly adopt extending collective agreements. Further, higher workforce skill polarization is related to the lower collective agreement in both the firms and industries in Germany
Hennebert et al. (2021)	13 trade unions in Canada	May 2017–July 2018	Digital ICTs do not significantly impact trade unions' roles
Lábaj and Vitáloš (2021)	10 European countries	1997–2016	Industrial robots used for welding, soldering, and dispensing significantly affect the replacement of workers
Lindstrom (2019)	France, Sweden, and the United Kingdom	2018	In the United Kingdom, trade unions put pressure on policymakers to keep workers' rights against the platform economy. In Sweden, trade unions try to include workers in the platform economy, and in France, trade unions are reluctant to preserve workers' platform economy
Parolin (2019)	15 OECD countries, 50 United States	1979–2013	Collective bargaining has a rather effect on wage growth of high routine occupations compared to less routine in the case of higher risk of automation
Payne et al. (2022)	Norway and the United Kingdom	April 2021–February 2022 (data taken from interviews with union representatives)	Trade unions try to integrate technology to increase the welfare of workers in two countries. Trade unions are interested in the impact of digitalization on job losses in both countries. Trade unions are stronger in Norway, and implementing automated labor scheduling is rather hard. Trade unions can use technology to monitor and surveil employees
Scaramuzzino and Scaramuzzino (2020)	Sweden	January 2016–November 2017	Trade unions in Sweden are not prone to adopting new technologies
Haapanala et al. (2023)	27 European countries and the United States	1998–2019	In industries where robots are prevalent, higher union density reduces employment for younger and less educated workers, while lower union density leads to lower unemployment rates
Ivanitskaia (2022)	Iceland, Finland, Norway, Denmark, and Sweden	1991–2019	Digitalization has a negative effect on unemployment
Chen et al. (2022)	The United States	2013–2019	The displacement risk of AI negatively affects occupational wages and employment. However, digital skills mitigate the negative effects of AI

Source: Authors' compilation.

The literature view from Table 7.1 shows that only some studies focus on digitalization's impact on trade unions. The current literature mainly examines the effect of AI in terms of digitalization on unemployment; in contrast, just a few studies concentrate on the nexus among trade unions, collective bargaining, and technology. However, its reflection on trade unions should be a key research field in the era of rapid digital transformation. Because within the change of work structure along with digitalization, the protection of workers' rights increases the importance of trade unions and collective bargaining policies. Therefore, the answer to the rising question of how digitalization affects trade unions becomes vital for policymakers.

3. DATA AND METHODOLOGY

3.1. Data Description

In this study, the influence of digitalization on trade union density between 2000 and 2019 is empirically investigated using a sample of 25 OECD countries, including Austria, Belgium, Canada, Chile, Costa Rica, Czechia, Denmark, Estonia, Finland, Germany, Iceland, Ireland, Italy, Japan, Korea, Mexico, the Netherlands, New Zealand, Norway, Slovak Republic, Spain, Sweden, Switzerland, the United Kingdom, and the United States. Table 7.2 lists all of the variables utilized in the study along with their definitions, units, and sources.

3.2. Model Specification

This study constructs the theoretical model of the relationship between real GDP per worker, labor force, average annual wages, digitalization, globalization, institutions, and trade union density as follows:

$$\text{TUD}_{it} = f(\text{GDP}_{it}, \text{LAB}_{it}, \text{WAG}_{it}, \text{DIG}_{it}, \text{KOF}_{it}, \text{INS}_{it}) \quad (1)$$

where TUD is trade union density, GDP is real gross domestic product per worker, LAB is the labor force as a total, WAG is average annual wages, DIG is digitalization measured as ICTs index, KOF is globalization as KOF index, and INS is institutions index.

Table 7.2. Data Description.

Variable	Definition	Unit	Source
TUD	Trade union density	Percentage of employees	OECD (2024)
GDP	Gross domestic product	Real GDP per worker	Penn World Table (2024)
LAB	Labor force	Total	World Bank (2024)
WAG	Wages	Average annual	OECD (2024)
DIG	Digitalization	ICTs index	UNCTAD (2024)
KOF	Globalization	KOF index	Gygli et al. (2019)
INS	Institutions	Index	UNCTAD (2024)

Source: Authors' compilation.

The theoretical model in Eq. (1) can be transformed into an empirical model and expressed in full logarithmic form as follows to make it appropriate for econometric estimation:

$$\ln\text{TUD}_{it} = \alpha_0 + \alpha_1 \ln\text{GDP}_{it} + \alpha_2 \ln\text{LAB}_{it} + \alpha_3 \ln\text{WAG}_{it} + \alpha_4 \ln\text{DIG}_{it} \\ + \alpha_5 \ln\text{KOF}_{it} + \alpha_6 \ln\text{INS}_{it} + \varepsilon_{it} \qquad (2)$$

where β refers to coefficients, i and t are the cross-section (country) and the time (year), respectively, and ε_{it} is the error term.

3.3. Estimation Techniques

In this study, the following techniques are applied to measure the impact of digitalization on unionization in OECD countries in a stepwise manner: The first step is to analyze descriptive statistics, which provide a brief overview of the panel data. The second stage tests the cross-sectional dependence (CSD) of the panel series. The third stage evaluates the slope heterogeneity of the parameters. The fourth step tests the stationarity of the panel series. In the fifth step, long-run coefficients are estimated. In the sixth stage, causality relationships are examined. Fig. 7.3 shows the estimation techniques applied in this study.

It is important to test for the CSD to obtain consistent and robust results from panel data analyses. When $T > N$, the Breusch–Pagan Lagrange multiplier (LM) test developed by Breusch and Pagan (1980); when $T = N$, the scaled LM test developed by Pesaran (2004); when $T < N$, the CD test developed by Pesaran (2004); when $T >$ N and T $<$ N, the bias-corrected scaled (BCS) LM test developed by Baltagi et al. (2012) is appropriate to check the CSD. Since $T < N$ in our analysis, the BCS LM test is appropriate for our model and can be represented as follows (Baltagi et al., 2012):

$$\text{LM}_{\text{BCS}} = \sqrt{\left(\frac{1}{N(N-1)}\right) \sum_{i=1}^{N-1} \sum_{j=i+1}^{N} (T\hat{p}_{ij}^2 - 1) - \frac{N}{2(T-1)}} \qquad (3)$$

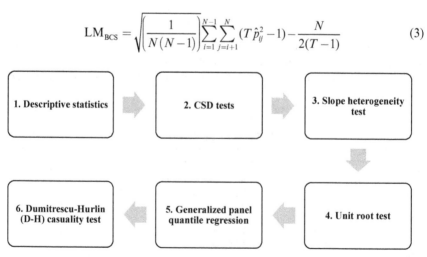

Fig. 7.3. Estimation Techniques. *Source*: Authors' compilation.

In Eq. (3), the binary correlation residual sample estimate is P_{ij}^2, and the variables T and N represent time and cross-sections, respectively. It is crucial to do the slope heterogeneity test after determining whether the CSD in the panel is present. This test can reveal a variety of variations among the participating nations. We employ the slope heterogeneity test developed by Pesaran and Yamagata (2008). The test's equation is as follows:

$$\tilde{\Delta}_{SH} = (N)^{\frac{1}{2}} (2K)^{-\frac{1}{2}} \left(\frac{1}{N} \tilde{S} - k \right) \quad (4)$$

$$\tilde{\Delta}_{ASH} = (N)^{\frac{1}{2}} \left[2K \left(\frac{T-k-1}{T+1} \right) \right]^{-\frac{1}{2}} \left(\frac{1}{N} \tilde{S} - k \right) \quad (5)$$

In Eq. (4), the delta tilde is represented by $\tilde{\Delta}_{SH}$, while the adjusted version is represented by $\tilde{\Delta}_{ASH}$ in Eq. (5). It would be reasonable to utilize the cross-sectional augmented Im-Pesaran-Shin (CIPS) unit root test, one of the second-generation unit root tests developed by Pesaran (2007), to ascertain the integration features of the variables if the CSD and slope heterogeneity are validated in the panel data. The cross-sectional augmented Dickey–Fuller (CADF) test is the source of the CIPS unit root test. The following is the CADF equation:

$$\Delta y_{it} = \varphi_i + \varphi_i Z_{i,t-1} + \varphi_i y_{t-1} + \sum_{l=0}^{p} \varphi_{il} \Delta \bar{y}_{t-l} + \sum_{l=1}^{p} \varphi_{il} \Delta y_{i,t-l} + \mu_{it} \quad (6)$$

The CIPS test statistic might be displayed as follows based on CADF (Faisal et al., 2023):

$$\text{CIPS} = \frac{1}{N} \sum_{i=1}^{N} t_i (N, T) \quad (7)$$

In Eq. (7), the t-statistics from the CADF regression are shown by the symbol $t_i(N,T)$. We use the generalized panel quantile method to estimate the long-run coefficients for the relationship between digitalization and trade union in OECD countries. The generalized panel quantile regression model is constructed as follows (Opoku & Aluko, 2021):

$$\ln \text{TUD}_{it} = \delta_\vartheta \acute{X}_{it} + \varepsilon_{it}; \quad \text{Quantile}_\vartheta (\ln \text{TUD}_{it} | X_{it}) = \delta_\vartheta \acute{X}_{it} \quad (8)$$

In Eq. (8), $\acute{X}$ denotes the vector of explanatory variables consisting of lnGDP, lnLAB, lnWAG, lnDIG, lnKOF, and lnINS. Also, $\text{Quantile}_\vartheta (\ln \text{TUD}_{it} | X_{it})$ stands for the ϑth quantile of lnTUD given X.

Finally, we use the D–H panel causality test to determine the causal links between digitalization and regressors in OECD nations. The D–H test specification is as follows (Dumitrescu & Hurlin, 2012):

$$y_{it} = \alpha_i + \sum_{i=1}^{K}\gamma_i^k y_{i,t-k} + \sum_{i=1}^{K}\beta_i^k x_{i,t-k} + \varepsilon_{it} \qquad (9)$$

In Eq. (9), K represents the lag length, t is the time period, β_i^k displays the slope coefficients, and α_i is the cross-sectional units. The null hypothesis is tested using the following statistics:

$$\overline{W} = \frac{1}{N}\sum_{i=1}^{N}W_i \qquad (10)$$

$$\overline{Z} = \sqrt{\frac{N}{2K}\left(\overline{W} - K\right)} \qquad (11)$$

Eqs. (10) and (11) display the $\overline{W}$ and $\overline{Z}$ statistics, respectively.

4. EMPIRICAL FINDINGS

This section reports the results of descriptive statistics, preliminary tests, generalized quantile regression, and the D–H panel causality test. Descriptive statistics, which provide a summary of the data, are given in Table 7.3.

As seen in Table 7.3, the variable with the highest mean value is lnLAB, followed by lnGDP, lnWAG, lnINS, lnKOF, lnDIG, and lnTUD. The CSD tests comprise the second step of the empirical study. The CSD test results are displayed in Table 7.4.

Table 7.4 proves that the null hypothesis $H0$ is rejected at a 1% statistical significance level for all variables in the model. Hence, there is a CSD in the countries in the sample. Table 7.4 also reports the results of the slope heterogeneity test. Accordingly, the argument that the slope is homogeneous is rejected. Based on the findings from the CSD test, the analysis continues in the third step with the CIPS, a second-generation unit root test.

Table 7.3. Descriptive Statistics.

Variable	Observation	Mean	Maximum	Minimum	Standard Deviation	Skewness	Kurtosis
lnTUD	500	3.198	4.535	1.504	0.670	0.295	2.315
lnGDP	500	11.268	12.306	10.238	0.350	−0.885	3.830
lnLAB	500	15.778	18.934	12.040	1.503	−0.077	2.864
lnWAG	500	10.657	11.283	9.564	0.405	−0.909	2.795
lnDIG	500	4.096	4.391	3.025	0.231	−1.553	5.740
lnKOF	500	4.386	4.510	4.051	0.097	−1.092	3.680
lnINS	500	4.427	4.605	3.820	0.149	−1.483	5.483

Source: Authors' compilation.

Table 7.4. The CSD and Slope Heterogeneity Tests Results.

		The CSD Tests Results		
Variable	LM	CD_{LM}	CD	LM_{adj}
lnTUD	3,369.365 (0.000)	125.306 (0.000)	35.430 (0.000)	124.648 (0.000)
lnGDP	4,532.499 (0.000)	172.791 (0.000)	65.094 (0.000)	172.133 (0.000)
lnLAB	4,509.523 (0.000)	171.853 (0.000)	64.179 (0.000)	171.195 (0.000)
lnWAG	3,484.641 (0.000)	130.012 (0.000)	49.153 (0.000)	129.355 (0.000)
lnDIG	5,643.937 (0.000)	218.165 (0.000)	75.093 (0.000)	217.507 (0.000)
lnKOF	4,426.689 (0.000)	168.471 (0.000)	63.458 (0.000)	167.814 (0.000)
lnINS	1,540.811 (0.000)	50.656 (0.000)	2.718 (0.006)	49.998 (0.000)

	Slope Heterogeneity Test Results		
Delta ($\tilde{\Delta}$)		Delta ($\tilde{\Delta}$)$_{adj}$	
Test statistics	p-Value	Test statistics	p-Value
10.277	0.000	13.268	0.000

Source: Authors' compilation.
Note: Those in parentheses indicate probability values.

Table 7.5 shows the CIPS unit root test outcomes. According to the results, lnTUD and lnLAB are stationary at the first difference in both trend and trend&constant models, and lnGDP is stationary at the first difference in the constant model. However, it is stationary at a level in the trend&constant model. Furthermore, lnWAG, lnDIG, lnKOF, and lnINS are stationary at the level in both trend and trend&constant models. In the next stage of our empirical analysis, we analyze the long-run coefficient estimates. Table 7.6 reports the estimation results of generalized panel quantile regression.

Table 7.5. The CIPS Unit Root Test Results.

Variable	Deterministic	CIPS Test Statistics (Level)	CIPS Test Statistics (First Difference)
lnTUD	Constant	−1.586	−3.082
	Constant & trend	−1.279	−3.232
lnGDP	Constant	−1.953	−4.095
	Constant & trend	−2.716	−4.202
lnLAB	Constant	−1.967	−3.544
	Constant & trend	−2.136	−3.840
lnWAG	Constant	−2.140	−3.629
	Constant & trend	−2.765	−3.647
lnDIG	Constant	−2.203	−4.107
	Constant & trend	−2.876	−4.240
lnKOF	Constant	−2.737	−4.584
	Constant & trend	−2.698	−4.631
lnINS	Constant	−2.214	−4.143
	Constant & trend	−2.579	−4.327

Source: Authors' compilation.
Note: The critical values for constant are −2.07, −2.15, and −2.32 at 10%, 5%, and 1%, respectively. The critical values for constant and trend are −2.58, −2.68, and −2.83 at 10%, 5%, and 1%, respectively.

Table 7.6. Generalized Panel Quantile Regression Results.

Variable	Low			Medium			High		
	Q01	Q02	Q03	Q04	Q05	Q06	Q07	Q08	Q09
lnGDP	−0.110	0.271	0.421	0.575	1.034	1.048	0.672	0.425	0.810
	(0.493)	(0.105)	(0.012)	(0.011)	(0.000)	(0.000)	(0.000)	(0.008)	(0.000)
lnLAB	−0.170	−0.246	−0.280	−0.227	−0.223	−0.231	−0.256	−0.281	−0.341
	(0.000)	(0.000)	(0.000)	(0.000)	(0.000)	(0.000)	(0.000)	(0.000)	(0.000)
lnWAG	1.271	1.030	0.969	0.808	0.655	0.602	0.556	0.459	−0.198
	(0.000)	(0.000)	(0.000)	(0.000)	(0.000)	(0.000)	(0.000)	(0.001)	(0.119)
lnDIG	−1.236	−1.146	−1.186	−0.944	−0.536	−0.562	−0.512	−0.423	−0.475
	(0.000)	(0.000)	(0.000)	(0.000)	(0.002)	(0.000)	(0.001)	(0.006)	(0.001)
lnKOF	1.597	0.326	0.204	−0.333	−1.204	−1.159	−0.176	0.417	0.770
	(0.000)	(0.368)	(0.576)	(0.497)	(0.002)	(0.001)	(0.614)	(0.227)	(0.013)
lnINS	−2.034	−0.931	−0.863	−0.719	−0.992	−0.863	−0.698	−0.383	0.180
	(0.000)	(0.002)	(0.004)	(0.070)	(0.002)	(0.003)	(0.013)	(0.170)	(0.473)

Source: Authors' compilation.
Note: Those in parentheses denote probability values.

As shown in Table 7.6, the results of the generalized quantile regression show that digitalization (lnDIG) significantly negatively impacts trade union density (lnTUD) across all quantiles. Economic growth (lnGDP) has a positive and statistically significant effect on trade union density in the Q03–Q09 quantiles. Labor force (lnLAB) negatively affects trade union density in all quantiles. Average annual wages (lnWAG) positively affect trade union density in all quantiles except the Q09 quantile. Globalization (lnKOF) has a positive effect in the Q01 and Q09 quantiles and a negative effect in the Q05 and Q06 quantiles. Institutional quality (lnINS) has a negative impact on trade union density in the Q01–Q07 quantiles. Our empirical findings validate the opinion that since digitalization changes and transforms the job structure, it challenges the ability to act collectively and erodes the standard roles of trade unions. Following the long-run estimations, the D–H panel causality test is employed to ascertain the causal relationship among variables. The causality results are reported in Table 7.7.

Table 7.7. The D–H Panel Causality Test Results.

Null Hypothesis	$\overline{W}$ Statistics	$\overline{Z}$ Statistics	Probability	Results
lnLAB ↛ lnTUD	3.292	1.634	0.102	lnTUD → lnLAB
lnTUD ↛ lnLAB	4.728	4.162	0.000	
lnWAG ↛ lnTUD	3.426	1.869	0.062	lnWAG ↔ lnTUD
lnTUD ↛ lnWAG	3.902	2.707	0.007	
lnINS ↛ lnTUD	1.634	−1.285	0.199	lnTUD → lnINS
lnTUD ↛ lnINS	4.913	4.486	0.000	
lnKOF ↛ lnTUD	2.775	0.724	0.469	lnTUD ↔ lnKOF
lnTUD ↛ lnKOF	4.566	3.877	0.000	
lnGDP ↛ lnTUD	4.286	3.384	0.001	lnGDP ↔ lnTUD
lnTUD ↛ lnGDP	3.521	2.036	0.042	
lnDIG ↛ lnTUD	3.937	2.769	0.006	lnDIG ↔ lnTUD
lnTUD ↛ lnDIG	4.649	4.023	0.000	

Source: Authors' compilation.

Table 7.7 presents a two-way causality between trade union density (lnTUD) and annual average wages (lnWAG), trade union density (lnTUD) and economic growth (lnGDP), and trade union density (lnTUD) and digitalization (lnDIG) and a one-way causality running from trade union density (lnTUD) to labor force (lnLAB), institutional quality (lnINS), and globalization (lnKOF).

5. CONCLUSIONS

The world has experienced a rapid digitalization process in the last two decades. As emphasized in the report of the International Federation of Robotics (2023), industrial robots' operational stock reached around 4 million in 2022. Along with increased digitalization, although it is claimed that different opportunities have emerged, the labor market has exposed several challenges. Specifically, the transformation of jobs and the widespread gig economy cause a decline in the trade union density. From this point of view, this study aims to investigate the impact of digitalization on trade union density for a panel sample of 25 OECD countries covering the period 2000–2019. According to the panel quantile regression analysis, digitalization negatively affects trade union density in OECD countries. Similarly, the labor force has a negative effect on trade union density in all quantiles. Wage positively affects trade union density in all quantiles except Q09. Institutional quality negatively affects trade union density in the Q01–Q07 quantiles. Globalization has a positive effect in the Q01 and Q09 quantiles and a negative effect in the Q05 and Q06 quantiles. Economic growth positively impacts trade unions in the Q03–Q09 quantiles. Our empirical findings verify that since digitalization transforms the economic structure and nature of work, it causes a reduction in the importance of being a member of a trade union for the workers.

The results of our study have important implications for policy discussions on how digitalization is shaping the role of trade unions in the era of globalization. First, trade unions should expand their traditional roles to include workers in the digitalized sectors. In other words, they should advocate for regulatory reforms to protect workers' rights in the digital economy. Second, policies related to digital unionism should be broadened by utilizing technological tools. The use of new technologies can play a vital role in unionism. For example, with digital tools, the cost of trade union membership can be reduced, increasing the number of members. Additionally, using digital platforms can help reach more people and amplify workers' voices worldwide (Şimşek, 2023). Third, trade unions should invest in education and training programs to strengthen their members' adaptation to changing conditions.

NOTE

1. The latest data for trade union density are available for Chile, Czechia, Korea, New Zealand, and Switzerland in 2018. Hence, the missing data are completed by using the average value for these countries for 2019.

REFERENCES

Baltagi, B. H., Feng, Q., & Kao, C. (2012). A Lagrange multiplier test for cross-sectional dependence in a fixed effects panel data model. *Journal of Econometrics*, *170*(1), 164–177. https://doi.org/10.1016/j.jeconom.2012.04.004

Basualdo, V., Dias, H., Herberg, M., Schmalz, S., Serrano, M., & Vandaele, K. (2021). *Building workers' power in digital capitalism: Old and new labour struggles*. Friedrich-Ebert-Stiftung.

Breusch, T. S., & Pagan, A. R. (1980). The Lagrange multiplier test and its applications to model specification in econometrics. *The Review of Economic Studies*, *47*(1), 239–253.

Charles, L., Xia, S., & Coutts, A. P. (2022). *Digitalization and employment: A review*. International Labour Organization.

Chen, N., Li, Z., & Tang, B. (2022). Can digital skill protect against job displacement risk caused by artificial intelligence? Empirical evidence from 701 detailed occupations. *PLoS One*, *17*(11), e0277280. https://doi.org/10.1371/journal.pone.0277280

Demir, Ö., Cengiz, O., & Nas, Ş. (2023). The impact of digitalization and globalization on income distribution in emerging industrial economies. *Journal of Abant Social Sciences*, *23*(3), 1836–1853. https://doi.org/10.11616/asbi.1329669

Dittmar, N. (2022). *Collective bargaining and digitalization-crisis or revitalisation of trade unions?* Paper prepared for the 13th ILERA European Congress 2022. Retrieved February 1, 2024, from https://www.researchgate.net/publication/365853272_Collective_bargaining_and_digitalization_-crisis_or_revitalisation_of_trade_unions

Dumitrescu, E. I., & Hurlin, C. (2012). Testing for Granger non-causality in heterogeneous panels. *Economic Modelling*, *29*(4), 1450–1460. https://doi.org/10.1016/j.econmod.2012.02.014

Faisal, F., Rahman, S. U., Khan, A., Ali, A., Irshaid, M. A., & Amin, M. Y. (2023). Exploring the N-shaped EKC in the top tourist destinations. Empirical evidence from cross-country analysis. *International Social Science Journal*, *73*, 479–497. https://doi.org/10.1111/issj.12397

Gygli, S., Haelg, F., Potrafke, N., & Sturm, J. E. (2019). The KOF globalisation index-revisited. *The Review of International Organizations*, *14*, 543–574. https://doi.org/10.1007/s11558-019-09344-2

Haapanala, H., Marx, I., & Parolin, Z. (2023). Robots and unions: The moderating effect of organized labour on technological unemployment. *Economic and Industrial Democracy*, *44*(3), 827–852. https://doi.org/10.1177/0143831X221094078

Hennebert, M. A., Pasquier, V., & Lévesque, C. (2021). What do unions do ... with digital technologies? An affordance approach. *New Technology, Work and Employment*, *36*(2), 177–200. https://doi.org/10.1111/ntwe.12187

ILO. (2021). *World employment and social outlook: The role of digital labour platforms in transforming the world of work*. International Labour Organization.

Ivanitskaia, V. (2022). The impact of digitalization on unemployment: The case of the Nordic countries. In J. Juhász (Ed.), *Proceedings of the European Union's contention in the reshaping global economy* (pp. 55–67). Doctoral School in Economics, University of Szeged.

Jolly, C. (2018). Collective action and bargaining in the digital era. In M. Neufeind, J. O'Reilly, & F. Ranft (Eds.), *Work in the digital age: Challenges of the fourth industrial revolution* (pp. 209–221). Rowman & Littlefield.

Lábaj, M., & Vitáloš, M. (2021). Automation and labor demand: The role of different types of robotic applications. *Czech Journal of Economics & Finance*, *71*(3), 220–244. https://doi.org/10.32065/CJEF.2021.03.02

Lei, X., Shen, Z. Y., Štreimikienė, D., Baležentis, T., Wang, G., & Mu, Y. (2024). Digitalization and sustainable development: Evidence from OECD countries. *Applied Energy*, *357*, 122480. https://doi.org/10.1016/j.apenergy.2023.122480

Lindstrom, E. (2019). *Industrial relations in a digital age. Trade union reaction to the platform economy in France, Sweden and the United Kingdom*. Retrieved January 20, 2024, from https://www.inclusivegrowth.eu/files/Call-25/Lindstrom-Social-Dialogue-1.pdf

McKinsey Global Institute. (2019). *Twenty-five years of digitization: Ten insights into how to play it right*. Retrieved February 3, 2024, from https://www.mckinsey.com/capabilities/mckinsey-digital/our-insights/twenty-five-years-of-digitization-ten-insights-into-how-to-play-it-right

Meyer, B. (2019). Financialization, technological change, and trade union decline. *Socio-Economic Review, 17*(3), 477–502. https://doi.org/10.1093/ser/mwx022

Meyer, B., & Biegert, T. (2019). The conditional effect of technological change on collective bargaining coverage. *Research & Politics, 6*(1), 1–9. https://doi.org/10.1177/2053168018823957

Moreno, A. D., López, M. D. M. M., Limón, M. G., & Fernández, M. R. (2024). Digitalization and the impact on the labour relations. In J. Lubacha, B. Mäihäniemi, & R. Wisła (Eds.), *The European digital economy: Drivers of digital transition and economic recovery* (pp. 83–100). Routledge.

Mwamadzingo, M., Kisonzo, S., & Chakanya, N. (2021). Digitalize, adapt and innovate: Challenges and opportunities for trade unions amidst the COVID-19 pandemic and the recovery period. *International Journal of Labour Research, 10*(1/2), 107–123.

OECD. (2019). *OECD employment outlook 2019: The future of work*. OECD Publishing. https://doi.org/10.1787/9ee00155-en

OECD. (2023). *OECD employment outlook 2023: Artificial intelligence and the labour market*. OECD Publishing. https://doi.org/10.1787/08785bba-en

OECD. (2024). *Trade union density*. Retrieved February 2, 2024, from https://www.oecd.org/en/data.html

Opoku, E. E. O., & Aluko, O. A. (2021). Heterogeneous effects of industrialization on the environment: Evidence from panel quantile regression. *Structural Change and Economic Dynamics, 59*, 174–184. https://doi.org/10.1016/j.strueco.2021.08.015

Øvretveit, J. (2020). Impact of digitalization on employment and working conditions. In A. Larsson & R. Teigland (Eds.), *The digital transformation of labor automation, the gig economy and welfare* (pp. 334–336). Routledge.

Parolin, Z. (2019). *Automation and occupational wage trends: What role for unions and collective bargaining?* [LIS Working Paper Series No. 767]. Luxembourg Income Study (LIS), Luxembourg.

Payne, J., Lloyd, C., & Jose, S. (2022). *Trade unions and digitalisation in Norway and the UK: Findings from the grocery retail sector*. UDIG: De Montfort University and Cardiff University. https://udig.powi.dmu.ac.uk/

Penn World Table. (2024). *Penn world table version 10.01*. Retrieved February 5, 2024, from https://www.rug.nl/ggdc/

Pesaran, M. H. (2004). General diagnostic tests for cross section dependence in panels. The Institute for the Study of Labor (IZA) Discussion Paper No. 1240, 1–39.

Pesaran, M. H. (2007). A simple panel unit root test in the presence of cross-section dependence. *Journal of Applied Econometrics, 22*(2), 265–312. https://doi.org/10.1002/jae.951

Pesaran, M. H., & Yamagata, T. (2008). Testing slope homogeneity in large panels. *Journal of Econometrics, 142*(1), 50–93. https://doi.org/10.1016/j.jeconom.2007.05.010

Qehaja, D., & Zhushi, G. (2021). Macroeconomic policy changes and its impact on trade unions, an empirical study on OECD countries for the period 2001–2020. *International Journal of Sustainable Development and Planning, 16*(8), 1575–1582.

Raj-Reichert, G., Zajak, S., & Helmerich, N. (2021). Introduction to special issue on digitalization, labour and global production. *Competition & Change, 25*(2), 133–141. https://doi.org/10.1177/1024529420914478

Scaramuzzino, G., & Scaramuzzino, R. (2020). Membership in the digital era: Swedish trade unions' use of Internet and social media. *Sociologisk Forskning, 57*(1), 43–66. https://doi.org/10.37062/sf.57.20171

Şimşek, G. Y. (2023). Yeni teknolojik değişimler bağlamında sendikacılık. *Ünye İktisadi ve İdari Bilimler Fakültesi Dergisi, 5*(2), 27–46.

The IMD World Competitiveness Center. (2024). *World Digital Competitiveness Ranking*. Retrieved February 1, 2024, from https://www.imd.org/centers/wcc/world-competitiveness-center/rankings/world-digital-competitiveness-ranking/

The International Federation of Robotics. (2023). *World robotics 2023 – Industrial robots*. IFR Statistical Department.

The World Bank. (2023). *Working without borders: The promise and peril of online gig work*. World Bank Publications.

UNCTAD. (2024). *Statistics and data*. Retrieved February 2, 2024, from https://unctad.org/statistics

Voss, E., & Bertossa, D. (2022). Collective bargaining and digitalization: A global survey of union use of collective bargaining to increase worker control over digitalization. *New England Journal of Public Policy*, *34*(1), 1–35. https://scholarworks.umb.edu/nejpp/vol34/iss1/10

World Bank. (2024). *World development indicator*. Retrieved February 5, 2024, from https://databank.worldbank.org/source/world-development-indicators

Xia, L., Baghaie, S., & Sajadi, S. M. (2024). The digital economy: Challenges and opportunities in the new era of technology and electronic communications. *Ain Shams Engineering Journal*, *15*(2), 102411. https://doi.org/10.1016/j.asej.2023.102411

CHAPTER 8

THE ROLE OF INTERNAL COMMUNICATION AND EMPLOYEE PARTICIPATION IN CREATING HEALTH AND SAFETY CLIMATE: A MONOGRAPHIC STUDY

Elif Sungur[a], Nevin Kılıç[b] and Çiğdem Vatansever[c]

[a]*Communication Faculty, Maltepe University, İstanbul, Türkiye*
[b]*Faculty of Humanities and Social Sciences, Fatih Sultan Mehmet Foundation University, İstanbul, Türkiye*
[c]*Labor Economics and Industrial Relations Department, Tekirdağ Namık Kemal University, Tekirdağ, Türkiye*

ABSTRACT

This study has been conducted to understand the elements of the employee health and safety climate in a steel factory with 1,200 employees, the focus was on employee participation and communication, which are at the center of the ISO 45001 Occupational Health and Safety (OHS) Management System standard. The main aim has been to provide the framework to manage OHS risks and opportunities. Data were obtained through 14 focus group (FG) interviews with 133 blue- and gray-collar workers, including foremen, assistant foremen, shift supervisors, and engineers, in February 2023. The data were analyzed using the MAXQDA 2022 qualitative data analysis program. It was aimed to create a unique inductive model from the data collected under nine themes, and the model was created with grounded theory based on detecting, defining, and integrating meaning categories in the qualitative research literature. Analyses focused on the themes of communication and participation, modeled as "intervening variables" in the study conducted with a qualitative method. The results revealed that effective communication, including providing direct information to employees and establishing trust-based relationships, training and development programs and interventions strengthening employees' approaches related to OHS are required. Employee participation in work and decisions, as an act of doing–learning–understanding related to real life, has the power to transform employee behavior more than issues that are "known on paper." Additionally, in terms of social sustainability, it is important to underline for employees to be heard in the process of creating successful workplaces that ensure employee well-being.

Keywords: Health and safety management; safety climate; employee participation; internal communication; social sustainability

1. INTRODUCTION

This study has focused on the safety climate in a steel factory in Turkey. According to updated International Labour Organization (ILO) statistics of 2024, Turkey ranks 11th in the world in non-fatal workplace injuries and 10th in workplace deaths. Accordingly, in Turkey, 2,459 people out of 100,000 employees are injured annually due to their work, and 6.3 out of 100,000 employees die because of their work (ILOSTAT, 2024). On the other hand, the steel industry is ranked as fifth in the most dangerous jobs according to Occupational Health and Safety Administration (OSHA) in the United States (Christy Bieber, 2023) as in Turkey (TMMOB Makina Mühendisleri Odası, 2020).

In the third National OHS Policy Document and Action Plan, prepared by the National OHS Council for the last time for the period 2014–2018, targets are defined to cope with the large number of accidents in the metallurgical sector (Turkish Republic, Ministry of Labour and Social Security, 2014). According to this, "reducing the rate of occupational accidents for each of the metal, mining and construction sectors" and "spreading the culture of occupational health and safety in society" are stated among the seven improvement goals (National Policy Document–III and Action Plan on Safety and Health at Work 2014–2018). In order to prevent work accidents and occupational diseases in the metal sector and to raise awareness in working life within the Ministry of Labor and Social Security, a metal unit was established in June 2022 within the Department of Sectoral Risk Management, and the work accidents experienced in the Casting Sector in the last five years were statistically examined (Strategy Development Directorate, 2023, p. 90).

Although the steel industry is one of the highest risk sectors, it is also one of the key industries in producing economic value. According to economic indexes of 2021, world steel production increased by 3.7% in 2021 compared to 2020, reaching 1.95 billion tons. But Turkey's steel production increased by 12.7% in 2021, reaching 40.4 million tons and was recorded as the highest production amount of all time (General Directorate of Industry, 2021). Therefore, the Turkish steel industry has maintained its seventh place in the world and ranked as first place in Europe. This ranking is considered as an important success of the Turkish steel industry despite the protectionist policies initiated in 2019 by America and Europe, the stagnation in the economy due to the Covid-19 epidemic, the contraction in demand and not receiving any government aid. The iron and steel sectors are the most important locomotive sectors in the basic metal sectors which also include steel pipe, casting, aluminum, copper, and galvanization and provide basic inputs and raw materials to the machinery, automotive, electronics, chemistry, defense, aviation, mining, and transportation sectors. Additionally, the sector provides direct and indirect employment to 55,000 people in Turkey (General Directorate of Industry, 2021). Although the report of the World Steel Association (WSA, 2023) points out that lost time accidents follow a downward trend in the trend analysis of 2013 and 2022, the same trend is not observed in the metal sector in Turkey, and accidents are increasing. Since the number of sectoral fatal accidents included in the annual reports of the Social Security Institution has not been disclosed since 2018, it is not possible to obtain precise information about the number of accidents in the metallurgy sector. Since 2013, the reports on the number of fatal accidents across the country, published annually by the Worker Health and Occupational Safety Council (https://www.isigmeclisi.org), a voluntary monitoring organization, are based on data obtained through scanning newspaper news and denunciations. According to these reports (Annual Reports, 2013–2023), there is no downward trend in the number of fatal accidents in the metallurgical sector in Turkey in recent years, as seen in the world.

On this occasion, it would be appropriate to mention an important organization organized by the sector with the theme "worth to employees," where it focuses entirely on worker health and safety. Employee Safety and Wellbeing Symposium in Metallurgy Sector, organized for the first time by Chamber of Metallurgical and Materials Engineers Training Center, was held on November 16–17, 2023 (https://www.esws-mtm.com). Therefore, protecting and improving the health and safety of heavy industry workers must be one of the main objectives in Turkey.

2. EMPLOYEE HEALTH AND SAFETY (EHS)

There are various work-related environmental factors that negatively affect the health of employees in working environments, causing the development of occupational diseases, occupational accidents, permanent damage to employees, and/or death for these reasons (Esin, 2006, pp. 75–88). Therefore, hazards in the workplace must be identified and risks must be managed. The goals of protecting and improving employee health by minimizing these environmental factors have been transformed into standards that require their implementation in workplaces.

The purpose of the ISO 45001 OHS Management System, published by the International Standards Organization (ISO) in April 2018, is to provide the framework to manage the risks and opportunities of occupational health and safety. ISO 45001 replaces the OHSAS 18001 standard published by the British Standards Institute. Organizations were given a three-year transition period to transition from the previous standard, OHSAS 18001, and due to the Covid-19 pandemic, the period was extended for another six months and came into effect in September 2021. The purpose of the ISO 45001 standard is to provide the framework to manage OHS risks and opportunities. Unlike the previous OHSAS 18001, the standard emphasizes the organizational context in ISO 45001 (International Organization for Standardization, 2018).

3. EHS CULTURE

The organization puts several measures in place to predict the hazardous situations that are likely to occur and set up the barriers necessary to contain them: procedures, automated systems, protections, etc. This is called rule-based safety; it is based on anticipating what can be planned for. No matter how good this anticipation is, situations regularly occur that had not been planned for in the details (work-as-done deviates from work-as-imagined). In this case, safety will depend on the skills of the people at the scene and the individual and collective actions they take; this is called managed security. These two dimensions are not mutually exclusive: managed safety can include the adoption of formal rules and the decision to use them as is or to "adapt" them to situations perceived as exceptional; it also relies on "rules of custom" (solidarity, mutual assistance between colleagues) and on "rules of experience," based on a range of situations experienced by the individual themselves or in the history of the occupation (ICSI – Industrielle Institut Pour Une Culture De Sécurité, 2018, p. 62).

The aim should be an integrated safety culture: for most companies that are advanced around safety, the way forward lies in shifting from a bureaucratic safety culture to an integrated safety culture which considers both what experts and management anticipate as risky situations and what front-line staff have to say about the reality at the sharp end. An integrated safety culture requires everyone (managers and sharp-end workers) to share the responsibility of ensuring the safety of the system when performing their work and to interact with all other actors concerned with this goal in mind. This approach requires strong leadership from management, increased participation of employees and their safety representatives, a redefinition of the role of health, safety, environment (HSE) experts, and effective communication between departments and with contractor companies. Developing management's leadership and giving them freer rein is often the first step to creating the conditions for this shift (ICSI – Industrielle Institut Pour Une Culture De Sécurité, 2018, p. 18).

Parallel with OHS literature (Burke et al., 2008; Geller, 1996; Koivupalo et al., 2015; Williams, 2008), there are six safety and health principles for the steel industry (WSA, 2023):

(1) All injuries and work-related illnesses can and must be prevented.
(2) Managers are responsible and account for safety and health performance.

(3) Employee engagement and training are essential.
(4) Working safely is a condition of employment.
(5) Excellence in safety and health drives excellent business results.
(6) Safety and health must be integrated into all business management processes.

Board of members believe that clearly defined principles will result in an enhanced safety and health culture, as well as improved business results across the industry. Companies need to apply the six principles to the following four focus areas to ensure comprehensive safety and health management: "Safety Culture and Leadership," "Process Safety Management," "Occupational Safety Management," and "Occupational Health Management."

The safety culture of an organization is the product of individual and group values, attitudes, competencies, and patterns of behavior that determine how people and systems act and respond in relation to risks and opportunities. Safety culture and leadership evolve gradually over time as people go through various changes, adapt to environmental conditions, and solve problems. To create a truly robust safety culture, organizations need to proactively position safety as an integrated value for all workers. To attain this level of safety culture, significant commitment and a drive toward continuous improvement are required.

It can be said that safety culture is rooted in organizations in time and can be felt through a safety climate. The safety climate is defined as the support of the employees for raising the occupational safety at the organization, along with their perception about the management concerns toward this issue (Wills et al., 2006). In that sense, a safety climate is a psychological concept.

4. HEALTH AND SAFETY CLIMATE IN STEEL INDUSTRY

Zohar (1980) uses the concept of safety climate in his pioneering work and examines the effect of climate on safety. He states organizational safety climate dimensions as "the perceived importance of EHS training," "how the management's attitude towards EHS is perceived," "how the impact of occupational safety management on promotion is perceived," "how the risk level in the workplace is perceived," "the effect of work pace on occupational safety," "the status of the occupational safety professional," "the effect of safe behavior on social status," and "how the status of the occupational safety committee is." He also revealed that the two most important dimensions in determining the level of safety climate are how employees perceive management attitudes toward safety and their perceptions of the importance of safety in production processes.

In a series of studies which investigate the employees' perceptions about the organization and the management relevant to the organizational outcomes, the topics of company incident rates, self-reported occupational incident involvement, self-reported occupational inquiry frequency and severity, safety performance and behavior, and the compensation claims are studied relating to the safety climate (see Wills et al., 2006). Wills et al. (2006) claim that safety climate in the organizations is a strong predictor of the safety-related outcomes. Researchers tested this claim through investigating the relations between traffic behaviors and organizational climate. The concept, safety climate, is composed of the factors of "communication and procedures," "work pressures," "relationships," "driver training," and "management commitment." Safety climate refers to employees' perceptions of how much safety is valued in an organization. These perceptions are formed over time as people use safety systems, listen to what others say, and particularly what they do when it comes to safety. When positive perceptions of safety are consistent across the organization, a positive safety climate exists, and employees are more likely to act safely (www.worksafe.qld.gov.au, 2023).

On the other hand, Cooper (2016) states that attitude and safety climate research has demonstrated weak relationships with actual safety outcomes, published studies have not assessed relationships between values or norms, and situational and behavioral factors have not shown strong and consistent relationships with actual safety outcomes. The use of psychological factors alone (e.g., attitude or safe climate research) for safety culture is highly flawed, and research evidence suggests that efforts to improve safety culture should focus on safety-related managerial behaviors.

Guldenmund (2007) states that safety culture research should be separated from climate research, because it is a situational (instant) indicator that emerges in employees' perception of the organizational atmosphere and is more superficial and generally get through questionnaire surveys. He also points out that the surveys used in safety culture research can be distributed and collected quickly from many people, therefore, the data are subject to undesirable effects, can be "dirty," and "the survey can direct people's opinions." Climate is generally researched through attitude surveys (questionnaire surveys), and these studies try to reveal people's perceptions that are thought to be related to safety. The second type of climate research is confirmatory studies.

It is known that creating a positive safety climate requires close relationships and trust between leaders and employees, rather than threats or fear. Only when there is trust and closeness, communication regarding occupational safety improves, the manager's visible commitment to safety increases, and, in this way, injuries due to work accidents decrease (Morgeson & Hofmann, 1999, p. 41).

Kılıç et al. (2014) examined whether three different perceived leadership styles of managers (transformational, transactional, paternalistic) affected the perception of OHS in the current workplace and the role of communication in this relationship. According to the findings, transformational leadership, communication, and perception of management are among the factors that predict the safety climate in the workplace. Communication functions as an intervening variable between leadership styles and perceived safety.

5. THE ROLE OF COMMUNICATION AND EMPLOYEE PARTICIPATION IN CREATING HEALTH AND SAFETY CLIMATE

Strong communication is not only one of the determining factors of corporate culture, but also very important for EHS. A study developed a safety communication and recognition program designed to promote the improvement of physical working conditions and hazard reduction in construction (Dennerlein & Sparer-Fine, 2018). The program demonstrated how well both the work site and individual subcontractors controlled hazards on site. Workers in intervention areas noted increased levels of safety awareness, communication, and teamwork compared to control areas, with managers stating that subcontractors worked together and enabled workers to communicate and receive data. The program has led to many positive changes, including improvements in safety climate, awareness, team building, and communication, reaching workers through effective communication infrastructures and creating a significant and positive impact on construction site safety (Dennerlein & Sparer-Fine, 2018).

There are many studies (e.g., Butler, 2005; Demirbilek, 2005; Kılıç et al., 2014; Mearns, 2009; Nordlöf, 2015; Williams, 2006, 2008) that pointed out the effects of various types of communication on safety culture and the importance of communication to ensure safety culture. Sungur (2020) makes a classification that categorically evaluates practices related to health and safety communication in production environments according to the target audience/receiver (decoder) in the basic communication model. Therefore, some communicational processes related to workplace health and safety issues within a person and between persons can be categorized as message sender and receiver. For example, in a communication process, persons can be both sender and receiver by encoding and decoding messages with their perceptions of safety and with the way of its expression. So, it can be said that the perception of safety can be evaluated in the category of self-communication as the importance given to safety in an organization, and subordinate-superior and colleague relationships can be evaluated in the category of interpersonal communication. Moreover, the way the safety is discussed (Kılıç et al., 2014; Naji et al., 2022; Nordlöf, 2015; Williams, 2008) and the perception of safety norms can be evaluated in the category of person-group-organization communication and group behaviors, and campaign studies (Naevestad, 2010) can be evaluated in the mass communication category.

Topics discussed within the communication dimension in the safety culture literature covers verbal and visual aspects of safety communication; perceptions regarding health and safety (Kılıç et al., 2014); native language barrier for migrant workers (Williams, 2008; WorkSafe Victoria, 2022); corporate safety language and discourse; health and safety training communication (Sungur et al., 2009); hazard communication; accident and near miss communication (Şerifoğlu & Sungur, 2007); interpersonal communication between workers, managers, and

EHS experts (Sungur, 2015); safety communication campaigns (Karamürsel-Taşkan et al., 2011); and the entire organizational structure, process, and tools designed to disseminate information and engage people in workplace safety issues. From that point of view, this study aimed to examine the role of communication in a steel industry factory in operation of HSE procedures within the framework of a basic communication model.

6. METHOD

6.1. Sample and Procedure

This monographic study was conducted in an iron and steel company focused on improving EHS performance in its main plant. In this context, a qualitative data collection methodology was followed to define the safety climate in the workplace in question in 2023. An informative message about methodology was sent to the employees and invited to FGs; 133 of 167 employees who were invited took part in FGs. Each FG consisted of 10–12 who worked at the same department and at the same level. The same questions were asked to the participants in a standard way in each group. The interviews were audio recorded with the consent of the participants.

6.2. Analyses and Results

After the audio recordings of the FG interviews were transcribed, they were examined and processed using the MAXQDA 2022 qualitative data analysis program. According to the purpose of the study and obtained data in FGs, the discourses were classified under general themes. The codes related to the themes were mostly coded in vivo (as expressed by the employees) and then they were reviewed by all researchers, and new code categories were created as needed. Following this analysis, code clouds, hierarchical code maps, code–subcode section models, single and double case models, and concept maps were arranged. Afterward, the phase of creating a theoretical model as the main product of the analysis was started. This unique model (grounded theory) is based on identifying and integrating "meaning categories" through data (Vatansever et al., 2015). Under the EHS service code, employee perceptions toward EHS unit and workplace health unit, the use of personal protective equipment, and thoughts about preventive efforts during the pandemic period were classified. There were 931 coded statements obtained from FG transcriptions in total. According to the general code map, there were 12 main themes which are labeled as Management, Recommendations, Trust, Risks, Benefits and Services, Training, Work Accident, Health and Safety Service, Communication, Employee Value, Engagement, and Perception of Health and Safety. The code frequency matrix of FGs can be viewed in Table 8.1.

Some examples of the expressions placed in the codes presented in Table 8.1 are given below.

Table 8.1. Code Frequency Matrix of FG Interviews.

	Management	Trust	Risks	Benefits and Services	Trainings	Work Accident	EHS Service	Communication	Employee Value	Engagement	Perception of EHS	Recommendations
FG 1	7	0	10	10	1	4	13	10	8	2	9	0
FG 2	9	6	13	25	3	4	11	17	12	0	0	0
FG 3	9	7	7	13	6	0	1	1	0	0	5	4
FG 4	14	8	3	8	6	5	7	7	3	1	2	0
FG 5	8	18	7	22	5	13	14	10	1	2	0	0
FG 6	3	4	18	47	13	11	20	18	9	3	9	6
FG 7	11	0	16	8	1	4	14	4	3	9	15	0
FG 8	3	1	2	4	3	0	2	0	0	0	3	0
FG 9	2	0	8	2	0	4	7	1	1	2	0	0
FG 10	2	1	4	3	2	4	6	2	1	1	0	0
FG 11	2	2	1	4	8	3	4	2	0	1	0	0
FG 12	15	7	4	13	8	3	0	41	4	0	0	3
FG 13	5	3	1	5	4	3	1	2	2	2	1	5
FG 14	12	4	5	21	1	5	13	6	2	0	3	0
Total	102	61	99	185	53	63	113	121	46	23	47	18

Management:
There will be no change unless the mentality that runs the system changes.

You cannot make an evaluation when you are not in charge of the job and do not see it.

Recommendations:
The information system needs to be established quickly. An application can be made that can be accessed by white and blue collar workers, where we can enter our registration number, and information and training can be provided.

Trust:
If the top management knew about these, they would not be reported.

Risks:
I'm afraid, we will concede a goal from here.

There are so many documents, what will the subordinate understand if I don't understand?

Benefits and Services:
Our main problem is the shuttles and cafeterias that we use to go to work.

Training:
Training, training only goes so far, as far as the other person understands.

Work Accident:
Two years later, the same accident happened again … Why didn't we do it at the Occupational Safety Board meeting? But after something happens, we always fall behind.

EHS Service:
Nobody wants to go to the infirmary: Don't go to the infirmary, things will get tense.

The only unit that listens to the worker is the occupational health and safety department, you say this is a bad part, they are trying to fix it.

Communication:
There's worse communication here than you'd imagine.

There are so many documents, what will the man below understand if I don't?

Employee Value:
Employees are not valued because they are not informed.

We are not machines, we are not robots. So we don't have buttons, we are humans. So they should value us a little.

Engagement:
Security is the responsibility of all of us, I am doing this for the brother I work with ….

Perception of Health and Safety:
We have gone through a revolution in the last five to ten years.

In order to ensure (psychosocial) job security, it is not asking whether you have boots, clothes or glasses, but whether there is a problem in your head ….

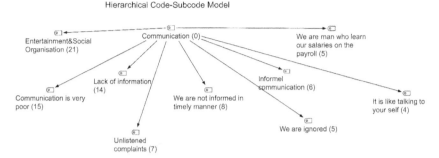

Fig. 8.1. Hierarchical Code–Subcode of Communication Map.

Fig. 8.2. Safety Climate Model as Grounded Theory.

The 121 expressions classified under the communication code were assigned to nine subcodes, most of which are in vivo codes. The hierarchical code map showing the subcodes connected to the communication code is presented in Fig. 8.1.

6.3. The Safety Climate Model According to Grounded Theory Obtained From FG Interviews

All the data obtained from FGs and conducted analysis according to the grounded theory have been constructed as the safety climate model (Fig. 8.2).

According to the model, communication is an intervening variable together with top management and EHS trainings; the value of employee, benefits and services, and health and safety services are antecedents; employee opinion and commitment are consequence variables.

7. CONCLUSIONS

Data regarding participation and communication filtered from the study were associated with the elements in the linear communication model. To strengthen communication, real, non-pretentious events that are structured together with the employees, where all parties can work together, will be valuable. Creating a positive health and safety culture or safety climate is only possible through finding multi-communication channels and keeping the employees in the communication loop. Employees' ideas should be involved in the process of finding these channels. Corporates must design internal communication opportunities and an effective communication process to create a health and safety culture. Creative ways should be found to involve the employees in the health and safety process. For this aim, employees have to be authorized, encouraged, and feel their contribution to the process is valuable.

The prominent statements include that for EHS services to become more acceptable in the shopfloor, it is important to share the reasons for the work done with employees in systematic ways, that the workplace health unit needs to be more present in the production area, and that the group providing EHS services should improve their skills on these issues by carrying out studies focused on EHS communication issues. It is evident from all FGs that it will contribute to improving the quality of work. The EHS training programs put forward in this study provide an important internal communication opportunity. We would like to point out that WSA measures and monitors the annual health and safety training hours per employee as one of the performance indicators related to the sustainability of the sector.

REFERENCES

Annual Reports. (2013–2023). *Health and safety labor watch Turkey*. Retrieved February, 2024, from https://www.isigmeclisi.org

Burke, M. J., Chan-Serafin, S., Salvador, R., Smith, A., & Sarpy, S. A. (2008). The role of national culture and organizational climate in safety training effectiveness. *European Journal of Work and Organizational Psychology, 17*(1), 133–152.

Butler, R. J. (2005). *Safety practices, firm culture and workplace injuries* (p. 18). W. E. Upjohn Institute for Employment Research.

Christy Bieber, J. D. (2023). *Forbes advisor*. Retrieved January, 2024, from https://www.forbes.com/advisor/legal/workers-comp/most-dangerous-jobs-america/#10_most_dangerous_jobs_in_america_section

Cooper, M. D. (2016). *Navigating the safety culture construct: A review of the evidence*. BSMS.

Demirbilek, T. (2005). *Güvenlik Kültürü*. Legal Yayıncılık.

Dennerlein, J. T., & Sparer-Fine, E. H. (2018). Improving employee involvement through safety communication. *Occupational Environmental Medicine* (p. A82–A83). Dublin. Ireland. Retrieved from https://oem.bmj.com/content/oemed/75/Suppl_2/A82.4.full.pdf.

Esin, A. (2006). *İş Sağlığı ve Güvenliği*. Yayın No. MMO/363/2. TMMOB Makina Mühendisleri Odası.

Geller, E. S. (1996). *The psychology of safety: How to improve behaviors and attitudes on the job*. Chilton Book Company.

General Directorate of Industry. (2021). *Demir-Çelik Sektör Raporu*. Retrieved January, 2024, from https://www.sanayi.gov.tr/plan-program-raporlar-ve-yayinlar/sektor-raporlari/mu1406011405

Guldenmund, F. (2007). The use of questionnaires in safety culture research: An evaluation. *Safety Science, 45*(6), 723–743.

ICSI – Industrielle Institut Pour Une Culture De Sécurité. (2018). *Safety culture from understanding to action*. ICSI.

ILOSTAT. (2024). *Occupational safety and health statistics (OSH) database*. ILOSTAT. Retrieved January, 2024, from https://ilostat.ilo.org/topics/safety-and-health-at-work/

International Organization for Standardization. (2018). *Occupational health and safety management systems – Requirements with guidance for use* [ISO Standard No. 45001:2018]. https://www.iso.org/standard/63787.html

Kılıç, N., Vatansever, Ç., & Işık, İ. (2014). Farklı Liderlik Tarzları Güvenlik İklimini Nasıl Etkiliyor? In M. Özdevecioğlu, T. Dedeoğlu & N. Çapar (Eds.), *2. Örgütsel Davranış Kongresi Bildiriler Kitabı* (pp. 293–301). Melikşah Üniversitesi.

Koivupalo, M., Sulasalmi, S., Rodrigo, P., & Vayrinen, S. (2015). Health and safety management in a changing organisation: Case study global steel company. *Safety Science, 74*, 128–139.

Mearns, K. K. (2009). Developing a safety culture measurement instrument for European air traffic control. In *Europe air traffic management research and development seminar*. EUROCONTROL.

Morgeson, F. P., & Hofmann, D. A. (1999). The structure and function of collective constructs: Implications for multilevel research and theory development. *Academy of Management Review, 24*(2), 249–265.

Naevestad, T. (2010). Evaluating a safety culture campaign: Some lessons from a Norwegian case. *Safety Science, 48*(5), 651–659.

Naji, G. M., Isha, A. S., Alazzani, A., Saleem, M. S., & Alzoraiki, M. (2022). Assessing the mediating role of safety communication between safety culture and employees safety performance. *Frontiers in Public Health, 10*, 1–17.

Nordlöf, H. W. (2015). Safety culture and reasons for risk-taking at a large steel-manufacturing company: Investigating the worker perspective. *Safety Science, 73*, 126–135.

Şerifoğlu, U. K., & Sungur, E. (2007). İşletmelerde sağlık ve güvenlik kültürünün oluşturulması: Tepe yönetimin rolü ve kurum içi iletişim olanaklarının kullanımı. *Yönetim Dergisi, 358*, 41–50.

Strategy Development Directorate. (2023). *T.C. Çalışma ve Sosyal Güvenlik Bakanlığı 2022 Yılı Faaliyet Raporu*. Retrieved January, 2024, from https://www.csgb.gov.tr/media/90634/2022-faaliyet-raporu.pdf

Sungur, E. (2015). Kişilerarası İletişim İşyerinde Sağlık ve Güvenliği Nasıl Etkiliyor? *8. Ulusal İşçi Sağlığı ve İş Güvenliği Kongresi* (pp. 315–322). TMMOB Makine Mühendisleri Odası, Yayın no: E/2015/635.

Sungur, E. (2020). *Çalışan Sağlığı ve Güvenliği Kültürünün Sürdürülebilirliği: Davranış Odaklı Yaklaşımın Rolü/Sustainability of employee health and safety culture: The role of behavior-based approach* [Unpublished PhD thesis]. Maltepe Üniversitesi, Lisansüstü Eğitim Enstitüsü, İstanbul.

Sungur, E., Vatansever, Ç., & Tiryaki, A. R. (2009). İş sağlığı ve güvenliği eğitimi etkili eğitim tasarımı ve eğitim etkinliğini değerlendirme. *Mühendis ve Makina, 50*(592), 10–22.

Taşkan, E. Wetzstein, A., Chilvers, C., Wittig, K., Friedl, W., & Kohstall., T. (2011). *Evaluation of prevention campaigns: Analyse the parts and see the whole better: Measuring the effects of campaigns of accident insurers* [Institut für Arbeit und Gesundheit der DGUV (IAG) Report 1/2011].

TMMOB Makina Mühendisleri Odası. (2020). *İşçi Sağlığı ve İş Güvenliği Oda Raporu, Ağustos 2020, Güncellenmiş 9. Baskı*, Yayın No. MMO/718, E-ISBN: 978-605-01-13778, Ankara. Retrieved February, 2024, from https://www.mmo.org.tr/sites/default/files/isgrapor_06082020.pdf

Turkish Republic, Ministry of Labour and Social Security. (2014). *National policy document – III and action plan on safety and health at work 2014–2018*. Art Ofset Matbaacılık Ltd.

Vatansever, Ç., Çalışkan, S., & Işık, İ. (2015). Bir dünya şirketinin Türkiye'deki çalışanlarına göre çeşitliliklerin yönetimi: Gömülü kuram analiziyle modelleme. *Yönetim Araştırmaları Dergisi, 12*(1–2), 29–61.

Williams, J. H. (2006, June). *Improving safety communication skills: Becoming an empathic communicator* [Conference title]. Proceedings of the annual professional development conference for the American Society of Safety Engineers, Seattle, WA.

Williams, J. H. (2008). Employee engagement improving participation in safety. *Professional Safety, 53*(12), 12–40.

Wills, A. R., Watson, B., & Biggs, H. C. (2006). Comparing safety climate factors of work-related driving behavior. *Journal of Safety Research, 37*, 375–383.

Worksafe.qld.gov.au. (2023). *Safety leadership at work: Choosing the right safety climate tool for your organisation*. Retrieved December, 2023, from https://www.worksafe.qld.gov.au/__data/assets/pdf_file/0018/21492/choosing-the-right-safety-climate-tool.pdf

WorkSafe Victoria. (2022). *Communicating occupational health and safety across languages* https://www.worksafe.vic.gov.au/resources/communicating-across-languages-your-health-and-safety-guide

WSA. (2023). *Safety and health in the steel industry: Data report*. World Steel Association. worldsteel.org

Zohar, D. (1980). Safety climate in industrial organizations: Theoretical and applied implications. *Journal of Applied Psychology, 65*(1), 96–102.

CHAPTER 9

IMPORTANCE OF CORPORATE SOCIAL RESPONSIBILITY (CSR) IN THE GLOBAL FOOD PROCESSING INDUSTRY

Małgorzata Wiktoria Paprocka

Warsaw University of Life Sciences (SGGW), Poland

ABSTRACT

In the global food processing industry, corporate social responsibility (CSR) is garnering increasing attention from companies, employees, consumers, and regulatory bodies. The purpose of this chapter is to identify areas insufficiently addressed in the existing literature, yet significant and specific to the food processing sector, and those exerting the greatest impact on global society. CSR initiatives in the global food industry are diverse, and companies in the food sector are increasingly recognizing the importance of CSR not only for ethical reasons but also to enhance competitiveness, consumer trust, and overall sustainable business development, including mitigating risks associated with the environmental, social, and governance (ESG) area. The methodology used includes a literature review and a critical analysis of the scientific literature. The research question identified by the author is: "Whether and why CSR is important in the global food processing industry from various perspectives and what key aspects require further analysis and research in this field?" Two hypotheses were delineated: H1*: *CSR is of paramount importance and possesses a vast scope of influence in the global food industry and* H2*: *Need for further analysis of key CSR aspects in the food industry. To identify research* areas of focus, the Scopus database was utilized. Due to insufficient literature, this chapter was enriched with additional sources of scientific literature. Stakeholder engagement, transparency, and compliance with standards are vital for effective CSR implementation. The role of independent verification and consumer awareness in enhancing companies' legitimacy lacks research. Insufficiently explored are also tools for all market participants to curb harmful practices and promote healthy competition and development on the market.

Keywords: Corporate social responsibility; CSR; environmental social governance; ESG; food processing sector; food industry

1. INTRODUCTION

In the global food processing industry, CSR initiatives have gained significant interest increasing among companies, employees, consumers, as well as regulatory legitimacy.

> Processed Foods industry entities process and package foods such as bread, frozen foods, snack foods, pet foods and condiments for retail consumer consumption. Typically, these products are made ready to consume, are marketed for retail consumers and can be found on food retailers' shelves. The industry is characterised by large and complex ingredient supply chains, because many entities source ingredients from around the world. Large entities operate globally, and international opportunities are driving growth. (Definition Food and Beverage Industry – Processed Foods, Sustainability Accounting Standards Board (SASB), 2023)

Fordham and Robinson (2018) present CSR as an evolving concept that reflects different perspectives and approaches on the relationship between companies and society. While as defined by the European Commission in 2011 in the document "Renewed EU strategy 2011–2014 for Corporate Social Responsibility" (COM (2011) 681; European Commission, 2011), CSR is "the responsibility of enterprises for their impacts on society." The emphasis on health as a CSR strategy in the food processing industry has become crucial. This is due to the general health of the population, diseases caused by processed food, the problem of world hunger, and many other important issues related to nutrition and its consequences in the world. Although CSR in this sector encompasses more than just health considerations. The complex impact of the food processing industry on ESG as a whole is well illustrated by the ESG risk materiality map. Based on SASB's materiality map for the areas most influenced by food processing companies, the following sections can be distinguished: Energy Management, Water and Wastewater Management, Product Quality and Safety, Customer Welfare, Selling Practices and Product Labeling, Product Design and Lifecycle Management, Supply Chain Management, Materials Sourcing and Efficiency (SASB, 2023). As evident, the impact of companies from this sector extends far beyond health issues, encompassing a broader spectrum, including environmental influence and business model dynamics. Considering the entire Food and Beverage Industry sector and its intricate supply chain connections (Nguyen et al., 2021), an image of a sector particularly close to human life emerges, both from the perspective of employees and consumers. The sector fulfills basic needs and shapes a landscape where threats and significant opportunities intertwine across various dimensions. CSR operationalizes ESG, which is expressed through indicators that can be measured and compared. In this chapter, these terms will be used interchangeably, but they always refer to the impact of business on stakeholders, including customers, employees, the natural environment, shareholders, and society as a whole.

The purpose of this chapter is to identify areas insufficiently addressed in the existing literature, yet significant and specific to the food processing sector, and those exerting the greatest impact on global society. In response to the research question, which is "Whether and why CSR is important in the global food processing industry from various perspectives and what key aspects require further analysis and research in this field?" the author presents two hypotheses *H1*: *CSR is of paramount importance and possesses a vast scope of influence in the global food industry and *H2*: *Need for further analysis of key CSR aspects in the food industry. The first hypothesis posits that CSR is highly important in the global food industry and significantly impacts society as a whole. The second hypothesis suggests that there is a need to continue research on key aspects of CSR in the food industry that may influence its development and society worldwide. These hypotheses can serve as a starting point for further research on CSR in the global food industry, and the research undertaken in this chapter can help identify areas that need more attention from researchers. The methodology used includes a literature review and a critical analysis of the scientific literature. Literature review was conducted using the Scopus database. The keywords used in the advanced search of scientific texts are identical to the keywords designated for this chapter. They are "corporate social responsibility," "csr," "environmental social governance," "esg," "food processing sector," and "food industry." The search was restricted to English-language texts and the disciplines of Business, Management and Accounting, as well as Economics, Econometrics, and Finance. Another limitation was articles published in journals. The search was conducted in February 2024, among titles, abstracts, and keywords, and the code used in the search is as follows:

> TITLE-ABS-KEY (("corporate social responsibility" OR "csr" OR "environmental social governance" OR "esg") AND ("food processing sector" OR "food industry")) AND (LIMIT-TO (SRCTYPE, "j")) AND (LIMIT-TO (DOCTYPE, "ar")) AND (LIMIT-TO (SUBJAREA, "BUSI") OR LIMIT-TO (SUBJAREA, "ECON")) AND (LIMIT-TO (LANGUAGE, "English"))

In total, 92 articles were found. Due to insufficient literature, the article was enriched with additional sources of scientific literature.

2. CHARACTERISTICS OF CSR IN THE GLOBAL FOOD PROCESSING INDUSTRY

In the literature, within the searched database, we observe an increase in the number of articles from the year 2004. However, after 2021, during which 13 documents were found, there was a decrease to 9 documents in 2022 and only 5 in 2023 (Scopus Database, 2024; Fig. 9.1). This trend is concerning due to the significance

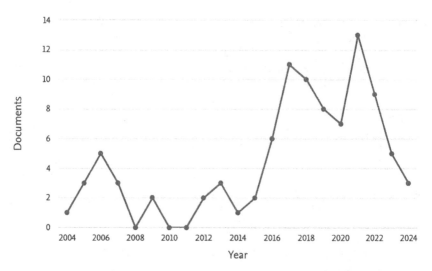

Fig. 9.1. Documents by Year. *Source*: Scopus Database (2024).

of corporate responsibility in the food processing sector, including its impact on public health, which will be addressed in subsequent parts of the article.

Another observation can be made regarding regulations, which are increasingly proliferating mainly through the European Commission. The most significant regulations concern the reporting obligation for an increasing number of companies. However, regulations related to greenwashing are also emerging, along with a range of best practices dedicated to specific sectors, thanks to the efforts of nongovernmental organizations, rating agencies, and entities specializing in ESG analysis. More and more companies are also subjecting themselves to ESG ratings, and the financial sector is increasingly offering and providing products where margins are tied to the improvement of a company's ESG performance (Sandberg et al., 2023).

Drawing from the literature, below are the key initiatives that companies in the food processing sector can undertake regarding CSR/ESG:

1. *Environmental*:
    - Sustainable sourcing of raw materials: companies focus on sourcing raw materials sustainably, minimizing negative environmental impact.
    - Energy efficiency: companies strive to reduce energy consumption and greenhouse gas emissions through investments in low-impact environmental technologies.
    - Waste management: large food processing companies take steps to minimize waste and increase recycling.

2. *Social*:
    - Equality and diversity: companies aim to promote gender equality, cultural diversity, and equal opportunities in the workplace.

- Worker safety: companies prioritize providing safe working conditions and ensure the physical and mental well-being of employees.
- Sustainable supply chain: food companies engage in sustainable development of local communities by supporting local economies and communities.

3. *Governance*:

- Transparency: food companies aim for greater transparency in management, including publishing information on finances, activities, and ESG-related goals.
- Stakeholder dialogue: companies aim to engage in open dialogue with stakeholders, including investors, customers, employees, and local communities.
- Board accountability: company boards focus on responsible management, ensuring compliance with legal regulations, ethical standards, and shareholder interests.

A specific aspect of CSR in this sector is that it encompasses a wide range of fields, not just focusing on social or environmental issues but also covering extensively the realm of social sciences and many specialized scientific disciplines (Scopus Database, 2024; Fig. 9.2). Therefore, research should be conducted interdisciplinarily. The division into individual disciplines is presented in Fig. 9.2.

Research illustrates the diversity of CSR aspects in the supply chain, encompassing issues related to animal welfare, biotechnology, environmental protection, fair trade, health and safety, as well as labor rights (Maloni & Brown, 2006). This underscores the multifaceted nature of activities undertaken by companies in the food processing sector, which must take into account a wide range of factors and the far-reaching scope of their impact when implementing CSR initiatives. However, a company's considerations do not end with the proper integration of initiatives. They must also understand their role in the economy and society while

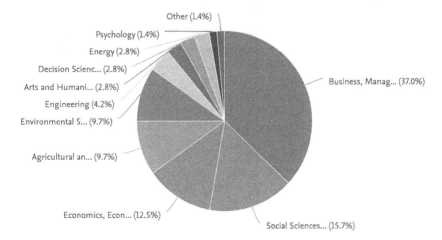

Fig. 9.2. Documents by Subject Area. *Source*: Scopus Database (2024).

simultaneously considering other issues related to the operations of each company, such as profitability, various types of risks, legal changes, and competitiveness, among many others.

Companies manufacturing processed food play a significant role in society by providing consumers with affordable and convenient sources of food. Through innovations in processed food, these companies offer efficient sources of essential nutrients in the diet for their consumers (SASB, 2015). Hence, on the one hand, trust in food manufacturing companies is of utmost importance, while, on the other hand, their responsibility toward every conscious or unconscious consumer is significant (Lombardi et al., 2015). The situation in the food processing sector is particularly intriguing due to its close proximity to a large segment of society. Therefore, the initiatives undertaken can significantly impact consumer awareness, as well as the understanding among employees of companies regarding the obligations of processing corporations toward society. Companies can use packaging information not only to provide guidance on consumption frequency, composition, or calorie content but also to promote eco-friendly solutions, such as packaging materials and waste segregation after consuming the products. CSR actions by leading food retailers play a significant role in supporting communities and well-being (Lee & Hammant, 2022).

Characterizing the food processing sector while considering ESG issues highlights the complexity of interconnections among various stages in food production. CSR initiatives across the entire sector stem not only from ethical motivations but also have a significant impact on dynamic changes in productivity, efficiency, and process improvement, underscoring the industry's role in environmental and societal contexts as well as in the economy (Kapelko & Guillamón-Saorín, 2020). Research by Partalidou et al. (2020) illustrates the relationship between financial outcomes and the implementation of CSR activities in the food industry, emphasizing that larger companies are more inclined to adopt CSR practices. On the other hand, smaller companies, lacking economies of scale, may aim to offer higher-quality food products at a higher cost to clients. Moreover, all these aspects are also regulated by procedures and regulations. From a business perspective, there has been a noticeable surge in investor interest in ESG issues in recent years, accompanied by a growing awareness among companies regarding the necessity of incorporating ESG considerations into their business strategies. Many companies in the food and beverage sector are striving to integrate ESG principles not only for social benefit and mitigating negative environmental impact but also to enhance shareholder value and ensure long-term company success. The role of CSR in crisis management within the food industry is also emphasized, highlighting the necessity for companies to develop robust ESG/CSR strategies (Assiouras et al., 2013).

The implementation of CSR initiatives in the food processing sector, especially in export-oriented industries, is crucial for adhering to standards concerning labor practices and food safety. ESG considerations are highly important in the context of global sustainable production, as in areas where the law does not reach, companies must collaborate internationally in spirit of upholding human rights, labor rights, and principles of occupational health and safety (Nguyen et al., 2019). In emerging markets, such as the food industry, CSR has emerged as a critical factor for companies operating within global supply chains (Klerkx et al., 2012).

There are several reasons why CSR has evolved and gained significant traction. The diversity of actions and initiatives undertaken is a response to increasing societal awareness, regulatory pressure, political and ideological influences, as well as the financial and reputational benefits associated with integrating stakeholders into business strategy. There is a rising interest among consumers and governments in understanding the social and environmental impact of the food industry, highlighting the growing importance of CSR within this sector (Lerro et al., 2018).

3. KEY ASPECTS OF CSR IN THE FOOD INDUSTRY ON WHICH THERE IS STILL A LACK OF FULL UNDERSTANDING

The adoption of CSR practices in the food industry is increasingly common, as indicated by the regular release of CSR bulletins by companies (Ikram et al., 2020). The reporting of ESG issues in the food sector directs our analysis toward cases where the levels or quality of reported indicators are somehow unclear, uncertain, or manipulated. These instances prompt us to delve deeper into the transparency and accuracy of reported data, shedding light on potential discrepancies or inconsistencies that may exist within companies' disclosures. Larger firms are required to demonstrate greater transparency, yet they also have greater potential for manipulation. The lack of transparency, along with practices such as greenwashing and social washing, whereby companies manipulate their image to appear socially responsible when they are not, have been investigated but still lack sufficient exploration (Montero-Navarro et al., 2021). Regulations addressing green-social-washing are emerging in the market, yet there are few studies on how consumers can also on their own exclude non-transparent companies from the market or how to identify manipulating firms or at least on how to avoid their harmful products.

There are studies confirming the proposition that the implementation of CSR practices positively impacts financial performance. These findings highlight the correlation between CSR initiatives or CSR reporting and various financial metrics, indicating that companies that prioritize CSR tend to achieve better financial outcomes (Buallay, 2022). This is one of the reasons why companies may manipulate their non-financial reports. Research has demonstrated that CSR can have an impact on the financial performance within the food and agribusiness sector (Ali, 2023). However, there are no definitive studies indicating that companies in the food processing sector will undoubtedly experience better financial results after implementing socially responsible practices. This is because it is challenging to demonstrate the direct impact of CSR amid numerous other market factors affecting a range of composite indicators. Another reason could be the costliness of investments and process changes, which may not yield immediate profits in the short term. However, the positive value for the company is often seen in increased consumer trust, greater resilience to ESG risks, reduced employee turnover, and, in the long term, improvements in the business model, process optimization, and ultimately stable financial liquidity and at the end increased profits. Certainly, investor interest also increases, stemming from the belief that companies engaging in CSR practices are better positioned to manage risks and capitalize on opportunities in the long term. As a result, investors may view these companies as more attractive investment opportunities, leading to a positive impact on the company's market value and potentially prompting increased demand for its shares. The impact of CSR practices on the financial realm of companies in the food processing sector is certainly an area that can provide fertile ground for further research, mainly to encourage companies to integrate CSR practices into their business strategies effectively.

Some studies have focused on integrating CSR initiatives with food supply chain management to improve relationships between producers and customers (Chen et al., 2021). Companies in the food processing sector, particularly those involved in export industries, are progressively prioritizing CSR demands such as implementing sound labor practices and adhering to food safety standards to align with consumer expectations (Nguyen et al., 2019) and also legal requirements. However, consumer's perspectives on CSR in the food industry are not an easy or researched topic, as research indicates that consumers have different preferences regarding CSR initiatives. Regardless of preference, the essence here is open communication and building consumer trust. Research indicates that the implementation of CSR activities in agri-food companies is crucial for improving business reputation and consumer trust (Lerro et al., 2018). The evolution of CSR initiatives in the food industry has led to the adoption of new communication strategies via social media platforms, representing another area of research on how companies in the sector can most effectively engage with their customers (Mądra-Sawicka & Paliszkiewicz, 2020).

Emerging regulations and societal shifts indicate a growing apprehension regarding the health and safety aspects of processed food items. Furthermore, there is increasing concern about the environmental and social impacts stemming from the production and sourcing processes of these products and their ingredients. These factors pose a risk to a company's social legitimacy to conduct its operations (SASB, 2015). When it comes to other fields of study, it is also imperative to thoroughly investigate topics related to health impact, encompassing research on issues such as microplastics in food, carcinogenic substances, hazardous pasteurizing agents, food colorants, and similar concerns. However, due to the scope of this article, the author does not provide specific recommendations in this regard, while emphasizing the need for an interdisciplinary approach to the subject.

4. CONCLUSIONS

In the area of CSR in the food processing industry, there is a research gap in understanding all the relationships, both from the perspective of the company and its stakeholders. Managing material sustainability issues can potentially affect a company's valuation, impacting sales, earnings, reputation, assets, liabilities, and cost of capital (SASB, 2015). While research has shown that the adoption of CSR strategies by major food corporations offers significant benefits to communities and enhances public health (Richards et al., 2015).

CSR in the global food industry is not only a moral imperative but also, perhaps primarily, a strategic business aspect. Companies that implement CSR practices can enhance their reputation, mitigate risks, and make a positive contribution to society and the environment, potentially improving their performance, including financial results. The synthesis of these studies emphasizes the importance of CSR in shaping the sustainable future of the food industry. However, there is a temptation to act and receive results solely for the purpose of acquiring or retaining customers or for immediate financial gains, rather than in synergy and as a result of sustainable business development. While new regulations regarding green and social washing address many risks, there is a lack of research highlighting the role of self-regulation of companies and consumer awareness in enhancing companies' legitimacy. In research, there is also a lack of presenting specific tools that all market participants can utilize to curb practices that degrade public health and the environment, as well as promote healthy competition in the market. By "specific tools," the author means identifying which ESG indicators should be prioritized to increase financial profit or determining the most effective communication channels, for example, in digital space to engage with customers (Lingur et al., 2022). For society, this could involve, for example, the development of new technologies to help identify product compositions or educational programs on harmful chemical ingredients, advising on what to avoid and what to choose.

To sum up, incorporating stakeholder engagement, transparency, and compliance with standards are vital factors for companies to address when implementing and disclosing CSR initiatives within the food industry. The source of the food processing sector's motivation to undertake CSR activities is secondary here. Even if a company does not do it for ethical reasons, it has such a large impact on society that research should focus on presenting specific benefits and tools for achieving them for both companies and society to pursue their interests in synergy, regardless of beliefs and approaches to ESG topics.

The presented chapter consists of an introduction, a section dedicated to the characterization of CSR in the food processing sector based on the reviewed literature, and a part addressing areas requiring attention from researchers, along with a concluding section summarizing findings and offering suggestions for future research. This study confirmed two hypotheses. Based on the literature review, it was observed that CSR holds significant importance and has a broad impact in the sector under examination. Additionally, a research gap was identified, indicating the need for comprehensive analyses in areas insufficiently addressed in existing literature yet crucial and specific to the food processing sector, influencing the global society. Thus, this chapter effectively achieved its objective. In contemporary times, there should be no room for lack of transparency in the actions of companies regarding CSR. This can exert pressure on company management, leading to the establishment of market operation principles specific to this sector. Furthermore, by collectively increasing awareness among consumers, employees, society as a whole, regulatory bodies, and governmental authorities, stakeholders should seek tools to regulate the operations of food processing companies, thereby ensuring they adhere to the principles of CSR, directly impacting the health and well-being of the global population (Iazzi et al., 2022). CSR in the global food industry is not just ethical but strategic, offering reputation enhancement, risk mitigation, and positive societal and environmental contributions, potentially improving financial performance. However, prioritizing immediate gains over sustainable development is a risk. While regulations address some risks, the role of independent verification and consumer awareness in enhancing companies' legitimacy lacks research. Tools for all market participants to curb harmful practices and promote healthy competition and development in the market are also insufficiently explored. Stakeholder engagement, transparency, and compliance with standards are vital for effective CSR implementation. Regardless of the sector's motivations, research should focus on presenting specific benefits and tools for both companies and society to pursue their interests synergistically.

REFERENCES

Ali, J. (2023). Does mandatory corporate social responsibility expenditure affect the financial performance of food and agribusiness firms? Evidence from India. *European Business Review*, *35*(4), 520–533. https://doi.org/10.1108/ebr-09-2022-0193

Assiouras, I., Özgen, Ö., & Skourtis, G. (2013). The impact of corporate social responsibility in food industry in product-harm crises. *British Food Journal*, *115*(1), 108–123. https://doi.org/10.1108/00070701311289902

Buallay, A. (2022). Sustainability reporting in food industry: An innovative tool for enhancing financial performance. *British Food Journal*, *124*(6), 1939–1958.

Chen, T., Huang, Y., Weng, M., & Do, M. (2021). Two-stage production system pondering upon corporate social responsibility in food supply chain: A case study. *Applied Sciences*, *11*(3), 1088. https://doi.org/10.3390/app11031088

European Commission. (2011). *Renewed EU strategy 2011–2014 for corporate social responsibility* (COM (2011) 681). https://www.europarl.europa.eu/meetdocs/2009_2014/documents/com/com_com(2011)0681_/com_com(2011)0681_en.pdf

Fordham, A. E., & Robinson, G. M. (2018). Mapping meanings of corporate social responsibility – An Australian case study. *International Journal of Corporate Social Responsibility*, *3*(1), 6. https://doi.org/10.1186/s40991-018-0036-1

Iazzi, A., Ligorio, L., Vrontis, D., & Trio, O. (2022). Sustainable development goals and healthy foods: Perspective from the food system. *British Food Journal*, *124*(4), 1081–1102.

Ikram, M., Qayyum, A., Mehmood, O., & Haider, J. (2020). Assessment of the effectiveness and the adaption of CSR management system in food industry: The case of the South Asian versus the Western food companies. *SAGE Open*, *10*(1), 215824401990125. https://doi.org/10.1177/2158244019901250

Kapelko, M., & Guillamón-Saorín, E. (2020). Corporate social responsibility and dynamic productivity change in the US food and beverage manufacturing industry. *Agribusiness*, *37*(2), 286–305. https://doi.org/10.1002/agr.21645

Klerkx, L., Villalobos, P., & Engler, A. (2012). Variation in implementation of corporate social responsibility practices in emerging economies' firms: A survey of Chilean fruit exporters. *Natural Resources Forum*, *36*(2), 88–100. https://doi.org/10.1111/j.1477-8947.2012.01440.x

Lee, C., & Hammant, C. (2022). Corporate social and community-oriented support by UK food retailers: A documentary review and typology of actions towards community wellbeing. *Perspectives in Public Health*, *143*(4), 211–219. https://doi.org/10.1177/17579139221095326

Lerro, M., Caracciolo, F., Vecchio, R., & Cembalo, L. (2018). Consumer's side of corporate social responsibility: A nonhypothetical study. *Journal of Consumer Affairs*, *52*(3), 689–710. https://doi.org/10.1111/joca.12182

Lingur, L., Martyniuk, O., Ivchenko, I., & Ivchenko, O. (2022). Creating a digital space of socially sustainable development for food enterprises. *Eastern-European Journal of Enterprise Technologies*, *4*(13(118)), 22–33. https://doi.org/10.15587/1729-4061.2022.263540

Lombardi, A., Caracciolo, F., Cembalo, L., Lerro, M., & Lombardi, P. (2015). How does corporate social responsibility in the food industry matter? *New Medit*, *14*(3), 2–9.

Mądra-Sawicka, M., & Paliszkiewicz, J. (2020). Information sharing strategies in the social media era: The perspective of financial performance and CSR in the food industry. *Information*, *11*(10), 463. https://doi.org/10.3390/info11100463

Maloni, M. J., & Brown, M. E. (2006). Corporate social responsibility in the supply chain: An application in the food industry. *Journal of Business Ethics*, *68*(1), 35–52. https://doi.org/10.1007/s10551-006-9038-0

Montero-Navarro, A., González-Torres, T., Rodríguez-Sánchez, J.-L., & Gallego-Losada, R. (2021). A bibliometric analysis of greenwashing research: A closer look at agriculture, food industry, and food retail. *British Food Journal*, *123*(13), 547–560.

Nguyen, P. M., Vo, N. D., Nguyen, N. P., & Choo, Y. (2019). Corporate social responsibilities of food processing companies in Vietnam from consumer perspective. *Sustainability*, *12*(1), 71. https://doi.org/10.3390/su12010071

Nguyen, T. T. H., Nguyen, T. T. T., & Phan, T. T. H. (2021). The effect of corporate social responsibility on supply chain performance. *Uncertain Supply Chain Management*, *9*(4), 927–940.

Partalidou, X., Zafeiriou, E., Giannarakis, G., & Sariannidis, N. (2020). The effect of corporate social responsibility performance on financial performance: The case of food industry. *Benchmarking: An International Journal*, *27*(10), 2701–2720. https://doi.org/10.1108/bij-11-2019-0501

Richards, Z., Thomas, S., Randle, M., & Pettigrew, S. (2015). Corporate social responsibility programs of big food in Australia: A content analysis of industry documents. *Australian and New Zealand Journal of Public Health*, *39*(6), 550–556. https://doi.org/10.1111/1753-6405.12429

Sandberg, H., Alnoor, A., & Tiberius, V. (2023). Environmental, social, and governance ratings and financial performance: Evidence from the European food industry. *Business Strategy and the Environment*, *32*(4), 2471–2489.

Scopus. (2024). *Documents by year*. Scopus Database. https://www.scopus.com.

Sustainability Accounting Standards Board (SASB). (2015). *Processed foods research brief*. FINAL-CN0103_Processed_Foods_Brief.pdf (ifrs.org).

Sustainability Accounting Standards Board (SASB). (2023). *Find industry topics*. Retrieved from https://sasb.ifrs.org/standards/materiality-finder/find/?industry%5B0%5D=FB-PF

INDEX

Affirmative factor analysis, 33
Artificial intelligence (AI), 114
Automation, 115

Bartlett's test, 34
Behavioral perspectives, 53–54
Beliefs, 4
BET20 index, 93
Bias-corrected scaled (BCS) LM test, 120
Big data, 114
Binary correlation residual sample estimate, 121
Blue collars, 48, 60, 67–68
Body of Expert and Licenced Accountants of Romania (CECCAR), 94
Bootstrap method, 39
Bootstrap research model estimates, 33
Bottom-up approaches, 48
Brand love, 4, 7–9
Brand trust, 4, 7–9
Breusch–Pagan LM test, 120
Bucharest Stock Exchange, 94
Business ethics, 73
Businesses, 4

Carbon disclosure project (CDP), 92
Career alternatives on career commitment, 17
Career commitment, 14–15
  career alternatives on, 17
  career investment on, 17–18
  career satisfaction on, 16–17
  professional self-efficacy on, 18
Career identity, 15
Career investment on career commitment, 17–18
Career resilience, 15

Career satisfaction on career commitment, 16–17
Career Satisfaction Scale, 20
Chief executive officer (CEO), 54
Civil servants, 17, 19
Classical "command and control" mentality, 47
Coda, 71–72
Coding process, 101–102
Communication, 135–136
Competitive strategy, 50
Confirmatory factor analysis (CFA), 34–36
Content analysis, 101
  coding process, 101–102
  deep analysis, 103–105
  drivers for ESG reporting, 105
  ESG reporting framework, 106
  implications on business, 106
  long-term value creation and sustainable business strategy, 105–106
  portrait of documents, 102–103
  stakeholders management, 105
Contingency Theory of Management, 67
Cooperation, 74, 76
Coordination, 74, 76
Corporate citizenship, 73
Corporate social responsibility (CSR), 4, 8, 73, 92, 144
  in global food processing industry, 145–149
  initiatives, 144
  key aspects, 149–150
Corporate sustainability reporting (CSR), 92
Corporate Sustainability Reporting Directive (CSRD), 92–93
Creativity, 73

Cronbach's alpha coefficient, 33–34
Cross-sectional augmented Dickey–Fuller (CADF) test, 121

Delayering, 71
Dependence, 16
Descriptive analysis, 20
Descriptive statistics, 120
Design school, 47
Determinist perspectives, 51–52
D–H panel causality test, 122
Digital content production, 114
Digital financial activities, 114
Digital labor platforms, 115
Digital tools, 114–115
Digitalization, 114
   data description, 119
   empirical findings, 122–125
   estimation techniques, 120–122
   literature review, 117–119
   model specification, 119–120
Division of labor, 66
Dynamic capabilities, 51

E-commerce, 114
E-marketing, 114
Eco-labeling, 6
Employee Health and Safety (EHS), 131–132
   culture, 132–133
   method, 136–139
Employee participation, 135–136
Employee satisfaction, 31
Employment relations, 114
Environment, social, and governance (ESG), 92, 146–147
   considerations on ESG disclosure, 94–95
   drivers for ESG reporting, 105
   reporting framework, 106
Environmental changes-based view, 76–77
Environmental conditions, 52
Estimation techniques, 120–122
Ethics, 4, 8
European Green Deal (EGD), 93

European Union (EU), 93
Exploratory factor analysis (EFA), 33–34
External incentives, 30
External motivation, 29
Extrinsic motivation, 28, 30
   policy implications of, 40
Extrinsic religiosities, 5

Firms, 67, 97
Food industry, 145
Food processing sector, 148
Formalization, 66
Fragmentation, 66

Gig work, 115
Global ESG Monitor (GEM), 93
Global Reporting Initiative (GRI), 92
Globalization, 115, 124
Gray collars, 48, 60, 67–68
Greenhouse gas (GHG) emission reductions, 93
Gross domestic product (GDP), 114

Hard devices, 115
Health and safety climate in steel industry, 133–134
Human capital, 51
Human resource (HR), 28

Inclusion, 55
Indeterminist perspectives, 51–52
Information and communication technologies (ICTs), 115
Informational software, 115
Integrated value creation (IVC), 96
Internal communication, 140
Internal motivation, 30
International Standards Organization (ISO), 131
Internet of Things, 114
Intrinsic motivation, 28, 31
   policy implications of, 39–40
Intrinsic religiosities, 5
Investment model theory, 15–16
Isha Shoppe, 5
Islamic banks, 6

Index

Job description indicators (JDIs), 30
Job insecurity, 18–19
Job satisfaction, 30–32
   policy implications of, 41–42

Kaiser–Meyer–Olkin (KMO) test, 34

Labor market, 114
Learning school, 48
Life cycle assessment (LCA), 95
Lithuanian civil servants, 17
Long-term value creation, 105–106
Low-level managers, 48
Luxury brands, 5

Machine learning, 114
Management science, 66
Management theories, 60
   critical approaches to extant management theories, 70–73
   dimensions of new management theories, 74–79
   extant management theories, 65–70
   method for theoretical advancement, 62–64
   theory for empirical inquiry and advancement, 64–65
Materiality matrix, 97
MAXQDA software, 101–102
Meta-literature analysis, 94
Ministry of Finance, 94
Moderation effect of perceived economic conditions, 18–19

National OHS Policy Document and Action Plan, 130
Networking software, 115
New Public Management (NPM) theory, 14
Non-executors, 48
Non-managerial workers, 51
Non-managers, 66
Nonfinancial disclosure, 92
Nonfinancial reporting directive (NFRD), 93

Occupational Health and Safety Administration (OSHA), 130
OECD, 115
Organizations, 75

Participation, 46
Patanjali, 5
People-Planet-Profit (3P) model, 96
Perceived economic conditions, moderation effect of, 18–19
Planning school, 47–48
Policy implications, 39
   of extrinsic motivation, 40
   of intrinsic motivation, 39–40
   of job satisfaction, 41–42
   of work efficiency, 40–41
Poly-cantered society, 73
Poly-contextual society, 73
Positioning school, 49–50
Practice, 49
Process-orientated legitimation, 100
Professional self-efficacy on career commitment, 18
Public servants, 14
   conceptual model, 20
   development of preposition, 16–19
   literature review, 15–16
   sampling and measuring, 20–21
Purchase intention, 9

Radicalism, 73
Rational/analytic perspectives, 53–54
Resource-based view (RBV), 50–51
Response–purchase decision, 9
Romania, 93
   literature review, 94–97
   research methodology, 97–101
   research results, 101–108
Routinization, 66
Rule-based safety, 132

Safety climate, 130, 133–134, 139
Safety culture
   of organization, 133
   research, 134

Satisfaction, 16
Scientific inquiry, 64
Self-determination theory, 28–29
Self-efficacy, 18
Self-organization, 71
Semi-structured interviews, 100
Short-term work, 115
Small-and medium-sized enterprise (SME), 94
Social Action Perspective (SAP), 69
Software company, 28
Specialization, 66
Spiritual brands, 4–5
   impact of, 5
   attributes, 4, 8
   core elements, 4
   previous studies, 5–6
   research model proposal, 7–9
Spiritual gurus, 6
Spiritual leaders, 4
Spirituality, 4
Sri Tattva, 5
Stakeholder management theory, 67, 105
Steel industry, 130
Stimulus–organism–response (SOR) theory, 6–7
Strategic management (SM), 46
   cognitive literature, 53–54
   content literature, 49–52
   process literature, 47–49
Strategic management, 66–68
Strategic objectives, 47
Strategy as Practice (SAP), 48–49, 68
Structural equation modeling (SEM), 20, 33
"Structure follows strategy" view, 50
Sustainability, 92
Sustainability Accounting Standards Board (SASB), 92
Sustainable business strategy, 105–106
Sustainable Business Value Creation (SBVC), 95–97
Sustainable development goals (SDGs), 92

Sustainable Finance Disclosure Regulation (SFDR), 93
System and contingency theories of management, 66
Systems theory, 67

Task Force on Climate-related Financial Disclosures (TCFD), 92
Taylorist Scientific Management, 66
Testing models and research hypotheses, 37–38
Theories of management, 66
Theory X, 66
Theory Y, 66, 72
Top managers, 50, 52, 54
Top-level management, 50
Trade unions, 115
Triple bottom line (TBL) model, 96
Turkish steel industry, 131

United Nations (UN), 92
Universalistic-based view, 75–76
Unskilled labor, 51
Upper Echelon Theory, 68

Value creation, 93
Value-based view, 78–79

Work efficiency, 29–30
   policy implications of, 40–41
Work environment, 28
Work motivation, 28–29
   data analysis and results, 33–42
   participants, 33
   research methodology, 33
   scale, 33
   theoretical framework and research model, 28–32
Work structure, 114
Worker, 114
Worker Health and Occupational Safety Council, 131
World Steel Association (WSA), 131

www.ingramcontent.com/pod-product-compliance
Lightning Source LLC
Jackson TN
JSHW011908160425
82743JS00004B/7